The Reader's Digest Good Health Cookbooks

Desserts, Cakes and Breads

The Reader's Digest Good Health Cookbooks

DESSERTS, CAKES AND BREADS

PUBLISHED BY THE READER'S DIGEST ASSOCIATION LIMITED LONDON SYDNEY CAPE TOWN

Contents

How to use The Good Health Cookbooks   6

The Diets   7–9

Recipes   10–73

    FRUIT-BASED DESSERTS   10
    BAKED AND STEAMED PUDDINGS   49
    CUSTARDS AND ICES   52
    PASTRIES   56
    CAKES AND BREADS   60

Buying for Quality   74–79

    FRUIT   74

Basic Cooking Methods   80–98

    PREPARATION OF FRUIT   80
    SWEETS AND PUDDINGS   82
    PASTRY   85
    BAKING WITH YEAST   90
    CAKE-MAKING   93
    HOME FREEZING   96
    GARNISHES AND DECORATION   98

A to Z of Cookery Terms   99

Index   100

How to use
The Good Health Cookbooks

Dieting need not be dreary. Whatever diet you may follow, you can still enjoy the classic dishes. Often, all you need are alternative ingredients that suit the recipe and suit the requirements of your diet. This book gives you the recipes for those classic dishes from *The Cookery Year*. It also gives you those vital alternatives. It has, in fact, several features unique in cookery books. In the special "Alternatives" column on each page, we identify how high each recipe is in salt, sugar, fat, cholesterol and fibre. We also give the calorie count. We check if it is gluten-free and wholefood. Then we suggest how you could adapt the recipe to any diet you, your family, or your guests might want to follow.

We do not lay down what diet you should follow. That is your decision. The book assumes that you yourself know what you want to do and tries to help you to do it by making suggestions (not commands), some or all of which you may want to follow. Perhaps you have been told to cut down drastically on salt; perhaps you have been thinking for some time that you should eat a little less sugar; perhaps you have a friend coming to a meal who cannot eat gluten or who is avoiding food high in cholesterol. You do not have to buy a new cookbook for each diet. You do not have to produce alternative meals for every guest. With these books, you can simply adapt the existing recipes to suit your needs.

You will find that we make use of a few conventions. This is mainly in order to avoid constant repetition. **The asterisk** (*) is used as follows:

1) Salt* indicates that this item may be omitted for those on a low-salt diet; the salt level of the recipe as given in the "Alternatives" column is calculated on the assumption that this salt has been omitted and that any ingredients that sometimes contain salt and sometimes don't (e.g. tinned tomatoes) have been bought in their salt-free version.

2) Gluten-free* indicates that the recipe is free of gluten so long as gluten-free flour (or bread or breadcrumbs) is used where appropriate.

3) Wholefood* indicates that the recipe is wholefood if wholemeal flour (or bread or breadcrumbs), brown rice and unrefined sugar are used where appropriate.

The levels of salt, **sugar**, **fat**, **cholesterol** and **fibre** for each recipe are denoted by symbols in the "Alternatives" column:

For definitions of what constitutes a high threshold level of any one of these, see under the appropriate diet on the following pages. Less than half this threshold level is considered low.

Calorie counts are given, firstly for the recipe as a whole and secondly as an indication of how many calories may be avoided as a result of following particular alternative suggestions.

Calories are automatically lost when either sugar or fat is significantly reduced. The calculations for calorie-loss can be no more than approximate, and occasionally are omitted, as so many factors can vary: the fat level of fish and meat at different times of the year, the exact amount of fat trimmed off a cut of meat, or the amount of sugar that will make a dish acceptably sweet to a particular palate.

To convert calories to kilojoules, multiply the figure for calories by 4·18.

Cooking hints on when it is appropriate or helpful to use a pressure cooker, slow cooker, food processor, freezer or microwave are indicated by a tick, together with any further information required. With a microwave it is always essential that you also consult the manufacturer's instructions, as cooking times vary from cooker to cooker.

Measurements are expressed in both imperial and metric units. The figures are rounded up or down as necessary. As this is an international publication, we have borne in mind that teaspoons and tablespoons vary in capacity from country to country, but in any recipe where we have used these measurements, the dish should not be affected by such variations. For a check on the comparative values of these measures, consult the tables on the inside of the book's covers.

With practice you should find that the technique and alternatives recommended in this book will work with recipes from other books. In this way it becomes simple to adapt recipes so that they are both healthy and delicious. That is how it ought to be.

The Diets

Low-salt diet

Sodium is acknowledged to be a contributory factor in hypertension (high blood pressure) and thus in coronary heart disease and strokes; it can also be involved in some kidney disorders.

By far the most concentrated source of sodium is common salt (sodium chloride), and many processed foods contain a lot of added salt.

Diets which are very severely restricted in sodium are on occasion prescribed, but we are not concerned with them here. A certain minimum of both sodium and chloride is essential to good health, and the majority of salt-conscious people will simply want to cut out excessive consumption.

While setting an exact figure is very difficult, as the total level of salt in a meal depends on the combination of foods eaten, a target of 5 grams a day (generally considered to be not excessive) can usually be reached by cutting down on cooking or table salt as well as on monosodium glutamate. Foods such as salted or cured pork products and most cheeses should be eaten only in small quantities. Then the sodium occurring naturally in meat and

fish, even in sodium-rich shell-fish, need not be avoided.

It is important to check the labels on tins. Some tomatoes, for instance, are canned with added salt, others not. Egg whites and dried fruit are also relatively high in sodium and should not be overindulged in.

Salt substitutes are available but we do not specify them: they do not taste like salt and anyone suffering from heart or kidney disease should not take them without medical approval.

Many of those wishing to cut down on salt will also want to combine this with cutting down on fat. Therefore, for example, although double cream contains much less sodium than single cream or milk does, we do not advocate replacing milk with double cream.

Salt is used to to mean both common salt (sodium chloride) and sodium in general. Where the level of salt in the recipe is given, this takes into account sodium occurring naturally in the ingredients; in the list of ingredients, salt refers, as usual, to the sodium chloride commonly used for seasoning.

The salt content of a recipe is taken to be high if it contains the equivalent of more than 2 egg whites or $\frac{1}{2}$ pint (300 ml) of milk per person.

Low-sugar diet

Sugar is "empty calories": it provides no nutrients, but concentrated calories for a very little weight of food.

Sugar is the first thing to go if you are on a calorie-controlled diet. It is also known to encourage tooth decay; and high consumption, especially of refined sugar, has been correlated with certain diseases.

Refined sugar is pure sucrose, the form of sugar which is the least desirable. Sugar occurs naturally in other forms – for example, fructose in fruit, lactose in milk, dextrose (glucose) and maltose. These do not always have the same harmful effect on the body as sucrose, and are not eaten in anything like the same sort of quantity.

A low-sugar diet, therefore, usually aims at cutting out as much refined sugar as possible. This can be done simply by using less of it and deliberately cultivating a less sweet tooth, or by replacing it to some extent with other forms of sugar. Honey, for instance (which is mainly fructose and glucose, with little sucrose) is sweeter than sugar so less of it is needed. In this way you can cut down on both sucrose and the total quantity of sugar. Molasses, although a form of sucrose, has a very strong taste and again a teaspoon of it can sometimes be used instead of a tablespoon or more of sugar.

In this book, when the level of sugar in a recipe is indicated, it takes into account both the general level of sugar, including all its various forms – sucrose, fructose, glucose etc. – as well as any added sugar specified in the recipe. In the list of ingredients, sugar refers to the added sugar which is virtually pure sucrose. The suggestions for decreasing the sugar content of a recipe almost always refer to sucrose.

We are not concerned here with sugar substitutes nor with special diabetic sweeteners and jams. We do not aim to preserve an ultra-sweet taste. What we aim to do is to cut down the amount of refined sugar and to make more use of fruit and of small quantities of honey and molasses. The results will be definitely less sweet but still delicious.

The sugar content of a recipe is taken to be high if it contains the equivalent of more than 1 tablespoon of sugar per person.

Low-fat and low-cholesterol diets

One of the most common reasons for eating less fat and cholesterol is that there appears to be an undisputed link between the presence of cholesterol in the blood and liability to heart attacks.

Populations who eat less fat have lower levels of heart disease, although their consumption of oil may be high, as in many Mediterranean countries. The exact link has not yet been established, and it appears that other foods, for example garlic, onions and polyunsaturated fat, as well as fibre, have the ability to lower blood cholesterol. However, more and more people are coming to the conclusion that cutting down on fats, especially saturated fats, cannot do them any harm. Certainly it will help calorie control: fat contains twice as many calories per ounce as protein or carbohydrate.

Whether you want to lose weight or reduce the risk of a heart attack, low-fat and low-cholesterol diets are similar in many ways. Both encourage cutting down on the saturated fats which contain cholesterol.

Saturated fats are usually of animal origin but not always: coconuts, for example, have a saturated fat content of 83%. Unsaturated fats are mainly of vegetable origin and are further divided into monounsaturated and polyunsaturated fats. (These terms refer to the way in which their molecules are chemically bonded.) They are generally liquid at room temperature.

Monounsaturated fats (the most usual example is olive oil, which is 73% monounsaturated fat) have no effect on the level of cholesterol in the blood. Polyunsaturated fats can in fact, as stated above, actually lower the blood cholesterol level. There are a few foods which are very high in cholesterol relative to their fat content, notably shellfish, fish roes, and organ meats such as liver, kidney, brains and sweetbreads.

Those on a low-fat diet will want to cut down on all fats and oils. Those aiming at a low-cholesterol intake will want to eliminate as far as possible all saturated fats and will be cautious about eating shellfish and offal. This book shows you how to do either or both of these.

However the book does not purport to give a diet which actually lowers blood cholesterol. For instance, in the recipes olive oil is often specified. Those on such a diet will replace olive oil with safflower, soya or sunflower oils. Nor does this book attempt to give a fat-free diet. Such a diet should only be attempted under medical supervision, and even then it is bound to have a minimal fat content. Some fat is necessary in our diet, particularly linoleic acid, an essential fatty acid, which cannot be manufactured by the body: it is found in vegetable oils, particularly safflower oil.

Some particular foods that will be found useful in both low-fat and low-cholesterol diets are:
- skimmed milk, both liquid and dried
- low-fat cheese, particularly cottage cheese and low-fat curd cheese, such as quark or fromage blanc
- smetana (5–10% fat as opposed to 18% in sour cream)

For low-cholesterol diets:
- safflower, soya, sunflower and walnut oils
- (for frying over high heat): corn or peanut oils. It is, however, better to avoid frying over high heat as far as possible, since this changes the composition of the oils into something resembling saturated fat
- soft margarines with a high percentage of polyunsaturated oils (all margarines labelled "all vegetable" are virtually cholesterol-free)

The fat and cholesterol content of eggs is found only in the yolks, but in many cases yolks can be decreased or omitted, sometimes with a proportionate increase in the number of whites used.

The fat content of a recipe is taken to be high if it contains the equivalent of more than any 2 of the following per person:
$\frac{1}{2}$ oz (1 tablespoon) double cream or oil
$\frac{1}{4}$ oz (7 grams) butter, lard, suet or margarine
1 egg yolk
$\frac{1}{2}$ oz (10–15 grams) ham, bacon, pork or cheese

The above applies also to the cholesterol content of a recipe, except that unsaturated oils are freely allowed, and over $\frac{1}{2}$ an egg yolk is considered to be high.

Fibre

The importance of fibre in the diet is now widely recognised, and many people pursue a high-fibre diet.

Since one of the best and easiest ways of increasing fibre intake is to eat a slice or two of wholemeal bread with your meal, the recipes themselves have not (except in one or two cases) been modified to include more fibre. The original versions of the recipes are always based on fresh ingredients, including vegetables, fruit and nuts (most of which are high in fibre), and wholefood adaptations are available for almost all the recipes, thus helping to increase the fibre level.

Gluten-free diet

As coeliac sufferers are being identified more and more frequently, so the need for a gluten-free diet for them and for other gluten-sensitive patients is becoming widely recognised.

A gluten-free diet involves complete exclusion of gluten (a protein, found mainly in wheat but also, in a different form and to a lesser extent, in rye, barley and oats). Commercial gluten-free flour is available and can be used successfully for bread, and some pastry and cakes; if it is difficult to find or expensive to buy just for one recipe, there are other flours, many of which are familiar to those on wholefood diets, which are gluten-free. Chick pea flour, brown rice flour, cornflour, potato flour and soya flour are perhaps the best known.

All labels on tins and jars must be carefully read, as wheat flour is a common ingredient not just in the obvious breads, biscuits, cakes, pastries and many cereals, but in packet soups, baking powder, sausages, stock cubes, bottled sauces and baked beans as well as in some brands of mustard, ground white pepper, curry powder and cheap chocolate.

Gluten-free grains include rice, maize, millet and buckwheat. Cornflour, chick pea flour and split pea flour are all suitable for making white sauces. For soufflés, cornflour and potato flour (the latter is denser than wheat flour and half the amount given in the recipe is usually enough) can be used. Any of these will do for coating food which is to be fried. Millet flakes make a good gluten-free alternative to a breadcrumb coating.

As a gluten-free diet is often low in fibre, it is advisable to eat plenty of brown rice, other whole grains and potatoes. Pectin (available dried from specialist suppliers) can be used as a binding agent in doughs and batters; grated fresh apple can also sometimes be used.

Intolerance of gluten is often associated with an inability to digest fats, so that a low-fat diet may also need to be followed.

Wholefood diet

Since the recipes in this book are based firmly on fresh seasonal produce, they need little alteration to be acceptable to lovers of wholefood.

The main items to avoid are refined flour and sugar. Wholemeal flour and bread, and brown rice or sugar, can be used instead as desired. When buying brown sugar, look for the name of the country of origin on the packet. If this is not given, the sugar may be white sugar that has been coloured brown with caramel.

In the case of sugar, it may also be necessary to follow any suggestion given for reducing the total amount. A high level of even the comparatively unrefined brown sugar is not usually considered wholefood. Anything other than this will be covered in the Alternatives column. Where quantities or proportions are affected, as for instance in baking, this will also be covered.

FRENCH APPLE FLAN

The open flans or tarts with a sweet filling of fruit or jam originate in the Alsace region of France. Remove the metal flan ring which holds the pastry in shape before serving the flan.

PREPARATION TIME: *1 hour*
COOKING TIME: *45 min*
INGREDIENTS *(for 4–6):*
2 lb (900 g) cooking apples
2 red-skinned dessert apples
6 oz (175 g) plain flour
Salt*
4 oz (100 g) unsalted butter
6 oz (175 g) caster sugar
1 large egg yolk
Juice of a lemon
1 level tablespoon apricot jam

Sift the flour and a pinch of salt into a mixing bowl. Cut 3 oz (75 g) of the butter into small knobs and rub it into the flour until the mixture resembles breadcrumbs. Mix in ½ oz (10 g) caster sugar. Make a well in the centre of the flour, drop in the egg yolk and mix to a stiff dough with a little cold water.

Wrap the pastry in greaseproof paper and leave to rest for 30 minutes. Meanwhile, peel and core the cooking apples and cut them up roughly. Melt the remaining butter in a saucepan and add the apple pieces and 3½ oz (90 g) of sugar. Cover with a lid and cook gently for 10 minutes. Strain the apples, saving the juice. Rub the cooking apples through a coarse sieve, then allow this purée to cool. Wash the dessert apples; core them before cutting them into ¼ in (½ cm) rings. Sprinkle with a little lemon juice to prevent them going brown.

Roll out the pastry, ¼ in (½ cm) thick, on a floured surface and use to line a 7 in (18 cm) flan ring set on a greased baking tray. Trim the pastry edges and prick the base with a fork. Spoon the apple purée over the pastry and smooth the top. Arrange the apple rings in an overlapping pattern on top.

Put the apple juice, 2 tablespoons lemon juice, and jam and remaining sugar in a saucepan. Cook over low heat until the sugar has dissolved, then bring to the boil and boil briskly for 4 minutes. Brush a little of this glaze over the apple slices.

Bake the flan for 45 minutes in the centre of an oven pre-heated to 400°F (200°C, mark 6). If the apple slices brown too quickly, cover the flan with foil. Remove the flan from the oven, brush with the remaining glaze and serve it hot or cold, with a jug of cream.

APPLE PIE

An alternative filling for this traditional pie could be 1 lb (450 g) apples and ½ lb (225 g) blackberries. Other fruits, such as halved and pitted apricots, plums, peaches, pears, black currants or blueberries, also make good pies.

PREPARATION TIME: *20 min*
COOKING TIME: *35 min*
INGREDIENTS *(for 4–6):*
6–8 oz (175–225 g) shortcrust pastry (page 85)
1½ lb (700 g) cooking apples
2–3 oz (50–75 g) caster or Demerara sugar
Milk

Peel and core the apples and cut them into chunky slices. Place a pie funnel in the centre of a 1½ pint (900 ml) pie dish, arrange half the apple slices in the dish, sprinkle over the sugar and add the remaining fruit with 3 tablespoons of water.

Cover the pie with the rolled-out pastry, decorate it and brush the top with milk. Dust with caster sugar. Make a slit in the centre of the pastry lid for the steam to escape. Set the pie on a baking tray and bake in the centre of the oven pre-heated to 400°F (200°C, mark 6) for 35–40 minutes. If the pastry browns too quickly, cover it with a double layer of moistened greaseproof paper.

For variation, the water may be replaced with orange juice and the grated rind of half an orange mixed with the sugar.

Gluten-free pastry
This is slightly adapted from an original recipe which also includes raw cane sugar.

INGREDIENTS
2 oz (50 g) polyunsaturated soft margarine
4 oz (100 g) ground brown rice
1 small eating apple
1 oz (25 g) ground almonds

Blend the margarine and ground rice, using a fork. Grate the apple and work it in together with the ground almonds. This makes an excellent shortcrust for sweet pies and pastries. It needs to be pressed into a dish as it is very difficult to roll, so it is suitable for flans and tarts, not double-crust or covered pies. It is simple to make and does not go hard or tough. The pectin in the apple binds it and moistens it, and the texture is slightly crunchy, like shortbread.

FRENCH APPLE FLAN

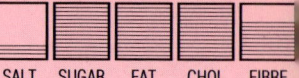

SALT SUGAR FAT CHOL FIBRE

GLUTEN-FREE* WHOLEFOOD*
TOTAL CALORIES: ABOUT 2567

To reduce the **sugar** content to low, use dessert apples throughout. Cook and purée them, then sweeten to taste with about 2 tablespoons honey or fruit sugar (fructose), both of which tend to give more sweetness for the same weight than ordinary sugar. (Calories lost: up to 293.)
The pastry is high in both **fat** and **cholesterol**. The cholesterol can be avoided completely by using vegetable fat, preferably soft margarine, in place of butter. To reduce the fat by more than a quarter is difficult without losing the properties of shortcrust pastry, but you could use the recipe for low-fat pastry on page 23. (Calories lost: up to 1082.)
The **fibre** level is moderate, as given, if 6 are served, but high if 4 are served.
Gluten-free flour can be used, or you can use the gluten-free recipe suggested on this page.

Freezing: ☑ up to 3 months.

APPLE PIE

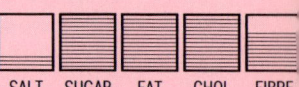

SALT SUGAR FAT CHOL FIBRE

GLUTEN-FREE* WHOLEFOOD*
TOTAL CALORIES: ABOUT 2175

Reduce the **sugar** content to moderate by using eating apples rather than cookers. The variation using orange juice will help to reduce the need for sugar, and a tablespoon of honey could replace up to 2 tablespoons sugar. (Calories lost: up to 253.) See notes on the previous recipe for **fat** and **cholesterol** levels and for **gluten-free** pastry. (Calories lost: up to 1229.) Wholemeal flour makes delicious pastry for a **wholefood** diet. The dough may need slightly more water than when refined flour is used.

Freezing: ✓ up to 3 months if unbaked, 6 months if baked.

APPLE AND ALMOND PARADISE PUDDING

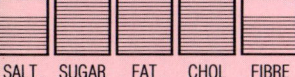

| SALT | SUGAR | FAT | CHOL | FIBRE |

GLUTEN-FREE   WHOLEFOOD*
TOTAL CALORIES: ABOUT 2081

For low **sugar**, use 1 tablespoon honey to sweeten the rice. Choose eating apples rather than cookers and poach them in half the amount of water, not in syrup; sweeten with 1 tablespoon of honey. Use apricot jam made without added sugar for the base of the pudding. One tablespoon of sugar will be enough for the topping. (Calories lost: up to 486.)

Reduce **fat** and **cholesterol** to low by substituting skim milk or soya milk; use quark or smetana instead of double cream. (Calories lost: up to 391.)

Using brown rice will make this **wholefood:** cook it in twice its volume of water for 30 minutes; or use millet, cooked as white rice.

APPLE AND ALMOND PARADISE PUDDING

The combination of creamed rice, fruit and crisp topping makes this pudding a great favourite with children. Pears or other autumn fruit can be used instead of apples.

PREPARATION TIME: *30 min*
COOKING TIME: *35 min*
INGREDIENTS *(for 4):*
2 oz (50 g) long grain or pudding rice
¾ pint (425 ml) milk
¼ teaspoon vanilla essence
4–5 oz (100–150 g) caster sugar
1½ lb (700 g) cooking apples
3 fluid oz (75 ml) double cream
3–4 rounded tablespoons apricot jam
TOPPING:
1 large egg white
2 level tablespoons ground almonds
2 level tablespoons caster sugar
2 tablespoons flaked almonds

Put the rice and milk in a heavy-based saucepan and bring slowly to simmering point. Cover with a lid, and cook over low heat for about 25 minutes or until the rice is cooked, but still slightly nutty in texture (pudding rice needs only about 15 minutes). Stir frequently during cooking to prevent sticking. Sweeten the rice to taste with vanilla essence and a little sugar. Leave to cool.

Peel, core and slice the apples. Put 4 oz (100 g) of sugar with ½ pint (300 ml) of water in a saucepan over low heat and stir until all the sugar has dissolved. Bring this syrup to simmering point, then add the apple slices. Cook gently for 5 minutes or until just tender and retaining their shape. Lift the slices carefully into a colander to drain and cool.

Whip the cream lightly and fold it into the cooled rice. Spread the apricot jam over the base of a shallow, 7 in (18 cm) wide oven-proof dish or pie plate. Cover the jam with apple slices and spoon over creamed rice.

Beat the egg white for the topping until stiff. Mix together the ground almonds and caster sugar and fold in the egg white. Spoon this mixture over the rice and scatter the flaked almonds on top. Put the dish under a hot grill for a few minutes until the almonds are crisp and golden. Serve at once.

APPLE-RUM MERINGUE

Meringue is a favourite topping for many sweets. In this recipe, it covers tart cooking apples over rum-soaked ratafia biscuits. Macaroons or sponge fingers may be used instead of ratafias.

PREPARATION TIME: *30 min*
COOKING TIME: *15 min*
INGREDIENTS (*for 6*):
4 oz (100 g) ratafia biscuits
4 tablespoons white rum
1½ lb (700 g) cooking apples
1 oz (25 g) unsalted butter
½ level teaspoon cinnamon
4 oz (100 g) soft brown sugar
3 egg whites
¼ level teaspoon salt★
3 oz (75g) granulated sugar
3 oz (75 g) caster sugar

Cover the base of a china flan dish with the ratafias, and pour the rum over them. Peel, core and thinly slice the apples into a saucepan; add the butter, cinnamon, brown sugar and 2–3 tablespoons water. Simmer for 10–15 minutes or until the apples are just cooked. Leave to cool, then spoon the apples over the ratafias.

Beat the egg whites with the salt until stiff, but not dry. Stir in the granulated sugar and beat for about 2 minutes or until the meringue mixture is smooth and glossy. Fold in the caster sugar, and immediately spoon the meringue over the apples in the flan dish. Swirl the meringue into soft peaks with a spatula.

Bake the flan for 10–15 minutes, in the centre of an oven pre-heated to 350°F (180°C, mark 4) until the meringue is pale beige. Serve hot or cold with a bowl of cream.

Macaroons

PREPARATION TIME: *10 min*
COOKING TIME: *15 min*
INGREDIENTS (*for 24 biscuits*):
Rice paper
4 oz (100 g) ground almonds
6 oz (175 g) caster sugar
2 egg whites
1 level tablespoon cornflour
¼ teaspoon vanilla essence
12 blanched almonds

Line two or three baking trays with rice paper. Mix the ground almonds with the sugar and add the unbeaten egg whites, setting 1 tablespoon aside. Using a wooden spoon, work the mixture until the ingredients are evenly blended. Stir in the cornflour, vanilla essence and 2 teaspoons of water. Spoon the mixture into a forcing bag fitted with a ½ in (1 cm) plain nozzle. Pipe the biscuits on to the rice paper in large round buttons; top each with half an almond. Brush lightly with the remaining egg white.

Bake the macaroons just above or in the centre of a pre-heated oven, at 375°F (190°C, mark 5), for about 15 minutes or until lightly browned, risen and slightly cracked. Cut the rice paper to fit round each macaroon and leave to cool on a wire rack. This recipe makes double the quantity required for the apple-rum meringue, but the macaroons will keep for a day or two in a tightly closed tin, although they are best if eaten on the day of baking.

APPLE TURNOVERS

These apple turnovers, sold ready-made in most French 'boulangeries', or pastry shops, provide an easily made sweet.

PREPARATION TIME: *25 min*
COOKING TIME: *30 min*
INGREDIENTS (*for 4–6*):
2 large cooking apples
½ oz (10 g) unsalted butter
¼ teaspoon grated lemon rind
2 oz (50 g) caster sugar
1 level tablespoon sultanas
12 oz (350 g) prepared puff pastry
1 egg
Icing sugar

Peel, core and thinly slice the apples. Melt the butter in a saucepan, add the apples and lemon rind. Cover with a lid and cook over low heat until the apples are soft. Beat the apples to a purée, add sugar and sultanas. Set aside until cold.

Roll out the puff pastry ¼ in (½ cm) thick. Using a 3 in (7½ cm) round, fluted pastry cutter, stamp out circles from the pastry; gently roll each circle with a rolling pin to form an oval about ⅙ in (a little under ½ cm) thick. Spoon the apple mixture equally over half of each pastry shape. Brush the edges with beaten egg and fold the pastry over. Press the edges firmly to seal. Slash the top of each pastry with a knife, brush with beaten egg and leave for 15 minutes.

Bake the pastries on wet baking trays, above the centre of an oven pre-heated to 425°F (220°C, mark 7), for 10 minutes. Lower to 375°F (190°C, mark 5) and continue baking until golden brown. Dust with sifted icing sugar and serve warm or cold with cream.

APPLE-RUM MERINGUE

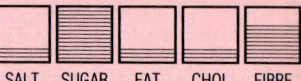

SALT SUGAR FAT CHOL FIBRE

GLUTEN-FREE WHOLEFOOD★
TOTAL CALORIES: ABOUT 1850

For a medium **sugar** level choose eating apples and use honey to sweeten as in the notes on the previous recipes. Make the meringue using only 2–3 oz (50–75 g) sugar. (Calories lost: up to 664.)

MACAROONS

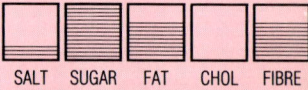

SALT SUGAR FAT CHOL FIBRE

GLUTEN-FREE WHOLEFOOD★
TOTAL CALORIES: ABOUT 1140

Reduce the **sugar** to moderate by using only 4 oz (100 g). The results, though unconventional, will still be very good. (Calories lost: up to 296.)

Freezing: ☑ up to 3 months.

APPLE TURNOVERS

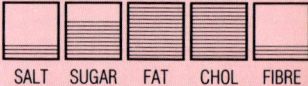

SALT SUGAR FAT CHOL FIBRE

TOTAL CALORIES: ABOUT 4332

The **sugar** can be reduced to very low by substituting a tablespoon of honey for the caster sugar and using eating apples; instead of dusting the finished pastries with icing sugar, brush with a little apple juice concentrate or apricot jam made without added sugar. For extra sweetness use up to one extra tablespoon sultanas. (Calories lost: up to 225.)

The problem with both **fat** and **cholesterol** is mainly in the puff pastry – the butter content in the apple mixture could be omitted but is hardly enough to worry about, and the whole egg can be replaced with just white of egg. But puff pastry needs a large quantity of fat, for which there is no substitute. An alternative is the strudel dough in the next recipe. (Calories lost: up to 2530.)

Freezing: ☑ up to 3 months if unbaked, 6 months if baked.

APPLE AND NUT STRUDEL

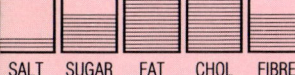

SALT	SUGAR	FAT	CHOL	FIBRE

WHOLEFOOD*
TOTAL CALORIES: ABOUT 2522

The **sugar** content can be reduced to fairly low by using a tablespoon of honey instead of the sugar and eating apples instead of cookers. (Calories lost: up to 166.)
Fat levels can be reduced to low by using only 1 tablespoon of oil for making the dough and a further tablespoon – or ½ oz (15 g) butter – for brushing it. Toast the breadcrumbs in the oven and mix with 2 oz (50 g) ricotta or cottage cheese. (Calories lost: up to 549.)
Cholesterol can be reduced by reducing fat as above, or eliminated by using oil and vegetable margarine.
Strudel dough can never be **gluten-free** as gluten is needed to give it its characteristic stretch; but a **wholefood** version using strong wholemeal flour is excellent.

Freezing: ☑ up to 3 months if unbaked, 6 months if baked.

APPLE AND NUT STRUDEL

Austria, and particularly Vienna, is renowned for its rich pastries and cakes. Among them all, the strudel recipe is probably the most popular. This famous pastry should be almost transparent, or as the Austrians say, 'thin enough to read your love letters through'.

PREPARATION TIME: *1 hour*
COOKING TIME: *40 min*
INGREDIENTS *(for 6):*
4 oz (100 g) plain flour
2½ tablespoons vegetable oil
Flour for rolling out
Oil for brushing
2 oz (50 g) unsalted butter
FILLING:
2 oz (50 g) unsalted butter
3 oz (75 g) fresh breadcrumbs
2 oz (50 g) hazel nuts or walnuts
1 lb (450 g) cooking apples
1 level teaspoon ground cinnamon
2 oz (50 g) caster sugar
2 oz (50 g) sultanas
Grated rind of half lemon

Sift the flour into a warmed bowl; make a well in the centre and stir in the vegetable oil mixed with 2½ tablespoons warm water. Work the mixture into a soft dough, adding more warm water as required. Knead the dough thoroughly on a lightly floured surface, then roll it into a long sausage shape. Pick up the strudel dough by one end and hit it against the pastry board. Repeat this lifting and hitting process, picking it up by alternate ends, for about 10 minutes or until bubbles appear under the surface of the dough.

Knead the elastic strudel dough into a ball and leave it to

rest on a plate for 30 minutes under an inverted, warm bowl.

Meanwhile, heat the butter for the filling, and gently fry the breadcrumbs until golden. Chop the nuts roughly. Peel, core and roughly chop the apples.

Spread a large, clean tea towel over the table top and sprinkle it evenly with flour. Roll out the strudel dough on the cloth, as thinly as possible, and brush it with a little warm oil to keep it pliable. Place the hands under dough and stretch it over the backs of the hands by pulling them away from each other until the dough is paper-thin. Work on one area at a time, until all the dough is nearly transparent.

When the dough is thin enough, trim off the uneven edges with a sharp knife or scissors. Melt the remaining butter; brush it over all the dough; spread the fried breadcrumbs on top. Cover these with the chopped apples to within 2 in (5 cm) of the edges. Mix the cinnamon and sugar, and sprinkle over the apples, together with the chopped nuts, sultanas and grated lemon rind. Fold the lower edge of the dough over the filling, then lift the edge of the cloth and roll the strudel up like a Swiss roll. Seal the join with water, and tuck under the ends.

Lift the strudel and roll it off the cloth on to a greased baking tray, with the join underneath. Curve the strudel into a horseshoe shape and brush the top with the remaining melted butter. Bake in the centre of a pre-heated oven, at 425°F (220°C, mark 7), for 10 minutes, then lower the heat to 400°F (200°C, mark 6) for about 30 minutes or until golden brown.

Serve the strudel hot or cold, dredged with sifted icing sugar.

Fruit-based Desserts

![Apple Crumble in a white oval baking dish on a yellow cloth]

APPLE CRUMBLE

A simple but well-loved and always popular sweet. The crisp and crunchy topping contrasts with the soft apple filling.

PREPARATION TIME: *25 min*
COOKING TIME: *45 min*
INGREDIENTS *(for 4–6):*
1½ lb (700 g) cooking apples
1 oz (25 g) caster sugar
Grated rind of half lemon
TOPPING:
6 oz (175 g) plain flour
3 oz (75 g) margarine
2 oz (50g) caster sugar
½ oz (10 g) Demerara sugar

Peel, core and slice the apples thinly. Put them, sprinkled with sugar, into a 3 pint (1¾ litres) pie dish; top with lemon rind.

For the topping, sift the flour into a mixing bowl, cut up the margarine and rub it lightly into the flour with the tips of the fingers. Mix in the caster sugar. Spoon the crumble mixture over the apples and press it down lightly. Sprinkle the Demerara sugar on top. Place the dish on a baking tray and bake in the centre of the oven at 400°F (200°C, mark 6) for 45 minutes.

Wholefood topping
Use wholemeal flour, and 1 oz (25 g) soft light brown sugar mixed with ½ oz (10–15 g) Demerara sugar. This makes a wonderfully satisfying, nutty-flavoured topping which will be preferred by many people who are not necessarily wholefood addicts themselves. Another excellent addition is 2 tablespoons of sesame seeds. This is the topping shown in the picture.

Ground almonds can be used instead of some or all of the sugar, with a little butter.

APPLE CRUMBLE

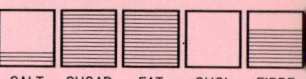

SALT	SUGAR	FAT	CHOL	FIBRE

GLUTEN-FREE* WHOLEFOOD*
TOTAL CALORIES: ABOUT 1755

For low **sugar** level use eating apples, half the sugar used to sweeten, and ground almonds in place of sugar in the topping. (Calories lost: up to 129.)
The **wholefood** topping is also very low in **fat**. (Calories lost: up to 203.)
Millet flakes make a good **gluten-free** alternative to flour in the topping.

Freezing: ✓ up to 3 months.
Microwave: ✓ except for browning the top.

CHEESY APPLE PIE

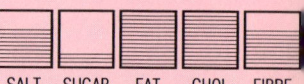

SALT	SUGAR	FAT	CHOL	FIBRE

GLUTEN-FREE* WHOLEFOOD*
TOTAL CALORIES: ABOUT 2436

The **salt** content comes from the cheese, which is essential. The **sugar** can be reduced still further by using eating apples and no added sugar, or perhaps a little honey or apple juice concentrate. (Calories lost: up to 77.)
To reduce the **fat** to low, use a scone dough (page 70) or the very low-fat pastry on page 23. Use reduced-fat Cheddar, or substitute Edam. This will also reduce **cholesterol** to low, especially if you glaze with skim milk. (Calories lost: up to 890.) See page 10 for a **gluten-free** pastry.

Freezing: ✓ up to 3 months if unbaked, 6 months if baked.

APRICOT SORBET

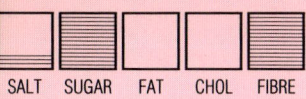

SALT SUGAR FAT CHOL FIBRE

GLUTEN-FREE WHOLEFOOD*
TOTAL CALORIES: ABOUT 2652

The very high **sugar** content of this recipe can easily be reduced to low: as dried apricots have quite a lot of sweetness, there is no need to poach them in a sugar syrup. Instead, use 12 fluid oz (350 ml) water and 2 tablespoons of apple juice concentrate. (Calories lost: up to 1761.)
Wholefood: if you are using sugar, it is important to crush it as finely as possible.

Food processor: ✓ to purée the apricots.

Freezing: ✓ up to 6 months.

BRANDY APRICOT TRIFLE

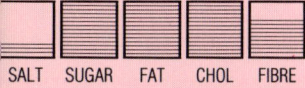

SALT SUGAR FAT CHOL FIBRE

GLUTEN-FREE WHOLEFOOD
TOTAL CALORIES: ABOUT 2437

To reduce the **sugar** to moderate, use a tablespoon of apple juice concentrate to sweeten the liquid in which the apricots cook, and use the honey ratafias on page 55. (Calories lost: up to 191.)
For low levels of both **fat** and **cholesterol**, use the low-fat custard recipe suggested on pages 32–33. Omit the whipped cream or substitute a low-fat curd cheese, beaten with 2–4 tablespoons apricot jam, preferably made without added sugar. (Calories lost: up to 494.)

CHEESY APPLE PIE

In Yorkshire, housewives by custom serve chunks of cheese with apple pie. This pie is a variation on that theme; the cheesy taste is more prominent if the apples are slightly sour.

PREPARATION TIME: *30 min*
COOKING TIME: *35–40 min*
INGREDIENTS *(for 4–6):*
8 oz (225 g) plain flour
*½ level teaspoon salt**
4 oz (100 g) unsalted butter
4 oz (100 g) Lancashire or Cheddar cheese
2 lb (900 g) cooking apples
1 level tablespoon sugar
1 egg
1–2 tablespoons milk

Sift the flour and salt into a mixing bowl. Cut the butter into small knobs and rub them into the flour until the pastry mixture is crumbly. Grate the cheese, blend it into the flour and knead the pastry to a stiff dough with a little cold water. Divide the pastry in half, roll out one half on a floured surface and use to line a 7 in (18 cm) pie plate. Peel, core and slice the apples. Pile them over the pastry and sprinkle with the sugar.

Roll out the remaining pastry; moisten the edge of the lining and cover the pie with pastry. Press the edges well down to seal, and use the trimmings to decorate the pie. Make an air vent in the centre. Beat the egg lightly with 1–2 tablespoons of milk and brush over the pie to give it a glaze. Bake for 35–40 minutes in the centre of the oven pre-heated to 425°F (220°C, mark 7).

Serve the pie cold.

APRICOT SORBET

A tart, beautifully flavoured sorbet is a perfect dessert after a heavy meal.

PREPARATION TIME: *2½ hours*
FREEZING TIME: *2 hours*
INGREDIENTS *(for 6):*
1 lb (450 g) dried apricots
1 lb (450 g) sugar
2 tablespoons cognac, apricot liqueur, or kirsch

Cover the apricots in warm water and soak for 2 hours. Drain. Cook the sugar in 8 fluid oz (225 ml) water until the mixture boils; boil for 10 minutes. Add the apricots and cook an additional 10 minutes. Put the apricots and the liquid through a food mill or purée them in a blender. Add the cognac, apricot liqueur, or the kirsch.

Pour the mixture into freezer trays and place in the freezer compartment of the refrigerator. When the mixture has become partially frozen, remove it from the refrigerator and turn into a chilled bowl. Beat thoroughly with a whisk or heavy fork. The mixture should be almost thin enough to pour; if it is too thick, whisk in a little ice water. Return the mixture to the trays. Put in the freezer until firm but not hard, or freeze packed with ice and coarse salt in a crank freezer until the mixture is frozen but still soft.

BRANDY APRICOT TRIFLE

Fresh apricots form the basis of this rich dessert, suitable for a dinner party.

PREPARATION TIME: *20 min*
COOKING TIME: *30 min*
CHILLING TIME: *2 hours*
INGREDIENTS *(for 4–6):*
1 lb (450 g) fresh apricots
1 pint (570 ml) custard (page 83)
¼ pint (150 ml) white wine
2 oz (50 g) sugar
3 fluid oz (75 ml) brandy
8 oz (225 g) ratafia biscuits
¼ pint (150 ml) double cream

Prepare the custard and set aside to cool. Wash and dry the apricots, cut them in halves and remove the stones. Put the wine and sugar in a pan and bring slowly to the boil. When the sugar has dissolved, add the apricot halves and cook them in this syrup, over low heat, until softened; set aside to cool.

Put the apricots in a trifle or serving dish and pour over the syrup and brandy. Set aside 6–8 ratafia biscuits for decoration and crush the remainder with a rolling pin. Sprinkle them over the apricots and brandy, stirring carefully to let the biscuits absorb the liquid. Spoon the custard, which should now be almost at setting point, over the apricots and chill the trifle in the refrigerator for about 2 hours.

Just before serving, whip the cream until stiff and pipe it in swirls over the trifle. Decorate the top with the remaining ratafias.

CROÛTES AUX ABRICOTS

A croûte is a classic French garnish of bread. For a dessert, the croûtes should be sweet bread, and brioches (page 69) are the most suitable. Slices of currant bread or milk loaf can also be used.

PREPARATION TIME: *10 min*
COOKING TIME: *20 min*
INGREDIENTS *(for 6):*
12 ripe apricots
6 oz (175 g) sugar
3 brioches
6–8 oz (175–225 g) clarified butter
¼ pint (150 ml) double cream
1 liqueur glass kirsch (optional)
GARNISH:
Angelica

Cut the apricots in half and remove the stones. Bring the sugar and 2 tablespoons of cold water to the boil in a saucepan, then add the apricots and poach them gently for 6–8 minutes; they should be tender and retain their shape. Carefully lift out the apricots and keep them warm. Turn up the heat and boil the syrup rapidly until it has reduced to a thick syrup. Do not allow it to caramelise. Let the syrup cool.

Trim the crusts from the brioches or bread and cut into six slices, ½ in (1 cm) thick; fry them in clarified butter (page 99) on both sides until golden brown. Keep warm. Whip the cream lightly and flavour it to taste with the apricot syrup and kirsch.

To serve, arrange the fried bread on a dish and put four apricot halves on each slice. Top with a swirl of cream and garnish with finely chopped angelica.

POACHED APRICOTS

Apricots, like other fruit with a strongly characteristic taste, do not need elaborate cooking to show them at their best. This very simple recipe is an excellent way of presenting early apricots which are perhaps not quite ripe and sweet enough to eat raw. The cinnamon goes particularly well with apricots.

PREPARATION TIME: *10 min*
COOKING TIME: *15 min*
INGREDIENTS *(for 4):*
1 lb (450 g) fresh apricots
3–4 oz (75–100 g) granulated sugar
Lemon rind or cinnamon stick

Wash and dry the apricots. Put the sugar with ½ pint (300 ml) of water and thinly pared lemon rind or cinnamon in a saucepan and place over low heat until the sugar has dissolved. Bring to the boil and cook for 2 minutes. Strain this syrup through a sieve.

Cut the apricots in half with a small sharp knife. Twist the two halves to separate. Discard the stones. Return the syrup to the pan, place the apricot halves, rounded side down, in the syrup and bring slowly to the boil. Reduce the heat, cover and simmer gently until the fruit is tender, about 15 minutes. Leave to cool.

Cook plums or greengages in a similar way; they cook more quickly and should be poached for 10 minutes only.

CROÛTES AUX ABRICOTS

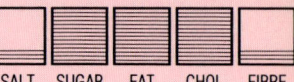

SALT	SUGAR	FAT	CHOL	FIBRE

TOTAL CALORIES: ABOUT 3711

Reduce **sugar** to moderate by using only 1–2 oz (25–50 g) with 1–2 tablespoons of honey for the syrup; omit the angelica. (Calories lost: up to 423.)
Both **fat** and **cholesterol** can be reduced to low if the bread is baked or toasted rather than fried, and smetana or low-fat thick yogurt is used instead of the whipped cream. Or, use apple purée sweetened with the apricot syrup for a sauce. (Calories lost: up to 2480.)
Gluten-free brioche dough is not successful; use an ordinary gluten-free bread.
Wholefood: as well as using wholemeal bread, omit the angelica.

POACHED APRICOTS

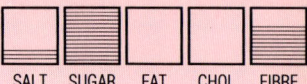

SALT	SUGAR	FAT	CHOL	FIBRE

GLUTEN-FREE   WHOLEFOOD*
TOTAL CALORIES: ABOUT 507

To reduce the **sugar** to moderate, use only 1 oz (25 g) and substitute apple or grape juice for the water. Dried apricots will be sweeter than fresh ones and can be successfully used instead. Soak them for an hour or two beforehand. Using dried apricots will increase the salt content slightly. (Calories lost: up to 187.)

Microwave: ✓ for poaching the apricots.

AVOCADO FOOL

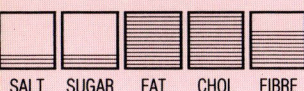

SALT	SUGAR	FAT	CHOL	FIBRE

GLUTEN-FREE WHOLEFOOD *
TOTAL CALORIES: ABOUT 1345

Although avocado pears are very high in **fat**, both this and the **cholesterol** can be reduced to low if the cream is replaced with low-fat curd cheese such as quark or fromage blanc, or with low-fat thick yogurt. (Calories lost: up to 395.)
The oatcakes on page 55 make a very good alternative to sponge fingers and are both low-fat and low-sugar.

Food processor: ☑ for blending to a smooth purée.

BANANA AND RHUBARB COMPÔTE

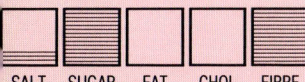

SALT	SUGAR	FAT	CHOL	FIBRE

GLUTEN-FREE WHOLEFOOD *
TOTAL CALORIES: ABOUT 946

This only needs a reduction in the **sugar** level to be a very healthy dessert. The amount of sugar given here makes it very sweet indeed, as bananas are naturally sweet. Try using only 2 oz (50 g) sugar or 2 tablespoons of honey, with a teaspoon or two of apple juice concentrate if you like the taste. You could replace up to half the rhubarb with chopped dried dates for extra sweetness: they go well with the rhubarb and bananas. (Calories lost: up to 369.)

AVOCADO FOOL

The origin of the word 'fool' to describe a purée of pressed fruit mixed with cream or custard goes back to the 16th century. It was a synonym for a trifling thing – of small consequence. This avocado fool is an unusual, refreshing sweet, best flavoured with lime.

PREPARATION TIME: *20 min*
CHILLING TIME: *2 hours*
INGREDIENTS *(for 6):*
3 large avocado pears
2 limes or 1 large lemon
1 rounded tablespoon icing sugar
4 fluid oz (100 ml) double cream

Peel the avocado pears and remove the stones. Dice the avocado flesh finely. Cut a thin slice from the middle of one lime or the lemon and divide the slice into six small wedges; set aside. Squeeze the juice from the fruit and put it into a liquidiser, together with the icing sugar.

After 30 seconds add the diced avocado and liquidise until the mixture has become a smooth purée. Whip the cream and fold it into the purée, adding more sugar and fruit juice to taste.

Spoon the avocado fool into six individual glasses and chill in the refrigerator for at least 2 hours. Garnish with the reserved lime or lemon wedges, and serve with sponge fingers.

BANANA AND RHUBARB COMPÔTE

Pink tender rhubarb is readily available early in the year. It should be cooked slowly to keep its shape for a compôte.

PREPARATION TIME: *15 min*
COOKING TIME: *35 min*
CHILLING TIME: 2 hours
INGREDIENTS *(for 4):*
1 lb (450 g) rhubarb
6 oz (175 g) sugar
Juice of an orange
1 lb (450 g) bananas

Trim tops and bottoms off the rhubarb, wash the stalks and cut them into 1 in (2½ cm) lengths.

Place in a casserole or ovenproof dish and add the sugar and strained orange juice. Stir to blend the ingredients thoroughly, and cover with a lid. Bake for 35 minutes in the centre of the oven pre-heated to 325°F (170°C, mark 3). Remove from the oven and leave the casserole to stand, covered, for 5–10 minutes.

Peel and thinly slice the bananas into a serving dish. Pour over the hot rhubarb and the juices. Cool and then chill in the refrigerator. A bowl of cream or vanilla ice cream could be served with the compôte.

BERRY LEMON PUDDING

The large cultivated blackberries now available go well with the lemon flavour of this pudding, which can be eaten hot or cold.

PREPARATION TIME: *25 min*
COOKING TIME: *45 min*
INGREDIENTS (*for 4*):
½ lb (225 g) blackberries
1 oz (25 g) unsalted butter
4 oz (100 g) caster sugar
1 lemon
2 eggs
¼ pint (150 ml) milk
1 oz (25 g) plain flour
¼ pint (150 ml) whipping cream

Cream together the butter and 2 tablespoons of the sugar in a mixing bowl. Wash the lemon and finely grate the rind into this mixture; squeeze the juice from the lemon and strain it in as well. Beat thoroughly.

Separate the eggs and beat the milk into the yolks. Add this little by little to the creamed mixture, alternately with the sifted flour and remaining sugar, beating until the mixture is thoroughly blended. Whisk the egg whites until stiff, but still moist, and fold them into the lemon mixture.

Hull the blackberries, setting a few large ones aside for decoration. Put the remaining berries in the base of a 1 pint (600 ml) soufflé dish. Pour the creamed mixture over the berries and set the dish in a roasting tin containing 1 in (2½ cm) of hot water. Bake the pudding in an oven pre-heated to 375°F (190°C, mark 5) for 40–45 minutes or until the top is golden brown and set. Test by pressing the top with a finger – the pudding is cooked if it leaves no imprint.

The top of the pudding will have set to a sponge-like mixture over a creamy lemon sauce covering the berries. If the pudding is served hot, sprinkle it generously with caster sugar and decorate with the remaining berries. Offer a bowl of whipped cream separately. For a cold dessert, pipe whipped cream over the top and garnish with the blackberries.

BLACKBERRY SWISS CHARLOTTE

The classic charlotte, which probably originated in France, is a cold dessert of cooked fruit, set in a mould of sponge fingers. In this version, cultivated blackberries are used, but autumn raspberries or loganberries are equally suitable. The Swiss meringue topping is crisp on top with a soft marshmallow texture underneath.

PREPARATION TIME: *40 min*
COOKING TIME: *25 min*
INGREDIENTS (*for 4–6*):
1 lb (450 g) cultivated
  blackberries
4 oz (100 g) caster sugar
1 tablespoon cornflour
2 small egg yolks
2½ fluid oz (65 ml) double cream
Lemon juice
4 oz (100 g) sponge fingers
MERINGUE TOPPING:
2 small egg whites
4 oz (100 g) icing sugar
2½ fluid oz (65 ml) blackberry
  syrup

Hull the blackberries and set aside a dozen large berries for decoration. Put the caster sugar and ½ pint (300 ml) of water in a pan over low heat until the sugar has dissolved to a syrup. Add the blackberries to the syrup and cook over very low heat for 10 minutes, or until tender but still whole. Drain the syrup into a measuring jug, and set the black-berries aside.

Put the cornflour into a small pan and gradually blend in ½ pint (300 ml) of the blackberry syrup; cook over low heat for 3–4 minutes, stirring constantly, until the mixture is clear and beginning to thicken. Remove from the heat.

Separate the eggs, setting the whites aside for the meringue. Beat together the yolks and cream and gradually stir this into the thick syrup mixture. Sharpen and sweeten to taste with lemon juice and caster sugar.

Cut a rounded end off each of the sponge fingers. Put a ½ in (1 cm) layer of the blackberry cream in the base of a 1 pint (600 ml) soufflé dish. Stand the sponge fingers, cut edge downwards, closely round the inside of the dish to make a casing. Put a single layer of blackberries over the cream, followed by another layer of cream and soon, finishing with a layer of blackberry cream.

For the meringue topping, put the egg whites in a mixing bowl with the icing sugar and blackberry syrup. Place the bowl over a pan of boiling water and whisk the mixture steadily until it stands in soft peaks. Remove the bowl from the pan and continue whisking until the meringue is cool. Swirl or pipe it over the blackberry cream.

Bake the charlotte in the centre of a pre-heated oven at 300°F (160°C, mark 2) for 20 minutes or until the meringue is delicately coloured. Serve the dessert cold, decorated with the reserved fresh blackberries.

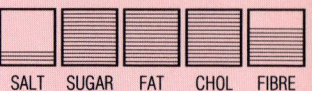

BERRY LEMON PUDDING

SALT · SUGAR · FAT · CHOL · FIBRE

GLUTEN-FREE*   WHOLEFOOD*
TOTAL CALORIES: ABOUT 1511

Reduce **sugar** to moderate by using only the 2 tablespoons that are creamed with the butter. Replace the rest of the sugar with 2 tablespoons honey. Using soya milk will give it a little extra sweetness. (Calories lost: up to 196.)
For moderate **fat** and **cholesterol**, use half the butter and only 1 egg yolk. Use skim milk or soya milk. (Calories lost: up to 255.) The cholesterol can be still further reduced by using vegetable margarine or oil instead of butter.
Cornflour is a suitable **gluten-free** flour to use here.

BLACKBERRY SWISS CHARLOTTE

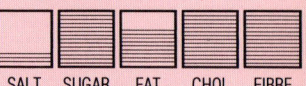

SALT · SUGAR · FAT · CHOL · FIBRE

TOTAL CALORIES: ABOUT 2077

For moderate **sugar**, use 1 tablespoon honey for the syrup and replace the water with apple juice. The meringue topping can be made quite successfully with half the quantity of sugar and syrup and could even be omitted altogether. (Calories lost: up to 443.)
For low **fat** and **cholesterol**, make the blackberry cream using only 1 egg yolk and skim milk (or soya milk, which will give a slightly creamy texture) instead of cream. If you are omitting the meringue topping and don't want a leftover egg

white, use one whole egg in order to thicken the cream. (Calories lost: up to 375.) The honey ratafias on page 55 make a good **gluten-free** and **wholefood** alternative to sponge fingers.

BLACK CURRANT AND MINT PIE

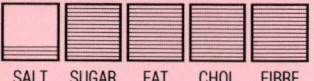

SALT	SUGAR	FAT	CHOL	FIBRE

GLUTEN-FREE*   WHOLEFOOD*
TOTAL CALORIES: ABOUT 2124

Half the amount of **sugar** will give a moderate sugar level and should be quite enough to sweeten the fruit, but you could also add 2–3 tablespoons of finely chopped dates. (Calories lost: up to 73.)
For a very low-**fat** pastry, see page 23; for low **cholesterol** and **gluten-free** alternatives to standard shortcrust, see notes on page 10.

Freezing: ☑ up to 6 months.

BLACK CURRANT AND MINT PIE

Fresh black currants are best when in season, but at any time of year whole frozen black currants can be used for this sharp, refreshing sweet.

Blueberries can be used in exactly the same way, but in this case you should omit the chopped mint.

PREPARATION TIME: *30 min*
COOKING TIME: *35–40 min*
INGREDIENTS *(for 6):*
1 lb (450 g) black currants
1 tablespoon chopped mint
4 oz (100 g) caster sugar
8 oz (225 g) shortcrust pastry
(page 85)

Top and tail the black currants and wash them in a colander, dipping it into several lots of cold water. Drain the black currants thoroughly and put them in a shallow, 7 in (18 cm) wide pie dish. Mix the finely chopped mint with the sugar and sprinkle it evenly over the black currants.

Roll out the prepared short-crust pastry on a floured surface, to a thickness of about ¼ in (½ cm). Cover the pie dish with the pastry and decorate with pastry leaves or flowers from the trimmings (pages 87 and 88).

Make a slit in the centre of the pastry for the steam to escape. Brush the surface lightly with water and sprinkle over a little extra caster sugar.

Bake the pie on the middle shelf of an oven pre-heated to 400°F (200°C, mark 6) for 35–40 minutes or until golden.

Serve the pie cold, with a jug of fresh cream or with vanilla or maple ice cream.

BLACK CURRANT BRÛLÉE

This can be made with other fruits: blueberries and cherries (stoned) are particularly successful. A tablespoon or two of liqueur can be added to the fruit if you like: crème de cassis is the obvious choice for black currants, kirsch for cherries.

PREPARATION TIME: *12 min*
COOKING TIME: *8–10 min*
INGREDIENTS *(for 4):*
½ lb (225 g) stripped black currants
3 oz (75 g) Demerara sugar
1½ level teaspoons arrowroot
¼ pint (150 ml) soured cream
Light soft brown sugar
Ground cinnamon

Simmer the stripped black currants in 4 tablespoons of water until tender; add the Demerara sugar, bring to the boil and simmer for a few more minutes. Blend the arrowroot with 1 tablespoon of water, stir it into the currants and boil gently, stirring all the time, for 1–2 minutes.

Cool the black currant mixture before spooning it into four small flameproof dishes. When it is quite cold, top the fruit with soured cream and cover with a thin layer of brown sugar mixed with a pinch of ground cinnamon. Put in the refrigerator for an hour or two to chill. Set the dishes under a hot grill for a minute or two until the sugar bubbles and caramelises. There should be a delicious contrast between the crunchy hot topping and the cool, refreshingly fruity base.

BLACK CURRANT SORBET

The taste of black currants is exceptionally refreshing in a sorbet or water ice. Blueberries can be used instead; both black currants and blueberries give a wonderful colour to the ice.

PREPARATION TIME: *30 min*
FREEZING TIME: *3–4 hours*
INGREDIENTS *(for 6):*
½ pint (300 ml) water
4 oz (100 g) caster sugar
½ lb (225 g) fresh or frozen black currants
1 teaspoon lemon juice
2 egg whites

Put the water in a saucepan together with the sugar. Heat over low heat until the sugar has dissolved, then bring to the boil and boil gently for 10 minutes. Set aside to cool.

Meanwhile, strip and wash the fresh black currants if you are using them. Put the fresh or frozen currants, with 2–3 tablespoons of water, in a pan and cook over low heat for 10 minutes. Rub the currants through a sieve and make up the purée with the sugar syrup and extra water to make a total of 1 pint (570 ml). Leave until quite cool. Stir in the lemon juice and pour the mixture into ice cube trays or a shallow freezing container. Place in the freezing compartment or the freezer until nearly firm.

Whisk the egg whites until stiff, but not dry. Turn the frozen mixture into a chilled bowl, break it down thoroughly with a fork, and carefully fold in the egg whites. Return the sorbet mixture to its container and freeze until firm. Take it out of the freezer and put into the refrigerator to soften slightly about half an hour before serving.

CLAFOUTI LIMOUSIN

A clafouti is a sweet pancake batter baked with fresh fruit. In the Limousin province of France, where the pudding originates, it is traditionally made with black cherries.

PREPARATION TIME: *15 min*
COOKING TIME: *30 min*
INGREDIENTS *(for 6):*
1½ lb (700 g) black cherries
3 eggs
3 level tablespoons plain flour
Salt*
5 level tablespoons caster sugar
¾ pint (425 ml) milk
1 tablespoon dark rum (optional)
2–3 level tablespoons unsalted butter

Remove the stalks from the cherries, stone, wash and drain the fruit thoroughly. Beat the eggs in a bowl; blend in the sifted flour and a pinch of salt before adding 3 tablespoons of sugar. Heat the milk until lukewarm and gradually pour it into the egg mixture, stirring continuously. Add the rum if used.

Butter a wide, shallow, fireproof dish thoroughly. Put in the cherries, pour the batter over them and dot with the remaining butter. Bake in the centre of an oven, pre-heated to 425°F (220°C, mark 7) for 25–30 minutes. When the dish is cooked, the cherries will have risen to the top and the batter will have set like a baked custard.

Sprinkle the pudding with the remaining caster sugar and serve lukewarm.

BLACK CURRANT BRÛLÉE

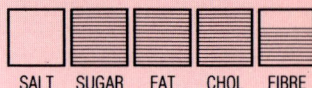

SALT SUGAR FAT CHOL FIBRE

GLUTEN-FREE   WHOLEFOOD
TOTAL CALORIES: ABOUT 813

Black currants do need some added sweetening; however, for low **sugar**, if apple juice is used instead of water (apples and black currants make a good combination) 1 oz (25 g) sugar or 1 tablespoon honey should be enough to sweeten the fruit. (Calories lost: up to 234.) For low **fat** and **cholesterol** substitute smetana for the soured cream. (Calories lost: up to 160.)

BLACK CURRANT SORBET

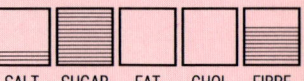

SALT SUGAR FAT CHOL FIBRE

GLUTEN-FREE   WHOLEFOOD
TOTAL CALORIES: ABOUT 487

As with the previous recipe, using apple juice instead of water and only half the quantity of **sugar** should make it quite sweet enough and will reduce the sugar level to moderate. You could also mix the fruit with 2 oz (50 g) dried apricots, cooked and beaten to a thick purée. (Calories lost: up to 89.)

Freezing: √ up to 6 months.

CLAFOUTI LIMOUSIN

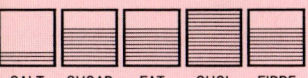

| SALT | SUGAR | FAT | CHOL | FIBRE |

GLUTEN-FREE* WHOLEFOOD*
TOTAL CALORIES: ABOUT 1544

The **sugar** level can be reduced to low quite easily: if soya milk, which is slightly sweet, is used for the batter, it will need no more than 1 tablespoon of sugar to sweeten it and another tablespoon for sprinkling over the top. (Calories lost: up to 177.)

The **fat** and **cholesterol** can be reduced to moderate by omitting one egg yolk, using skim milk (or soya milk) and using no more than ½ oz (10 g) butter for greasing the dish; omit the dotting with butter. For still lower cholesterol, replace the butter with vegetable margarine. (Calories lost: up to 442.)

Soya flour, fine cornmeal or a mixture of the two make good **gluten-free** alternatives to flour for the batter, but the cooking time may be longer. Test after about 25–30 minutes.

FRESH FIGS AND YOGURT

French or Italian purple-skinned figs with sweet red centres are available for a short season during the autumn. This refreshing sweet may evoke memories of the Mediterranean, especially if fig or vine leaves are arranged beneath the dessert glasses.

PREPARATION TIME: *15 min*
CHILLING TIME: *2 hours*
INGREDIENTS *(for 4)*:
8 fresh figs
¼ pint (150 ml) double cream
¼ pint (150 ml) natural yogurt
3–4 level tablespoons soft brown sugar

Put the figs in a large bowl of hot water for 1 minute. Drain them thoroughly, peel off the skins and quarter each fig. Whisk the cream lightly and blend it into the yogurt.

Spoon a little of the cream mixture into four small serving glasses. Top with a layer of figs, followed by more cream and figs and finish with a layer of cream mixture. Sprinkle each layer with brown sugar.

Chill in the refrigerator for at least 2 hours to allow the sugar to melt into the cream.

FIG PIE

In Lancashire, fig pie was traditionally served on Mothering Sunday in March. Also known as Laetare Sunday, this was the only day on which Lenten fasting could be broken.

PREPARATION TIME: *45 min*
COOKING TIME: *35 min*
INGREDIENTS *(for 6)*:
6 oz (175 g) shortcrust pastry (page 85)
½ lb (225 g) figs (fresh or dried)
2 level teaspoons cornflour
½ teaspoon ground mixed spice
1 oz (25 g) currants
2 teaspoons treacle or golden syrup

Roll out the pastry, on a floured surface, to a thickness of ⅛ in (¼ cm). Line a deep 8 in (20 cm) pie plate with the pastry. Cut the stalks off the figs and place the fruit in a shallow saucepan with just enough water to cover them; cook over low heat until tender. Fresh figs need 5–15 minutes, cooking time depending on their ripeness; dried figs should first be soaked for 12 hours with a squeeze of lemon juice before being stewed for 20 minutes in their soaking liquid.

Drain the figs and retain ½ pint (300 ml) of the liquid; top up with hot water if necessary. Pour a little of the juice into a basin, add the cornflour and mix until it resembles a thin smooth cream. Gradually add the rest of the liquid, stirring well. When well mixed, return it to the saucepan and place over moderate heat. Stir until thickened, then cook for another 2 minutes. Mix in the spice, currants and syrup and remove from the heat.

Arrange the figs over the

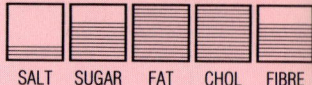
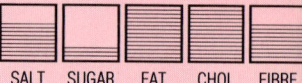

GOOSEBERRY FLAN

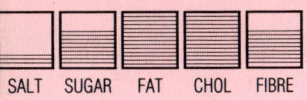

SALT	SUGAR	FAT	CHOL	FIBRE

GLUTEN-FREE * WHOLEFOOD *
TOTAL CALORIES: ABOUT 2404

For a low **sugar** level, choose very ripe, sweet gooseberries. Cook them in apple or grape juice instead of water, and sweeten them with 1–2 tablespoons of honey. (Calories lost: up to 287.)

You can eliminate the eggs and most of the butter, and thus reduce the **fat** and **cholesterol** in the filling to very low, by using tofu. Blend the gooseberry purée with about 11 oz (300 g) silken tofu to a smooth consistency. (Calories lost: up to 663.)

Try replacing 4 oz (100 g) of the gooseberries with the same weight of dried apricots, soaked for 30 minutes. The taste of apricots blends very well with tofu, and you may need a little less added sweetening.

For a very low-**fat** pastry, see this page; for low **cholesterol** and **gluten-free** alternatives to shortcrust, see notes on page 10.

Freezing: ☑ up to 3 months.

GRAPE JELLY

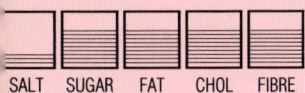

SALT	SUGAR	FAT	CHOL	FIBRE

GLUTEN-FREE WHOLEFOOD *
TOTAL CALORIES: ABOUT 818

To reduce the **sugar** to very low, use 1 tablespoon of honey. (Calories lost: up to 78.)

For low **fat** and **cholesterol**, use smetana or yogurt instead of cream. (Calories lost: up to 240.)

pastry; pour over the thickened fig liquid, making sure that the currants are evenly distributed. Bake the pie on the middle shelf of the oven heated to 400°F (200°C, mark 6) for 30–35 minutes.

Serve hot or cold, with cream or vanilla ice cream.

GOOSEBERRY FLAN

This sweet is based on an English recipe from the 18th century when puréed, wine-flavoured fruits were popular.

PREPARATION TIME: *1 hour*
COOKING TIME: *15 min*
INGREDIENTS *(for 6):*
1½ lb (700 g) gooseberries
4 oz (100 g) plain flour
1 rounded tablespoon icing sugar
5½ oz (155 g) unsalted butter
1 large egg yolk
3 large eggs
Caster sugar
3 teaspoons orange-flower water or 2 tablespoons muscat-flavoured white wine

Sift together the flour and icing sugar into a large bowl. Cut up 2½ oz (70 g) of the butter and rub into the flour until the mixture resembles fine breadcrumbs. Add one egg yolk and sufficient water to bind the pastry.

Roll the pastry out, on a lightly floured surface, to ¼ in (½ cm) thickness and use to line a buttered 7 in (18 cm) wide, loose-bottomed flan tin. Prick the pastry with a fork and bake it blind in the centre of a pre-heated oven, at 350°F (180°C, mark 4) for 15 minutes.

Wash and drain the gooseberries, but do not top and tail the fruit. Put them in a large saucepan with 2½ fluid oz (75 ml) of water.

Cover the pan with a lid and cook over low heat for 10 minutes, then increase the heat and cook until the gooseberries have burst and are soft.

Rub the gooseberries through a sieve and sweeten this purée with caster sugar to taste. Put the purée in a clean pan. Stir over low heat, adding the remaining butter in small pieces. Beat the eggs.

Remove the pan from the heat and stir in the eggs. Return the pan to the heat and cook, stirring continuously, until the purée thickens. It should not be allowed to boil. Cool slightly, then add orange-flower water or wine to taste.

If necessary, re-heat the flan case. Spoon the gooseberry purée into the pastry case and serve it warm, with cream.

Low-fat pastry
This recipe is similar to the wartime recipes evolved when butter was scarce. Although it does not have the same flavour as pastry made with fat, it is quite good if eaten hot. Using skim milk powder gives a slightly better result than using skim milk.

INGREDIENTS
4 oz (100 g) plain flour
4–5 tablespoons skim milk or 2 heaped tablespoons skim milk powder
1½ teaspoons baking powder
Salt ★

Mix all the ingredients together to a smooth dough. If you are using skim milk powder, add just enough water to bind the mixture. Do not try to roll out but press into a flan or tart tin.

GRAPE JELLY

A lovely, cool-looking sweet, this is even easier to make if you can find sweet seedless grapes.

PREPARATION TIME: *40 min*
SETTING TIME: *about 3 hours*
INGREDIENTS *(for 4):*
1¼ lb (550 g) large white grapes
Juice of 2 oranges
Juice of a lemon
2 level tablespoons caster sugar
4 tablespoons water
1½ level teaspoons powdered gelatine
¼ pint (150 ml) single cream

Dissolve the sugar with 2 tablespoons of water in a small pan over low heat, and dissolve the gelatine in a cup with the remaining water. Stir the hot sugar liquid into the gelatine, blend thoroughly and stir it all into the strained fruit juices. The liquid should now measure ½ pint (300 ml); make up with cold water if necessary. Leave to cool until it has gelled to the consistency of unbeaten egg white.

Peel and pip the grapes (page 80); this is easiest done by dipping the whole bunch in boiling water for 30 seconds, then stripping off the skin and extracting the pips from the stalk ends.

Divide the grapes equally between four sundae glasses, and spoon the jelly over them. Leave in the refrigerator until set, and just before serving float a thin layer of cream on top of each or serve the cream separately.

Fruit-based Desserts

GRAPEFRUIT IN BRANDY

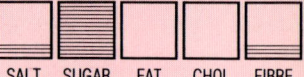

SALT	SUGAR	FAT	CHOL	FIBRE

GLUTEN-FREE   WHOLEFOOD*
TOTAL CALORIES: ABOUT 667

To reduce the **sugar** content to low, poach the grapefruit in water or grape juice to which 2 tablespoons of honey or fruit sugar (fructose) have been added. Pink grapefruits hardly need sweetening. (Calories lost: up to 314.)

Freezing: ☑ up to 6 months.
Microwave: ☑

GREENGAGES WITH APRICOT PURÉE

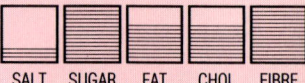

SALT	SUGAR	FAT	CHOL	FIBRE

GLUTEN-FREE*   WHOLEFOOD*
TOTAL CALORIES: ABOUT 1371

For low added **sugar**, use dried apricots: they are very sweet and will make it unnecessary to add sugar to the fruit purée. Use only 1 oz (25 g) vanilla sugar, or 2 tablespoons honey, on top of the greengages. (Calories lost: up to 197.)
To reduce the **fat** and **cholesterol** content, replace the bread-and-butter base under the fruit with a scone dough (see page 70). This should be baked at around 400°F (200°C, mark 6) for the first ten minutes, then continue at 350°F (180°C, mark 4). (Calories lost: up to 325.)
A **gluten-free** alternative to bread could be rice pudding, if the baking dish is well sealed with foil during baking to prevent a crust forming.

GRAPEFRUIT IN BRANDY

The slightly acid flavour of grapefruit is equally refreshing both before and after a rich main course. Slices of grapefruit, poached in syrup and doused with brandy, give a clean taste to the palate.

PREPARATION TIME: *12 min*
COOKING TIME: *8 min*
INGREDIENTS *(for 6):*
4 large grapefruit

4 oz (100 g) caster sugar
1 level teaspoon cinnamon
4 tablespoons brandy

Cut off all the peel and pith from the grapefruit and carefully poke out the pithy core with the little finger. Slice the fruit into ½ in (1 cm) thick rounds. Put the sugar in a large saucepan with ¼ pint (150 ml) cold water and the cinnamon. Cook over low heat, stirring frequently, until the sugar has dissolved, then boil this syrup briskly for 2 minutes. Lower the heat, add the grapefruit slices and poach them gently in the syrup for 6 minutes, turning once.

Arrange the grapefruit slices on a serving dish, pour over the brandy and serve hot or chilled.

Food processor: ✓ for the purée.
Freezing: ✓ up to 4 months for the purée.

QUICHE REINE-CLAUDE

| SALT | SUGAR | FAT | CHOL | FIBRE |

GLUTEN-FREE *   WHOLEFOOD *
TOTAL CALORIES: ABOUT 2637

It is easy to eliminate some of the **sugar** and reduce the level to low. Use the gluten-free pastry on page 10 which tastes sweet but does not include sugar; use greengage (or plum) jam made without added sugar; and try the alternative pastry cream suggested below. (Calories lost: up to 262.) For low **fat** and **cholesterol**, omit the accompanying cream and use the alternative pastry cream given. Use the very low-fat pastry on page 23 or a low-cholesterol one as suggested in the notes on page 10. (Calories lost: up to 726.)

ALTERNATIVE PASTRY CREAM
½ pint (300 ml) milk
2 tablespoons brown sugar
2 tablespoons soya flour
2 tablespoons cornmeal
1 large egg
Heat the milk in a pan over low heat. Blend together the sugar, soya flour, cornmeal and egg; gradually stir in the warm milk. Return the mixture to the pan over low heat and stir continuously until it thickens. Remove from the heat, pour into a bowl and cover with wetted greaseproof paper. Allow to become quite cold.

Freezing: ✓ up to 2 months.

GREENGAGES WITH APRICOT PURÉE

The small, round, golden-yellow greengages make their brief appearance in late summer. They are excellent as dessert fruits, and for puddings.

PREPARATION TIME: *25 min*
COOKING TIME: *30 min*
INGREDIENTS *(for 4)*:
1 lb (450 g) greengages
½ lb (225 g) fresh or 4 oz (100 g) dried apricots
1 oz (25 g) caster sugar
½ teaspoon grated lemon rind
4 slices bread
1½–2 oz (40–50 g) unsalted butter
1–2 oz (25–50 g) vanilla sugar (page 100)

Wash and dry the apricots, cut them in half and remove the stones. Leave dried apricots to soak overnight in cold water.

Put the apricots in a pan, cover with fresh cold water and cook until tender. Drain thoroughly and rub the apricots through a coarse sieve; flavour this purée with sugar and lemon rind.

Wash and dry the greengages, and cut them in half. Remove the stones. Cut the crusts from the bread and spread the slices with half the butter. Lay the slices, buttered side up, in a greased ovenproof dish. Arrange the greengages on top with a tiny knob of butter in each half; sprinkle with the vanilla sugar.

Bake in the centre of the oven, pre-heated to 350°F (180°C, mark 4), for about 30 minutes, or until the greengages are tender.

Serve the greengage pudding warm, and offer the warmed apricot purée separately.

QUICHE REINE-CLAUDE

Lorraine is the land of quiches and Alsace of guiches. Both are names for an open flan with a cream filling combined with sweet or savoury ingredients. This flan is filled with greengages (Reine-Claudes) on a base of crème pâtissière (confectioner's custard).

PREPARATION TIME: *40 min*
COOKING TIME: *30 min*
INGREDIENTS *(for 6)*:

1 flan case
½ lb (225 g) greengages
4 level tablespoons greengage jam
1 tablespoon lemon juice
¼ pint (150 ml) double cream

CRÈME PÂTISSIÈRE:
2 eggs
2 oz (50 g) caster sugar
1 oz (25 g) plain flour
½ pint (300 ml) milk
½ teaspoon vanilla essence or 4 teaspoons lemon juice

Bake or buy a 7 in (18 cm) flan case, made from sweet shortcrust or pâte sucrée pastry. Leave the baked flan to cool completely before assembling the sweet.

Make the crème pâtissière next as this too should not be used until quite cool: put 1 whole egg and 1 egg yolk in a mixing bowl (set aside the remaining egg white). Whisk the sugar with the eggs until creamy and near white, then whisk the sifted flour into the eggs, and gradually add the milk. Pour the mixture into a small saucepan and bring to the boil, whisking continuously.

Simmer this custard-cream over very low heat for 2–3 minutes to cook the flour. Flavour to taste with vanilla essence or lemon juice and pour the cream into a shallow dish to cool. Stir from time to time to prevent a skin forming.

Spread the cold crème pâtissière over the base of the flan case. Cut the greengages in half, remove the stones and arrange the fruit over the cream.

Put the greengage jam in a small, heavy-based pan, with 3 tablespoons of water and the lemon juice. Cook over low heat, stirring until the jam has dissolved and the mixture is clear. Increase the heat and boil rapidly to form a glaze. Do not over-boil— the glaze is ready when it will coat the back of the spoon and falls off in heavy drops. Rub the glaze through a coarse sieve.

Spoon the glaze over the greengages, covering them completely; brush the top edge of the flan with the remaining glaze to give a smooth finish. Set the flan in a cool place until the glaze has set.

Just before serving, whip the remaining egg white until stiff, but still moist. Whip the cream into soft peaks and fold in the white; sweeten to taste with a little sugar and serve in a separate bowl to accompany the quiche.

Fruit-based Desserts

LEMON MOUSSE

When shiny, firm lemons are plentiful and good value, they can be used for a light and refreshing mousse.

PREPARATION TIME: *30 min*
CHILLING TIME: *2 hours*
INGREDIENTS *(for 4)*:
Juice and rind of 2 large lemons
1 level tablespoon powdered
  gelatine
3 eggs
4 oz (100 g) caster sugar
¼ pint (150 ml) double cream
GARNISH:
¼ pint (150 ml) whipping cream

Sprinkle the gelatine over 2 tablespoons of water in a small pan and leave to soak for 5 minutes. Separate the eggs, putting the yolks into a large bowl and the whites into another. Finely grate the rind from the lemons, and mix it into the egg yolks, together with the sugar. Squeeze the lemons and strain the juice into the soaked gelatine. Place the saucepan over low heat, stirring continuously. Do not allow to boil, and immediately the gelatine has dissolved remove the pan from the heat.

Whisk the egg yolks and sugar until pale and creamy. Slowly pour in the dissolved gelatine, whisking all the time. Continue to whisk the mixture until it is cool and beginning to thicken. Lightly beat the double cream and fold into the mixture. Beat the egg whites until stiff, then blend them in evenly and lightly.

Spoon the mousse into a serving dish or individual dishes and chill until set. Serve a bowl of single cream separately or pipe whipped cream over the mousse.

LEMON SYLLABUB

In Elizabethan times, one of the favourite wines in Britain was a still dry wine produced around Sillery in the Champagne district of France. Bub was a slang term for a bubbly drink, and by association syllabub came to describe a drink or sweet made by mixing frothy cream with still wine.

PREPARATION TIME: *20 min*
STANDING TIME: *6 hours*
CHILLING TIME: *3 hours*
INGREDIENTS *(for 6)*:
1 lemon
1½–2 fluid oz (40–50 ml) brandy
3 oz (75 g) caster sugar
½ pint (300 ml) double cream
¼ pint (150 ml) sweet white wine
GARNISH:
Rind of a lemon

Peel the lemon thinly with a potato peeler. Squeeze out the juice and add enough brandy to make the liquid up to 2½ fluid oz (75 ml). Pour the liquid into a small bowl, add the lemon peel and leave to stand for at least 6 hours.

Strain the liquid through a fine sieve and stir in the sugar until it has dissolved completely. Whip the cream until it holds its shape. Mix the wine into the lemon and brandy, then add this liquid to the cream a little at a time, whisking continuously. The cream should absorb all the liquid and still stand in soft peaks. Pile the mixture into individual glasses and chill for several hours.

For the garnish, thinly peel the lemon rind and cut into narrow strips; blanch for 2–3 minutes.

Serve the syllabub with a cluster of drained lemon strips.

GLAZED LEMON TART

The fresh sharp flavour of this tart is welcome after a rich main course. Preparations for the tart, which can also be served as a pastry with morning coffee, should begin a day in advance.

PREPARATION TIME: *1¾ hours*
COOKING TIME: *25–30 min*
INGREDIENTS *(for 6)*:
4 oz (100 g) shortcrust pastry
  (page 85)
1 level tablespoon plain flour
2 oz (50 g) ground almonds
2 oz (50 g) unsalted butter
2 oz (50 g) caster sugar
1 egg
Rind of a lemon
TOPPING:
2 small lemons
1 vanilla pod
8 oz (225 g) caster sugar

Prepare the topping first: scrub the two lemons thoroughly in cold water, then cut them into slices about ⅛ in (¼ cm) thick. Remove the pips carefully and put the slices in a bowl. Cover with boiling water and leave to soak for 8 hours.

Drain the lemon slices, put them in a saucepan and cover with fresh cold water; bring briskly to the boil. Lower the heat, cover the pan with a lid and simmer gently for 1 hour or until the lemon slices are soft. Remove from the heat and let the slices cool in the liquid.

Roll the shortcrust pastry out on a lightly floured surface, to a circle about 9 in (23 cm) across. Line a 7–8 in (18–20 cm) flan tin with the pastry and prick the base lightly with a fork. Bake the tart blind for 5 minutes, then set it aside while preparing the filling.

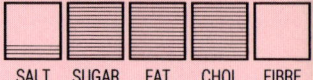
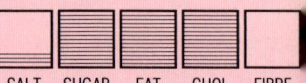

separately and then folding them into the mixture. (Calories lost: up to 641.)

GLAZED LEMON TART

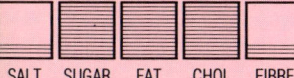

| SALT | SUGAR | FAT | CHOL | FIBRE |

GLUTEN-FREE *   WHOLEFOOD *
TOTAL CALORIES: ABOUT 2547

To reduce the amount of **sugar** in this dish involves changing the topping method completely. The easiest way to achieve this clear topping is to make a fruit juice jelly, using ½ pint (300 ml) of unsweetened, cloudy apple juice. Warm a little of this with 2 scant teaspoons gelatine or 1 of agar agar until completely clear, then mix with the remaining cold juice. Cool, taste, and add a teaspoonful or two of honey or fruit sugar if wished; then, when the jelly is thick in texture, spoon it over the tart. The lemon slices can be replaced with orange ones, poached as suggested, but not cooked in syrup as these are already sweet enough. In the filling use half the sugar. This gives a low sugar level. (Calories lost: up to 785.) The high **fat** level can only be reduced to medium by changing the shortcrust pastry to a scone dough base or using the very low-fat pastry on page 23; the filling cannot be altered substantially, although the **cholesterol** level can be reduced by exchanging some or all of the butter for soft vegetable margarine, and using only the egg white. (Calories lost: up to 502.) The **gluten-free** pastry on page 10 is excellent for this.

Freezing: ✓ up to 3 months.

Mix the flour and ground almonds; beat the butter and sugar until soft and light. Beat the egg lightly and blend in the finely grated lemon rind. Gradually stir the egg into the butter mixture, then add the flour and ground almonds. Spread this mixture evenly over the pastry base. Place the tart just above centre of a pre-heated oven at 375°F (190°C, mark 5) and bake for 25–30 minutes or until the tart has risen and is golden brown and firm to the touch. Remove from the oven and leave to cool.

Drain the liquid from the lemon slices, setting aside ½ pint (300 ml). Add the vanilla pod and the sugar to the lemon liquid and cook in a saucepan over low heat until the sugar has dissolved. Add the lemon slices and simmer gently for about 5 minutes, then carefully lift the soft lemon slices on to a plate. Continue to boil the syrup rapidly until the mixture sets – test by spooning a little on to a saucer. Arrange the lemon slices in a circular pattern over the tart. When the syrup is setting, draw the pan off the heat, remove the vanilla pod, and as soon as the bubbles have subsided, spoon all the syrup over the lemon slices.

Leave the tart to chill in the refrigerator before serving it cold, cut into wedges.

Fruit-based Desserts

LEMON MERINGUE PIE

A classic combination of pastry, tangy smooth lemon cream, and crisp airy meringue.

PREPARATION TIME: *30 min*
COOKING TIME: *40 min*
INGREDIENTS *(for 4–6):*
*4 oz (100 g) shortcrust pastry
    (page 85)
1 large thin-skinned lemon
2–3 level tablespoons granulated
    sugar
2 level tablespoons cornflour
2 eggs
½ oz (10 g) unsalted butter
4 oz (100 g) caster sugar*

Roll out the pastry and line an 8½ in (21 cm) pie plate or a 7 in (18 cm) flan ring. Bake the pastry case blind in the centre of a pre-heated oven, at 400°F (200°C, mark 6) for about 15 minutes or until the pastry is crisp and golden. When cold, remove the pastry from the pie plate or ease away the flan ring.

Meanwhile, peel the rind from the lemon in thin slivers, carefully omitting all white pith.

Squeeze the juice from the lemon and set it aside. Put the lemon peel, granulated sugar and ½ pint (300 ml) of water in a pan; cook over low heat until the sugar has dissolved, then bring this syrup to the boil. Remove the pan from the heat. Blend the cornflour in a bowl with 3 tablespoons lemon juice, then pour in the syrup through a strainer, stirring thoroughly. Separate the eggs, and beat in the egg yolks, one at a time, together with the butter. The mixture should be thick enough to coat the back of a wooden spoon; otherwise return it to the pan and cook for a few minutes without boiling. Spoon the lemon mixture into the cooked pastry case, set on a baking tray.

Whisk the egg whites until stiff, then add half the caster sugar and continue whisking until the meringue holds its shape and stands in soft peaks. Fold in all but 1 teaspoon of the remaining sugar, using a metal spoon.

Pile the meringue over the lemon filling; spread it from the edge towards the centre, making sure that the meringue joins the pastry edge to prevent the meringue 'weeping'. Sprinkle the meringue with the remaining sugar. Reduce the heat to 300°F (150°C, mark 2) and bake the pie in the centre of the oven for 20–30 minutes, or until the meringue is crisp. Serve the pie warm.

COLD LEMON SOUFFLÉ

The clean taste of lemon is particularly good in soufflés. It can be enhanced and given an unusual overtone by adding a few drops of fresh lime juice, if you have it.

PREPARATION TIME: *25 min*
CHILLING TIME: *1–2 hours*
INGREDIENTS *(for 4):*
*2 lemons
3 eggs
3 oz (75 g) caster sugar
2 level teaspoons gelatine
¼ pint (150 ml) double cream*

Grate the rind from the lemons and squeeze out the juice. Separate the eggs, and beat the egg yolks, sugar, lemon rind and juice in a bowl until thick.

In a small bowl, mix the gelatine with 2 tablespoons of cold water and set the bowl in a pan of hot water until the gelatine has dissolved and is clear. Allow the gelatine to cool slightly, then pour it into the lemon mixture. Beat the cream until it just holds its shape, then fold it into the lemon mixture. Whisk the egg whites until stiff and fold them carefully into the mixture when nearly set. Spoon the lemon soufflé into a prepared 6 in (15 cm) or 1½ pint (900 ml) soufflé dish and chill until set.

LEMON MERINGUE PIE

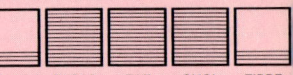

SALT   SUGAR   FAT   CHOL   FIBRE

GLUTEN-FREE*   WHOLEFOOD*
TOTAL CALORIES: ABOUT 1696

The high level of **sugar** added to the meringue topping can be reduced to 1 oz (25 g), reducing the sugar content of this recipe to low. (Calories lost: up to 295.)
The high **fat** content of the pastry cannot be reduced, except by substituting a scone dough or yeast pastry base, or the very low-fat pastry on page 23. However, if wished, 1 egg yolk only can be used in the filling, reducing the **cholesterol**; if you are using the shortcrust pastry base, cholesterol can be reduced to low by substituting vegetable fat, preferably soft margarine. (Calories lost: up to 502.)

Freezing: ☑ up to 2 months if you want to make the pie and filling in advance; the meringue itself does not freeze.

COLD LEMON SOUFFLÉ

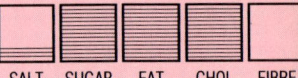

SALT   SUGAR   FAT   CHOL   FIBRE

GLUTEN-FREE   WHOLEFOOD*
TOTAL CALORIES: ABOUT 1263

The high **sugar** content can be reduced by half, to moderate; in this case use only 2 egg yolks. This will also reduce the **cholesterol** level to some extent, but it will still be high. (Calories lost: up to 308.)
To reduce the **fat** and cholesterol levels to low requires a change to the nature of the recipe, mixing 2 oz (50 g

double cream, whipped with 3 tablespoons of low-fat quark or fromage blanc, before folding in first the lemon mixture and then the beaten egg whites. (Calories lost: up to 412.)

Freezing: ☑ up to 2 months.

MELON ICE CREAM

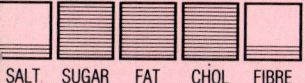

SALT	SUGAR	FAT	CHOL	FIBRE

GLUTEN-FREE   WHOLEFOOD *
TOTAL CALORIES: ABOUT 3004

The high **sugar** level can be reduced to low by finding a very sweet melon, and adding only 1 oz (25 g) sugar or honey to it. (Calories lost: up to 295.) The high **fat** and **cholesterol** level involved in the egg yolks and double cream can only be reduced by changing the nature of the recipe, although the lighter result can be tasty and refreshing. Use only 1 egg yolk added to the pulp, and only ¼ pint (150 ml) double cream, folding in as the recipe suggests. When mixture is mushy, beat smooth and fold in stiffly beaten egg whites. These changes reduce the fat and cholesterol levels to medium. (Calories lost: up to 379.)

Freezing: ☑ up to 3 months.

MELON ICE CREAM

The Italians introduced water ices or sorbets to Britain during the reign of Charles I, at least two centuries before cream ices became known. Today, virtually any sweetened fruit juice can be made into ice cream with egg custard and cream.

PREPARATION TIME: *30–40 min*
CHILLING TIME: *3 hours*
INGREDIENTS *(for 4)*:
1 large Ogen melon
4 oz (100 g) caster sugar
4 egg yolks
5 tablespoons ginger wine
2 tablespoons lemon juice
¾ pint (425 ml) double cream

A few hours before preparing the ice cream, set the refrigerator to its coldest setting.

Slice about 1½ in (4 cm) off the top of the melon; remove the seeds and fibres with a small spoon. Scoop all the melon pulp into a small saucepan, taking care not to pierce the shell. Add the sugar and place the pan over low heat until the sugar has melted into the melon, and the mixture is a soft pulp. Mash with a fork.

Beat the egg yolks until light and creamy, and add them to the melon pulp, stirring well. Continue cooking and whisking over low heat, so that the eggs will not curdle, until the mixture has the consistency of thin cream.

Pour the melon mixture into a bowl and leave it to cool completely. Stir in the ginger wine and lemon juice, mix thoroughly, then fold in the lightly whipped cream. Cover the bowl with foil and chill in the refrigerator for 30 minutes.

Spoon the melon cream into a freezing tray or container, cover with foil or the lid, and freeze for 2–3 hours. Stir the ice cream several times during freezing to prevent crystals forming.

Pile the ice cream into glasses or the chilled melon shell and serve at once. Any surplus ice cream can be stored for several months in the home freezer.

ORANGE SOUFFLÉS

A light fluffy soufflé is a good choice for rounding off a meal. These individual soufflés are baked in orange shells and should be served straight from the oven before they collapse.

PREPARATION TIME: *30 min*
COOKING TIME: *20 min*
INGREDIENTS *(for 4)*:
4 large oranges
1 lemon
1 oz (25 g) unsalted butter
1 oz (25 g) plain flour
1½ oz (40 g) caster sugar
3 eggs
GARNISH:
Icing sugar

Wash the oranges and cut them in half crossways. Take out all the orange flesh and remove the white pith; set the shells aside.

Squeeze the orange flesh to extract all the juice and strain it into a bowl together with the strained juice from the lemon. Melt the butter in a saucepan over low heat, stir in the flour and cook for a few minutes until this roux is lightly coloured. Gradually add the fruit juice, stirring continuously, until the mixture has thickened to a smooth sauce. Bring to the boil, simmer for 1–2 minutes, then take the pan off the heat. Stir in the sugar, and let the sauce cool slightly.

Separate the eggs, and beat one yolk at a time into the sauce, stirring well before adding the next (all these preparations can be made in advance). Whisk the egg whites until stiff, then fold them into the sauce carefully but thoroughly, using a metal spoon.

Fill the orange shells with the soufflé mixture, set them on a baking sheet (or in a tartlet tray to keep them steady). Bake the oranges in a pre-heated oven for 20 minutes at a temperature of 400°F (200°C, mark 6).

Serve the oranges immediately, dusted generously with sifted icing sugar.

FRUITS RAFRAÎCHIS

A fresh-fruit salad is easily prepared from a selection of fruit whose flavours and colours harmonise. Chill the salad for a few hours so that the flavours can develop.

PREPARATION TIME: *30 min*
CHILLING TIME: *2–3 hours*
INGREDIENTS *(for 6)*:
2 oranges
½ lb (225 g) black grapes
½ ripe honeydew melon
2–3 ripe pears
2 bananas
4 oz (100 g) caster sugar
5 fluid oz (150 ml) dry white wine
2 tablespoons kirsch

Choose a deep glass bowl as the serving dish, and arrange the prepared fruit in layers in the bowl.

With a sharp knife, cut a slice from the top and base of each orange, then cut down each orange in strips to remove the peel and all white pith. Ease out each orange segment and peel off the thin skin. Peel and halve the grapes and remove the seeds (page 80). Place in the bowl on top of the oranges and sprinkle with a little of the sugar. Remove the seeds from the melon, cut it in quarters lengthways, cut away the peel and dice the flesh. Add the melon to the bowl with another sprinkling of sugar. Quarter, peel and core the pears, then slice them thinly. Peel the bananas, cut them in half lengthways before dicing them. Put them in the bowl with the remaining sugar.

Mix the fruit carefully, pour over the white wine and the kirsch. As the fruit soaks in the liquid, press it down so that it is covered with juice and less likely to discolour.

Chill in the refrigerator for 2–3 hours. A jug of cream may be served separately.

CANDIED ORANGES GRAND MARNIER

A tangy dinner-party sweet becomes even more attractive to the hostess when it can be prepared the day before. It should be left to chill in the refrigerator.

PREPARATION TIME: *15 min*
COOKING TIME: *45 min*
CHILLING TIME: *2–3 hours*
INGREDIENTS *(for 6)*:
6 oranges
6 oz (175 g) caster sugar
Juice of half lemon
2 tablespoons Grand Marnier

Cut a slice from the top and bottom of each orange, so that it will stand upright. Slice downwards through the orange skin, cutting away the peel and all the white pith, leaving only the orange flesh. Cut the oranges crossways into slices and place them in a serving dish.

Select six of the larger pieces of peel and carefully cut away the pith. Shred the peel finely and put it in a saucepan. Cover with cold water, bring to the boil, then drain – this removes the bitter flavour of the peel. Cover the peel

ORANGE SOUFFLÉS

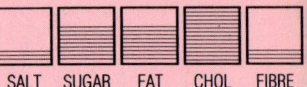

SALT SUGAR FAT CHOL FIBRE

GLUTEN-FREE * WHOLEFOOD *
TOTAL CALORIES: ABOUT 923

The **sugar** can be reduced to 1 tablespoon, a very low level, provided the orange juice is only briefly heated: it tends to go sour if cooked. (Calories lost: up to 99.)
The high **cholesterol** level can be reduced to low by using only 1 egg yolk in the soufflé, with all the whites. The **fat** in the soufflé roux cannot be reduced, but can be rendered cholesterol-free by using vegetable fat, preferably soft margarine. (Calories lost: up to 160.)

FRUITS RAFRAÎCHIS

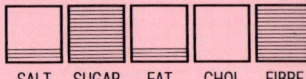

SALT SUGAR FAT CHOL FIBRE

GLUTEN-FREE * WHOLEFOOD *
TOTAL CALORIES: ABOUT 1030

The high added **sugar** level of this recipe can be reduced to nil, provided the fruit chosen is ripe. A small amount of sugar will be added by the kirsch, but too little to worry about. (Calories lost: up to 394.)

Freezing: ☑ if the bananas are omitted (they can be added just before serving).

CANDIED ORANGES GRAND MARNIER

SALT	SUGAR	FAT	CHOL	FIBRE

GLUTEN-FREE   WHOLEFOOD*
TOTAL CALORIES: ABOUT 1028

The high **sugar** content of this recipe can be reduced simply by serving less caramel with each portion. 2 oz (50 g) sugar will produce enough to give the dish a characteristic flavour. If wished, add a little more lemon or orange juice, or Grand Marnier, and use a deep dish which will allow more of the fruit to be immersed in the liquid. This will give a medium sugar level. (Calories lost: up to 493.)

with fresh cold water; bring to the boil and simmer for about 30 minutes or until the orange peel is tender. Drain and set aside.

Put the sugar into a heavy-based saucepan, then stir with a wooden spoon over moderate heat until the sugar has melted and turned to caramel. Remove from the heat and add ¼ pint (150 ml) of water: it will boil furiously. When the bubbling stops, return the pan to the heat and stir until the caramel has dissolved and a syrup has formed. Add the shredded peel and bring to the boil. Simmer for 2–3 minutes until the peel is glazed.

Draw off the heat, cool for a few moments, then add the lemon juice and the Grand Marnier.

Spoon the syrup and candied peel over the oranges. Set aside until cold, basting the oranges occasionally with the syrup. Chill for several hours before serving with vanilla ice cream (page 53).

CRÈME CARAMEL À L'ORANGE

Caramel custard is a favourite international dessert, especially after a rich or spicy main course. In this Spanish recipe, the caramel custard is given additional flavour by fresh or frozen orange juice.

PREPARATION TIME: *30–35 min*
COOKING TIME: *25 min*
CHILLING TIME: *2 hours*
INGREDIENTS (*for 4*):
Rind of an orange
½ pint (300 ml) orange juice
3 eggs plus 3 egg yolks
2 level tablespoons caster sugar
CARAMEL:
4 oz (100 g) caster sugar

Finely grate the rind from the orange and leave it to steep in the orange juice.

Meanwhile, warm but do not grease four dariole moulds (page 99) and make the caramel. Put the sugar and 1½ tablespoons of cold water in a small, heavy-based pan over low heat; stir gently until the syrup is clear. Turn up the heat and boil briskly, without stirring, until the syrup turns a golden caramel colour. Pour a little caramel into each dariole mould. Twist the moulds quickly until they are evenly coated with the caramel (use thick oven gloves to handle the moulds as they will be very hot).

Heat the orange juice and rind in a pan over low heat. Whisk the whole eggs, egg yolks and sugar until creamy and when the orange juice is on the point of boiling, strain it into the eggs, stirring briskly. Pour the orange cream into the prepared dariole moulds and set them in a roasting pan

with 1 in (2½ cm) of hot water.

Cover the moulds with buttered greaseproof paper and bake in the centre of a pre-heated oven at 350°F (180°C, mark 4) for about 30 minutes or until completely set.

Remove the moulds from the oven, leave them to cool and then chill in the refrigerator for at least 2 hours. Just before serving, unmould the caramel custards on to individual plates and serve with a jug of cream.

BAKED ORANGES

Orange sections are delicious baked in a rich, orange-flavoured custard.

MARINATING TIME: *overnight*
PREPARATION TIME: *15 min*
COOKING TIME: *50 min*
INGREDIENTS (*for 4*):
4 navel oranges, sectioned
4 oz (100 g) sugar
4 tablespoons orange liqueur
3 eggs
3 fluid oz (75 ml) double cream
⅛ teaspoon salt★

Sprinkle the orange sections with half the sugar and layer them in a rectangular 2½ pint (1½ litre) baking dish. Add the liqueur, cover, and refrigerate overnight.

Preheat the oven to 350°F (180°C, mark 4). Bake the oranges, covered, for 20 minutes. Drain and save ¼ pint (150 ml) of the juice. Beat the eggs with the cream, the remaining sugar, the salt, and the reserved juice. Pour this mixture over the oranges and bake, uncovered, for 25 minutes or until the custard is slightly thickened.

Serve this dessert warm, rather than hot or cold.

CRÊPES SUZETTE

Pancakes with lemon are traditionally served on Shrove Tuesday. For a small dinner party, Crêpes Suzettes are more interesting, especially cooked in a chafing dish.

PREPARATION TIME: *30 min*
COOKING TIME: *2–3 min*
INGREDIENTS (*for 6*):
4 oz (100g) plain or self-raising flour
Pinch of salt★
1 egg
½ pint (300 ml) milk
1½–2 oz (40–50 g) unsalted butter
2 oz (50 g) caster sugar
Juice of 2 oranges
Juice of half lemon
2–4 tablespoons orange liqueur

Sift the flour and salt into a large bowl. Using a wooden spoon make a hollow in the centre of the flour and drop in the lightly beaten egg. Slowly pour half the milk into the flour, gradually working the flour into the milk. When all the flour is incorporated, beat the mixture with a wooden spoon, whisk, or rotary beater, until it becomes smooth and free of lumps. Allow it to stand for a few minutes. Then add the remainder of the milk, beating continuously until the batter is bubbly and has the consistency of single cream.

It is not necessary to leave the batter to stand for a while before being cooked, although this may be done if you wish. The batter may be left, covered, at room temperature for any time up to 4 hours, or up to 24 hours in a refrigerator. It may be necessary to add a little more liquid to restore the batter to its original

CRÈME CARAMEL À L'ORANGE

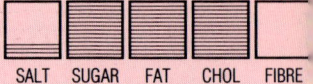

| SALT | SUGAR | FAT | CHOL | FIBRE |

GLUTEN-FREE   WHOLEFOOD★
TOTAL CALORIES: ABOUT 1091

The custard itself does not contain a large amount of **sugar**, although even this may be reduced by half if you prefer a less sweet flavour. The main sugar content, in the caramel, can only be reduced by putting less caramel in each small dish. A reasonable coating can be achieved with only 2 oz (50 g) sugar, but the total level for the dish is still fairly high. (Calorie lost: up to 256.)
The **fat** and very high **cholesterol** levels come from the eggs and extra yolks, and these can be reduced if wished to 3 whole large eggs – still fairly high levels. (Calories lost up to 195.)
Serve the dish with poached apricots in place of cream.

BAKED ORANGES

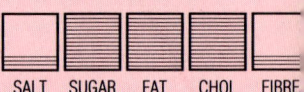

| SALT | SUGAR | FAT | CHOL | FIBRE |

GLUTEN-FREE   WHOLEFOOD★
TOTAL CALORIES: ABOUT 1351

The **sugar** level can easily be reduced to low by simply using only ½ tablespoon of brown sugar or honey or fruit sugar, sprinkled over the oranges before baking, and omitting sugar from the marinade. (Calories lost: up to 167.)
To reduce the **fat** and **cholesterol**, the egg-cream custard can be made less rich, using 2 eggs, ½ tablespoon sug-

or honey, and ¼ pint (150 ml) thick low-fat yogurt or smetana with the juice. If a more solid mixture is wanted, work 1 teaspoon cornflour or arrowroot into the mixture. Omit the salt. This gives the mixture a low fat and sugar content, but it still has a medium cholesterol level from the eggs. (Calories lost: up to 514.)

CRÊPES SUZETTE

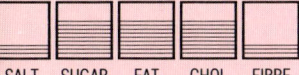

SALT	SUGAR	FAT	CHOL	FIBRE

GLUTEN-FREE*   WHOLEFOOD*
TOTAL CALORIES: ABOUT 1245

The amount of **sugar** can be reduced to low simply by adding only 4 teaspoonfuls to the sauce. (Calories lost: up to 117.)

To reduce the **fat** level to low, use skim milk in the batter, cook in a heavy pan brushed very lightly with oil and use only 1 teaspoon butter or vegetable margarine for the sauce. Make up the necessary volume of liquid with extra orange and lemon juice, if needed. (Calories lost: up to 246.)

For a strict low **cholesterol** regime, use the white of egg but not the yolk in making the pancakes. (Calories lost: up to 55.)

Gluten-free pancakes can be made by blending 6 tablespoons gluten-free flour with 2 tablespoons oil, 3 small eggs and about ½ pint (300 ml) skim milk, or enough to make a thin batter.

Freezing: ☑ up to 2 months.

pouring consistency.

To make the pancakes, use a 6 in (15 cm) heavy-based shallow frying pan with sloping sides. Add just enough butter to gloss the pan to prevent the batter sticking. Fierce heat is necessary, and the pan should be really hot before the batter is poured in.

Pour in just enough batter to flow in a thin film over the base – tilting the pan to spread it. Use a jug or ladle for pouring in the batter. The heat is right if the underside of the pancake becomes golden in 1 minute; adjust the heat to achieve this. Flip the pancake over with a palette knife or spatula, or toss by flicking the wrist and lifting the pan away from the body. The other side of the pancake should also be done in about 1 minute. (See the illustrations on page 84.)

Keep the pancakes hot between two plates over a saucepan of gently boiling water. Melt the butter in a large frying pan, stir in the sugar and cook gently until it is a golden-brown caramel. Add the strained orange and lemon juice and stir until the caramel has dissolved and become a thick sauce. Drop a flat pancake into the pan, fold it in half and then in half again. Push to the side of the pan and add the next pancake. When all the pancakes are in the hot sauce, add the orange liqueur and set it alight when hot. Shake the pan gently to incorporate the flamed liqueur evenly in the sauce.

Transfer the pancakes to a hot serving dish, pour over the sauce from the pan and serve at once.

PEACH MELBA

During the 1892–3 opera season Escoffier, then chef at the Savoy Hotel, London, created this now classic sweet for Dame Nellie Melba, the famous Australian opera singer. It originally consisted of peaches and vanilla ice cream, the raspberry purée being a later addition.

PREPARATION TIME: *12 min*
INGREDIENTS *(for 4):*
2 large peaches
8 oz (225 g) fresh raspberries
2 oz (50 g) caster sugar
¾ pint (425 ml) vanilla ice cream

Put the peaches in a bowl and cover with boiling water. Leave for no more than 1 minute, then drain and peel them. Cut the peaches in half, carefully remove the stones and set the fruit aside. Rub the raspberries through a fine sieve into a mixing bowl; sweeten the resulting purée with the sugar.

Assemble the sweet by placing two scoops of vanilla ice cream (page 53) in each individual serving glass; place one peach half on top, rounded side up, and spoon over part of the raspberry purée. Serve at once.

PEACHES IN WINE

A very simple way to prepare peaches or nectarines, but one of the best if the fruit is really ripe. Nectarines, of course, need no peeling.

PREPARATION TIME: *20 min*
CHILLING TIME: *20 min*
INGREDIENTS *(for 4):*
4 ripe yellow peaches
4 level teaspoons caster sugar
6–8 tablespoons sweet white wine

Peel the peaches, cut them in half and remove the stones. Slice the peaches into individual serving glasses, sprinkle with sugar and spoon the wine over them. Chill for about 20 minutes.

PEACHES WITH GINGER

A good sweet for a dinner party as it is unusual and can be prepared well in advance.

PREPARATION TIME: *15 min*
CHILLING TIME: *3 hours*
INGREDIENTS *(for 4):*
¼ pint (150 ml) freshly squeezed orange juice
2 tablespoons honey
Pinch of salt★
4 large, ripe peaches
2 tablespoons finely chopped candied ginger
Flaked coconut
Mint sprigs

Peel the peaches, cut them in half and remove the stones. Slice the peaches. Mix the orange juice, honey, and salt. Add the peach slices and ginger. Toss gently to mix. Cover and chill for about 3 hours. Spoon into sherbet glasses. Sprinkle with coconut and garnish with mint sprigs.

PEACH MELBA

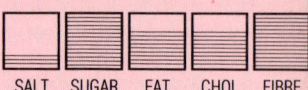

GLUTEN-FREE   WHOLEFOOD*
TOTAL CALORIES: ABOUT 1873

Added **sugar** can be omitted as raspberries are sweet enough alone for most tastes. (Calories lost: up to 197.)
For low-**sugar**, low-**fat** and low-**cholesterol** versions of home-made ice cream, see the notes on page 53, or serve with fromage blanc instead. (Calories lost: up to 548.)

Freezing: √ up to 6 months for the raspberry purée and ice cream.

PEACHES IN WINE

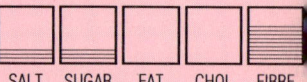

GLUTEN-FREE   WHOLEFOOD*
TOTAL CALORIES: ABOUT 353

You may prefer to omit the caster sugar, gaining any sweetness required from the wine, or replace it with clear honey drizzled over the peaches.

PEACHES WITH GINGER

GLUTEN-FREE   WHOLEFOOD
TOTAL CALORIES: ABOUT 387

To reduce the **sugar** level to low, halve the amount of honey added, or use only 2 teaspoonfuls. (Calories lost: up to 40.)

PEACHES WITH SOURED CREAM

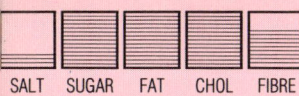

SALT	SUGAR	FAT	CHOL	FIBRE

GLUTEN-FREE   WHOLEFOOD*
TOTAL CALORIES: ABOUT 1968

The amount of **sugar** is difficult to calculate as the peaches will only absorb some of the sugar in the syrup in which they are poached. For a lower amount, poach peaches in a very little water (an ideal job for a microwave or pressure cooker), then, if they are not sweet enough, drizzle with a very little honey or fruit sugar before covering. (Calories lost: up to 807.)

In place of soured cream, which can be around 18% fat, use smetana (5–10% fat), or thick low-fat yogurt blended if wished half and half with quark. This will give low to medium **fat** and **cholesterol**. (Calories lost: up to 449.)

Freezing: ☑ up to 3 months.

BAKED STUFFED PEACHES

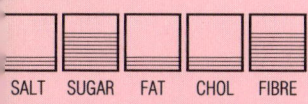

SALT	SUGAR	FAT	CHOL	FIBRE

GLUTEN-FREE*   WHOLEFOOD*
TOTAL CALORIES: ABOUT 980

The biscuits can be fairly high in **sugar** unless you make them yourself, using the recipe on page 55, which will give a moderate overall sugar level. (Calories lost: up to 328.)

PEACHES WITH SOURED CREAM

Golden firm peaches from Italy are at their best and least expensive in the summer. They make refreshing summer sweets – on their own, poached in white wine or cooked in a pastry case. Here, poached peaches are served lightly chilled with a soured cream topping.

PREPARATION TIME: *35 min*
CHILLING TIME: *30 min*
INGREDIENTS *(for 6):*
6 large peaches
8 oz (225 g) vanilla sugar (page 100)
Caster sugar
½ pint (300 ml) soured cream
GARNISH:
1 oz (25 g) Demerara sugar or 1 oz (25 g) toasted flaked almonds

Dissolve the vanilla sugar in ½ pint (300 ml) of water in a small pan and cook over moderate heat. Simmer this syrup for 5 minutes.

Wash and dry the peaches thoroughly, then poach them lightly in the syrup for 5–10 minutes, depending on the ripeness of the fruit.

Lift the peaches from the syrup, leave to cool slightly, then peel off the skin and cut the peaches in half. Remove the stones, and slice the peaches into a serving bowl, one layer at a time, sprinkling each layer with a little caster sugar. Strain the syrup and set aside for another use.

Cover the top of the peaches with a thick layer of soured cream and chill for 30 minutes. Just before serving, sprinkle the top with Demerara sugar or toasted flaked almonds.

BAKED STUFFED PEACHES

Traditionally this Italian sweet is made with amaretti – tiny macaroons made from apricot kernels or bitter almonds. If these are unobtainable, ratafia biscuits make a good substitute (see recipes on pages 12 and 55).

PREPARATION TIME: *20 min*
COOKING TIME: *20–30 min*
INGREDIENTS *(for 4–6):*
4 large peaches
4 level teaspoons caster sugar
1 level tablespoon unsalted butter
1 egg yolk
2 oz (50 g) amaretti or ratafia biscuits

Cream together the sugar, butter and egg yolk in a small bowl. Crush the biscuits with a rolling pin and add these to the creamed mixture.

Pour boiling water over the peaches and leave for 2–3 minutes. Peel off the skin, halve the peaches and remove the stones. Enlarge the cavities slightly by scooping out some of the flesh with a pointed teaspoon. Add this pulp to the egg mixture and blend well.

Pile the stuffing into the peach halves and arrange them in a buttered fireproof dish. Bake on the centre shelf of a pre-heated oven, at 350°F (180°C, mark 4), for 20–30 minutes or until the peaches are soft, but still shapely.

Serve the peaches warm, with a bowl of cream.

PEARS IN CHOCOLATE JACKETS

Large ripe winter pears, such as 'Comice', are ideal for this attractive dessert of chocolate-covered pears. It makes a good choice for a dinner party as it can be prepared a day in advance and left in the refrigerator.

PREPARATION TIME: *20min*
COOKING TIME: *20 min*
CHILLING TIME: *2–3 hours*
INGREDIENTS *(for 4):*
4 ripe dessert pears
½ oz (10 g) shelled walnuts
½ oz (10 g) glacé cherries
4 oz (100 g) dark plain chocolate
3 tablespoons cold black coffee
1 oz (25 g) unsalted butter
2–4 teaspoons rum
2 eggs
GARNISH:
Angelica, or whipped cream and chopped pistachio nuts

Peel the pears thinly and cut out the cores from the base of the fruit, leaving the stem and top intact. Cut a small sliver from the base of each pear so that it will stand upright. Roughly chop and mix together the walnuts and cherries and press a little of this mixture into the core cavities of the pears. Stand the pears upright in one large or four small shallow serving dishes.

Break up the chocolate and put it in a bowl with the coffee. Stand the bowl over a saucepan of boiling water and stir occasionally until the chocolate has melted. Remove the bowl from the heat and stir in first the butter and then the rum. Separate the eggs and beat the yolks, one at a time, into the chocolate mixture. Whisk the egg whites until stiff, but still moist, and fold them carefully into the chocolate. The consistency should be similar to that of a mousse.

Spoon the chocolate mixture over the pears until they are evenly coated. Soften the angelica strips in hot water, cut into ½ in (1 cm) lengths and slice them crossways into eight diamond shapes. Make a small slit on either side of each pear stalk and insert an angelica diamond, twisting them to resemble small leaves.

Chill the chocolate pears in the refrigerator for 2–3 hours or overnight.

Piped whipped cream and chopped pistachio nuts are also attractive garnishes.

PEARS IN CHOCOLATE JACKETS

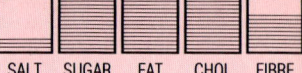

SALT SUGAR FAT CHOL FIBRE

GLUTEN-FREE
TOTAL CALORIES: ABOUT 1146

For a low added **sugar** content, omit the glacé cherries, which are preserved by heavy sugaring, and replace the chocolate (typically 56% sugar) with no-added-sugar carob. (Calories lost: up to 34.) These two changes will also render this dessert **wholefood**, as cherries are artificially coloured red. (Angelica is also coloured, but often remains uneaten.) The **fat** and **cholesterol** level can be limited to medium only by giving the pears a thinner coating. (Calories lost: up to 234.)

POIRES FLAMBÉES

SALT SUGAR FAT CHOL FIBRE

GLUTEN-FFREE   WHOLEFOOD
TOTAL CALORIES: ABOUT 733

The **fat** level can be reduced to low by replacing the double cream with 2 tablespoons smetana, quark, or soured cream. (Calories lost: up to 111.)
For low **cholesterol**, replace the cream as suggested above, and use 1 teaspoon of butter and 2 of vegetable margarine for cooking the pears.

CHINESE PEARS

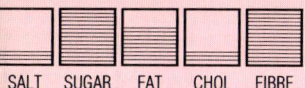

SALT	SUGAR	FAT	CHOL	FIBRE

GLUTEN-FREE   WHOLEFOOD
TOTAL CALORIES: ABOUT 1750

Most of the added **sugar** comes from the red currant jelly. To avoid this, make the sauce from puréed currants or raspberries, lightly sweetened with a very small amount of sugar or honey if necessary. The high-sugar ginger syrup can also be reduced, adding a little ground ginger or grated fresh root ginger if liked to step up the ginger flavour. This will give a low sugar level. (Calories lost: up to 315.)
The **fat** level comes mainly from the pine kernels, and these can be reduced by half if wished, giving a low fat level. (Calories lost: up to 241.)
Cholesterol can be eliminated or reduced by replacing butter with vegetable fat completely or in part.

POIRES FLAMBEES

This French recipe for pears in brandy is an ideal sweet to cook in a chafing dish at the table. Fresh firm peaches and apricots are also excellent cooked in this way.

PREPARATION TIME: *15 min*
COOKING TIME: *10 min*
INGREDIENTS *(for 4)*:
4 ripe firm dessert pears
4 pieces stem ginger
1 oz (25 g) unsalted butter
2 tablespoons brandy
1–2 tablespoons ginger syrup
2 tablespoons double cream

Peel the pears thinly, cut them in half and carefully scoop out the cores with a pointed teaspoon. Quarter each piece of stem ginger and set aside.
Heat the butter in a chafing dish, a shallow flameproof dish, or a frying pan over moderate heat. Fry the pears, cut side down, until golden brown. Turn the pears over and fry the other side. Fill a warmed tablespoon with brandy, set it alight and pour it over the pears. Repeat with the remaining brandy.
Arrange the pears on individual plates, placing two ginger pieces in each cavity. Add the ginger syrup and cream to the pan juices and stir over gentle heat until well blended and heated through. Spoon a little sauce over each portion and serve the pears immediately.

CHINESE PEARS

Despite its name this unusual and aromatic dessert is French in origin. It is sweet and rich, suitable for a dinner party. Williams or other squat dessert pears are excellent for this recipe.

PREPARATION TIME: *35 min*
COOKING TIME: *35 min*
INGREDIENTS *(for 6)*:
6 large ripe pears
3 oz (75 g) sultanas
3 oz (75 g) pine kernels
2 level tablespoons honey
1 oz (25 g) unsalted butter
¼–⅓ pint (150–200 ml) dry white wine
2 tablespoons ginger syrup
5 oz (150 g) red currant jelly

Peel the pears thinly and cut a small slice from the base of each, so that it will stand upright. Remove a ¾–1 in (2–2½ cm) lid from the top of each pear and scoop out the core and pips. Roughly chop the sultanas and pine kernels, mix with the honey and spoon the mixture into the pear cavities. Replace the lids.
Grease an ovenproof dish with the butter and stand the pears in the dish together with any remaining sultana mixture. Pour over the white wine and cover the dish with foil. Bake the pears in the centre of an oven pre-heated to 350–375°F (180–190°C, mark 4–5) for about 30 minutes or until tender – the time varies according to the type and ripeness of the pears.
When cooked, place the pears in individual serving bowls and keep them warm in the oven. Pour the cooking juices into a small saucepan and add the ginger syrup and red currant jelly. Boil over moderate heat until the jelly has dissolved. Pour this sauce carefully over the pears and serve at once.

FRUIT SALAD IN A PINEAPPLE

This uses the pineapple shell itself as a container which is very effective. Although the more homely apples and pears have not been used here, there is no reason why they should not be.

PREPARATION TIME: *30 min*
STANDING TIME: *1–2 hours*
INGREDIENTS *(for 6):*
4 oz (100 g) granulated sugar
2 tablespoons lemon juice
1 tablespoon orange liqueur or kirsch
½ lb (225 g) white or black grapes (optional)
1 pineapple
2 oranges
2 bananas

Put the sugar, with ¼ pint (150 ml) of water, in a small pan, heat gently to dissolve the sugar, then bring to the boil for 2–3 minutes. Set aside until cold, then add the lemon juice and liqueur and pour into a large serving bowl.

Peel the grapes if used and remove the pips (page 80). Add the grapes to the sugar syrup in the bowl. Peel and cut oranges into segments, and squeeze the orange membranes into the bowl. Peel and slice the bananas and add, with the oranges, to the bowl. Turn the fruit in the syrup. Cover and leave in a cool place, preferably not the refrigerator, for 1–2 hours to develop the flavours.

When fresh strawberries are available, include ½ lb (225 g) hulled and halved small strawberries. Stoned cherries, plums and greengages, halved apricots, sliced peaches and red currants are also good for fresh fruit salads, as are kiwi fruit, grapefruit and melon.

CRÊPES GEORGETTE

These pancakes with a rum-flavoured pineapple filling are said to have been created for Georgette Leblanc, close friend of the Belgian poet Maeterlinck.

PREPARATION TIME: *30 min*
COOKING TIME: *30 min*
INGREDIENTS *(for 6):*
½ pint (300 ml) pancake batter (page 84)
6 pineapple rings
½ pint (300 ml) vanilla-flavoured confectioner's custard (page 25)
3–4 tablespoons rum
2 oz (50 g) melted butter
Icing sugar

Prepare the pancake batter and use it to make 12 very thin pancakes. Drain and finely chop the pineapple rings. Make the confectioner's custard (crème pâtissière) and flavour it with 2–4 teaspoons rum. Mix the chopped pineapple into the cream. Put a tablespoon or so of the warm cream mixture in the centre of each pancake and fold the two sides over it.

Place the stuffed pancakes side by side in a well-buttered, warmed, flameproof dish. Brush them with melted butter, and dredge generously with sifted icing sugar. Heat a metal skewer and press it in a criss-cross pattern on to the sugar.

Set the dish under a hot grill for about 5 minutes to glaze the sugar topping. Just before serving, warm the remaining rum in a small pan, set it alight and pour it over the pancakes.

FRUIT SALAD IN A PINEAPPLE

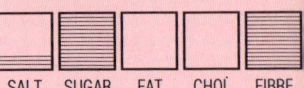

GLUTEN-FREE   WHOLEFOOD *
TOTAL CALORIES: ABOUT 936

Reduce the added **sugar** level to very low (only that contained in the liqueur) by omitting the sugar syrup, using apple juice to provide extra liquid if wished. (Calories lost: up to 394.)

Freezing: ☑ up to 2 months if bananas are not included.

CRÊPES GEORGETTE

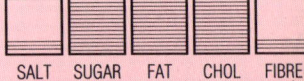

GLUTEN-FREE *   WHOLEFOOD *
TOTAL CALORIES: ABOUT 2329

For low **sugar**, make the alternative confectioner's custard or pastry cream suggested in the notes on page 25, and instead of dredging with icing sugar, trickle a little jam made without added sugar over the pancakes. Put under the grill for 5 minutes for the jam to melt and form a glaze. (Calories lost: up to 338.)
For low **fat** and **cholesterol**, see the notes on pancakes on page 33, and on pastry cream on page 25. Instead of brushing with the melted butter, use a tablespoon or two of smetana. (Calories lost: up to 739.)

Freezing: ☑ up to 1 month.

BAKED PINEAPPLE FLAMBÉ

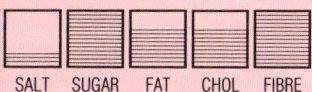

SALT	SUGAR	FAT	CHOL	FIBRE

GLUTEN-FREE   WHOLEFOOD
TOTAL CALORIES: ABOUT 1530

For low **sugar**, add only 1 oz (25 g) sugar to the mixture, and use marmalade made with no added sugar. (Calories lost: up to 290.)
The butter can be reduced to 1 tablespoon, giving an overall low **fat** and **cholesterol** content. (Calories lost: up to 259.)

Freezing: ☑ up to 2 months.

VICTORIA PLUMS IN WINE

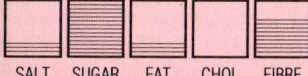

SALT	SUGAR	FAT	CHOL	FIBRE

GLUTEN-FREE   WHOLEFOOD*
TOTAL CALORIES: ABOUT 1161

For low **sugar**, poach the fruit in wine only, in two batches or more to enable the liquid to cover the fruit.
If wished, add a spoonful of honey to the wine and 2 tablespoons of water. Using this method, the syrup will not have the volume to require boiling down. As it will not thicken without sugar, stir in 1 heaped teaspoonful of arrowroot that has been moistened to a smooth paste with cold water, and simmer for a few minutes until mixture clears. (Calories lost: up to 246.)
Serve with low-fat yogurt or smetana in place of single cream.

Freezing: ☑ up to 2 months.

BAKED PINEAPPLE FLAMBÉ

A very successful combination of fruit. Any marmalade can be used, but grapefruit marmalade gives an interesting flavour. Greengages or apricots could be used instead of plums.

PREPARATION TIME: *30 min*
COOKING TIME: *20 min*
INGREDIENTS *(for 6):*
1 medium pineapple
1 lb (450 g) plums
4 tablespoons marmalade
Grated rind and juice of a lemon
½ level teaspoon ground cinnamon
4 oz (100 g) soft brown sugar
2 oz (50 g) unsalted butter
4 tablespoons white rum

Slice, peel and core the pineapple. Cut the slices in half. Cut the plums in half, and remove the stones. Place the pineapple and plums in a wide shallow casserole with a lid.
In a small pan, heat together the marmalade, lemon rind and juice, cinnamon, sugar and butter. Stir well and pour the mixture over the fruit. Cover and cook in a pre-heated oven at 400°F (200°C, mark 6) for about 20 minutes. Just before serving, place the rum in a warm ladle, ignite with a match and pour it flaming over the fruit.

VICTORIA PLUMS IN WINE

The slightly acid flavour of these home-grown plums makes them suitable for sweet compôtes and puddings. Their flavour is brought out to the full by poaching them in a syrupy wine and serving them while still warm.

PREPARATION TIME: *5 min*
COOKING TIME: *30 min*
INGREDIENTS *(for 6):*
1½–2 lb (700–900 g) firm Victoria plums
3 oz (75 g) caster sugar
½ pint (300 ml) tawny port, medium dry sherry or Madeira
2 tablespoons flaked almonds

Dissolve the sugar in ½ pint (300 ml) of water and simmer for 10 minutes. Stir in the wine and bring the syrup gently up to simmering point again.
Remove the stalks from the plums, wash and dry them. Add the plums, one at a time, to the simmering syrup. Cover the pan with a lid and remove from the heat. Leave the plums in the syrup for 10 minutes.
Lift out the plums with a perforated spoon and put them in a serving dish. Cover the dish with a plate or foil, and leave in a warm place. Boil the syrup over high heat until it has reduced by about one-third and thickened slightly. Pour it over the plums.
Meanwhile, toast the flaked almonds for about 5 minutes in the oven until golden. Scatter these over the plums and serve at once, with a jug of single cream.

PLUM AND CINNAMON PIE

You could also use fresh plums for this, poached in the same way as the apricots on page 16.

PREPARATION TIME: *5 min*
COOKING TIME: *40 min*
STANDING TIME: *1 hour*
INGREDIENTS *(for 6):*
8 oz (225 g) American stirred pastry (page 86)
2 tins (1 lb, 450 g) golden plums
1 level tablespoon fine tapioca
¼ level teaspoon powdered cinnamon
1 oz (25 g) butter
1 egg white
Granulated sugar

Drain the plums, reserving the syrup, and remove the stones. Blend the tapioca and cinnamon in a bowl with 6 tablespoons of the plum syrup and leave it to stand for 30 minutes.

Roll out half the prepared pastry and use it to line a 10 in (25 cm) pie plate. Mix the plums with the tapioca mixture and spoon it over the pastry base; dot with butter. Roll out the remaining pastry for the lid and cover the pie. Seal the edges, knock them up and make a slit in the lid. Brush the top with beaten egg white and dust generously with sugar. Chill for 30 minutes.

Set the pie on a heated baking tray and bake in the centre of a pre-heated oven at 400°F (200°C, mark 6) for about 40 minutes. Serve the pie warm, with whipped cream.

RASPBERRY YOGURT SORBET

A sorbet will be welcome on a hot summer's evening. One of the most delicious is made from raspberries. Adding yogurt to this sorbet enhances its flavour.

PREPARATION TIME: *15 min*
CHILLING TIME: *2–3 hours*
INGREDIENTS *(for 6):*
8 oz (225 g) raspberries
2–3 oz (50–75 g) caster sugar
½ pint (300 ml) natural yogurt
Juice of half lemon
½ oz (10 g) powdered gelatine
2 egg whites

Make a thick purée from the raspberries by rubbing them through a sieve and into a bowl. Sweeten to taste with the sugar. Stir the yogurt and the lemon juice into the sweetened purée.

Put 4 tablespoons of cold water in a small bowl and sprinkle the powdered gelatine over it. Leave the gelatine to stand for 5 minutes and then set the bowl over a pan of hot water. Stir until the gelatine has dissolved and the liquid clear.

Add the liquid gelatine to the raspberry purée. In a separate bowl, beat the egg whites until stiff but not dry, and then fold them into the purée.

Spoon the mixture into a container, cover with a lid and set in the freezing compartment of the refrigerator. When almost frozen, beat up the purée with a rotary whisk. Then allow the mixture to freeze firmly.

PLUM AND CINNAMON PIE

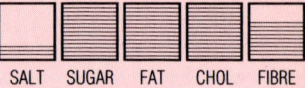

SALT   SUGAR   FAT   CHOL   FIBRE

GLUTEN-FREE*   WHOLEFOOD*
TOTAL CALORIES: ABOUT 3330

The high level of **sugar** typical of tinned fruit can be avoided by using fresh fruit, briefly poaching in a little water, then sweetening to taste with as little honey or sugar as possible. This should give a low to medium sugar level depending on how sweet the fruit is. Alternatively, poach with 4 oz (100 g) dates, stoned, which have been stewed and liquidised to a thick purée. These will give sweetness to the plums without adding sugar as such. Be sparing with sugar sprinkled on pie. (Calories lost: up to 446.) Stirred pastry has even more **fat** than shortcrust. To reduce, switch to shortcrust using 1 part fat to 2 of flour or use a scone dough instead. (Calories lost: up to 1105.)
If the fat used is vegetable, the dish will be low in **cholesterol**. Dotting with butter can be omitted. Using millet flakes would provide a more nutritious filling than tapioca.

Freezing: ✓ up to 6 months.

RASPBERRY YOGURT SORBET

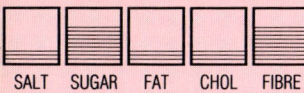

SALT	SUGAR	FAT	CHOL	FIBRE

GLUTEN-FREE   WHOLEFOOD*
TOTAL CALORIES: ABOUT 575

If wished, little or no **sugar** can be added to the raspberries, reducing the sugar level to low or nil. (Calories lost: up to 296.)

Freezing: ☑ up to 1 month.

HAZEL NUT GANTOIS

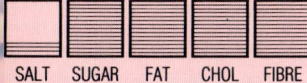

SALT	SUGAR	FAT	CHOL	FIBRE

GLUTEN-FREE*   WHOLEFOOD*
TOTAL CALORIES: ABOUT 2995

For a moderate **sugar** content, use only 1½ oz (40 g) sugar in the dough, and halve the amount used for the caramel topping. (Calories lost: up to 187.)
For low **fat** and **cholesterol**, use only 2 oz (50 g) butter (or replace some or all of it with vegetable margarine); use quark or fromage blanc instead of cream. (Calories lost: up to 950.)

Freezing: ☑ up to 3 months (biscuit layers only).

HAZEL NUT GANTOIS

A gantois, or Flemish pastry, consists of crunchy biscuits layered with fresh fruit and whipped cream. The pudding is topped with crisp golden caramel.

PREPARATION TIME: *1 hour*
CHILLING TIME: *30 min*
COOKING TIME: *25–30 min*
INGREDIENTS *(for 4–6):*
4 oz (100 g) shelled hazel nuts
4½ oz (125 g) plain flour
2 oz (50 g) plus 1 level teaspoon caster sugar
3 oz (75 g) unsalted butter
1 lb (450 g) raspberries or 6–8 peaches
½ pint (300 ml) whipping cream
CARAMEL TOPPING:
3 oz (75 g) caster sugar

Put the hazel nuts in the grill pan and grill under medium heat, shaking the pan frequently, until the nuts are toasted. Rub them in a colander with a dry cloth to remove the skins. Weigh off 1 oz (25 g) of the nuts, chop them coarsely and set aside. Grind the remainder in a coffee mill or chop them very finely.

Sieve the flour into a mixing bowl and add the ground nuts and the sugar. Rub in the butter until the mixture resembles fine bread-crumbs, then knead lightly for a few minutes. Chill the dough in a refrigerator for at least 30 min-utes, or until quite firm.

Meanwhile, pick over the raspberries and hull them, or peel the peaches and cut them into thin slices.

Shape the firm dough into a thick sausage, on a lightly floured board. Divide the dough into four equal pieces and roll each piece

out to a 7 in (18 cm) circle, about ⅛ in (¼ cm) thick. Lift the circles carefully on to greased baking trays. Bake in the centre of a pre-heated oven, at 350°F (180°C, mark 4) for 15 minutes or until the biscuits are golden brown and firm. Remove to a wire tray and leave to cool.

For the caramel topping, put 3 oz (75 g) sugar and 2 table-spoons water in a small pan over low heat. Stir until the sugar has completely dissolved. Turn up the heat and boil the syrup briskly, without stirring, until it is caramel-coloured.

Pour enough of the caramel over one biscuit circle to cover it, spreading it evenly with an oiled knife. Sprinkle the coarsely chopped nuts round the edge of the caramel-covered biscuit, and arrange a quarter of the rasp-berries or peach slices in the centre. Trickle over the remain-ing caramel or pull this into thin threads to make a spun sugar veil on top of the biscuit.

Whip the cream and sweeten to taste with a little sugar. Assemble the cake by spreading the cream in equal layers over the remaining three biscuits; arrange the fruit evenly on each layer. Put the biscuits on top of each other, finishing with the caramel-topped biscuit. Serve at once.

RASPBERRIES WITH COEUR À LA CRÈME

A classic French summer sweet is this combination of soft fruit and home-made cream cheese. Traditionally, the cheese is set in little heart-shaped moulds (which are now widely available) and served with cream poured over. Strawberries can be served in the same way.

PREPARATION TIME: *20 min*
CHILLING TIME: *12 hours*
INGREDIENTS (*for 4–6*):
2 lb (900 g) raspberries
*8 oz (225 g) unsalted cream cheese
  or cottage cheese*
½ pint (300 ml) double cream
4 level teaspoons caster sugar
2 egg whites
¼ pint (150 ml) single cream

Rub or press the cheese through a fine sieve and mix with the double cream before stirring in the sugar. (Cream cheese makes a richer, denser mixture than cottage cheese.) Beat the egg whites until stiff, but not dry, and fold them into the cheese and cream.

Line the heart-shaped moulds with the fine muslin (to make unmoulding easier). Alternatively, use a 6 in (15 cm) wide, shallow cake tin as a mould. Pierce a few holes in the base for draining, and line the tin with muslin.

Spoon the cheese and cream mixture into the prepared moulds and place them on a wide plate or in a sieve. Leave in the refrigerator overnight to drain and chill.

Just before serving, unmould the cream cheese on to a serving plate. Pour over the single cream, and serve with the fresh raspberries or other soft fruit, or with a sweetened fruit sauce.

RASPBERRY MOUSSE

The texture of this mousse is light and creamy; for a firmer set increase the gelatine to 4 level teaspoons.

PREPARATION TIME: *45 min*
SETTING TIME: *2 hours*
INGREDIENTS (*for 6*):
1 lb (450 g) raspberries
3 whole eggs
2 egg yolks
4 oz (100 g) caster sugar
*3 level teaspoons powdered
  gelatine*
3 tablespoons water
½ pint (300 ml) double cream
Grated chocolate

Set eight raspberries aside for garnish and put the remainder (hulled and washed) in a pan and simmer for about 5 minutes until soft. Rub the raspberries through a sieve – the purée should measure about ½ pint (300 ml).

Put the whole eggs and the egg yolks in a bowl, together with the sugar. Place the bowl over a pan of hot water and whisk the eggs until thick and fluffy. Take the bowl from the pan and set in a basin of chilled water or ice cubes. Whisk the egg mixture until cool.

Dissolve the gelatine in the water, stir it quickly into the raspberry purée, and then whisk this into the egg mixture. Whip the cream lightly and fold it into the raspberries when beginning to set. Spoon into a serving dish and chill until set.

Just before serving, sprinkle coarsely grated chocolate over the mousse and decorate with the whole raspberries.

SUMMER PUDDING

The origin of this classic English pudding is unknown, but as early as the 18th century it was served to patients who were not allowed rich pastry sweets. This does not in the least make it invalid food – it is a delicious composition of fresh summer fruits.

PREPARATION TIME: *30–40 min*
CHILLING TIME: *8 hours*
INGREDIENTS (*for 6*):
*6–8 slices stale, crustless bread,
  ½ in (1 cm) thick*
1½ lb (700 g) mixed soft fruits
4 oz (100 g) caster sugar

Strawberries, raspberries, red and black currants, as well as black cherries, are all suitable for this dish, and can be mixed according to taste and availability. The more varied the fruits, the tastier the result, but avoid using too many black currants as their flavour and colour will tend to dominate the pudding.

Line the bottom of a 1½-pint (900 ml) soufflé dish or pudding basin with one or two slices of bread to cover the base completely. Line the sides of the dish with more bread, if necessary cut to shape, so that the bread fits closely together.

Hull and carefully wash the fruit, and remove the stones from the cherries. Put the fruit in a wide heavy-based pan and sprinkle the sugar over it. Bring to the boil over very low heat, and cook for 2–3 minutes only, until the sugar melts and the juices begin to run. Remove the pan from the heat and set aside 1–2 tablespoons of the fruit juices. Spoon the fruit and remaining juice into the prepared dish and cover the surface closely

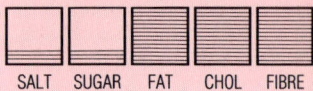
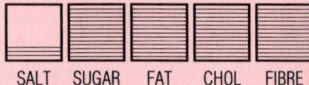

with the stiff egg whites making up the volume. For a lower fat dish, replace the remaining cream with quark mixed half and half with thick yogurt. (Calories lost: up to 1489.) Increase the amount of gelatine to 4 teaspoons to give a firmer set, as egg whites are less stable when beaten than cream.

Freezing: ☑ up to 2 months.

SUMMER PUDDING

SALT   SUGAR   FAT   CHOL   FIBRE

GLUTEN-FREE*   WHOLEFOOD*
TOTAL CALORIES: ABOUT 1290

To reduce the amount of added **sugar** to low or zero, replace 8 oz (225 g) of the fruit with 4 oz (100 g) dried apricots, stewed and puréed. This will sweeten the fruit without overpowering its flavour. Then taste and only add sugar cautiously if needed. (Calories lost: up to 172.)

Freezing: ☑ up to 2 months.

with the rest of the bread.

Put a plate that fits the inside of the dish on top of the pudding and weight it down with a heavy tin or jar. Leave the pudding in the refrigerator to chill for 8 hours.

Before serving, remove the weight and plate. Cover the dish with the serving plate and turn upside-down to unmould the pudding. Use the reserved fruit juice to pour over any parts of the bread which have not been soaked through and coloured by the fruit juices.

Fruit-based Desserts

SOFT FRUIT GÂTEAU

This dessert cake consists of a sponge case filled with fresh fruit and cream. It can be assembled to look like a jewellery box by setting the sponge lid at an angle and letting strawberries, raspberries or stalks of red currants appear over the edge.

PREPARATION TIME: *50–60 min*
COOKING TIME: *15 min*
INGREDIENTS *(for 6–8):*
4 eggs
4 oz (100 g) caster sugar
4 oz (100 g) self-raising flour
¼ level teaspoon salt
½–¾ lb (225–350 g) mixed soft fruit (strawberries, raspberries, red currants)
½ pint (300 ml) double cream
3 oz (75 g) icing sugar

Lightly grease and flour a rectangular sponge tin, approximately 14 in by 8 in (35 cm by 20 cm). Put the eggs and sugar into a deep mixing bowl, and whisk until the eggs are pale and thick enough for the whisk to leave a trail. Sift the flour and salt together, and fold gently into the creamed egg mixture.

Spoon this sponge mixture into the prepared tin, spreading

SOFT FRUIT GÂTEAU

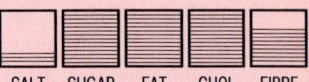

| SALT | SUGAR | FAT | CHOL | FIBRE |

GLUTEN-FREE* WHOLEFOOD*
TOTAL CALORIES: ABOUT 2818

To reduce the amount of **sugar** in this dish is impossible, as it is necessary to the structure of the sponge. Alternatives are to make a smaller sponge base, using 2 eggs, 2 oz (50 g) sugar and 2 oz (50 g) flour, and/or increase the amount of fruit topping.
This will give a low sugar content, and halves the **cholesterol** from the eggs. Most of the **fat** comes from the cream, and this can be replaced with quark, blended smoothly with honey to taste (about 1 lb (450 g) quark with 2 tablespoons honey), and a few drops of vanilla essence if wished. This gives a more cheesecake-like base. Some of the quark can be piped, just like cream, to decorate. These changes give a low-fat, low-cholesterol dish. (Calories lost: up to 1751.)
Gluten-free sponge cake can be made, using the same amount of sugar and eggs with 2½ oz (70 g) gluten-free flour.

Freezing: ✓ up to 6 months (sponge only).

RHUBARB CRUMBLE

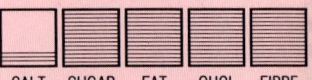

| SALT | SUGAR | FAT | CHOL | FIBRE |

GLUTEN-FREE* WHOLEFOOD*
TOTAL CALORIES: ABOUT 2633

The high level of added **sugar** can be reduced to low by these changes: mix 1½ lb (700 g) rhubarb with 8 oz (225 g) stewed dried apricots, dates or sultanas (4 oz, 100 g dried weight) that have been puréed. This will reduce the need for sugar to 1–2 tablespoons, with either honey or fruit sugar giving excellent results. Dates are the sweetest of the three. In the topping, the amount of sugar need only be 1 oz (25 g). (Calories lost: up to 315.) For a medium **fat** level rub only 1½ oz (40 g) fat into the flour. The remaining fat from the cream can be avoided by replacing this with quark, flavoured with honey and ginger, or for a softer consistency, mixed with low-fat yogurt. (Calories lost: up to 833.) If this is done, and vegetable fat (such as soft vegetable margarine) is used, the **cholesterol** will be very low.

Freezing: ✓ up to 3 months.
Microwave: ✓

STRAWBERRY SYLLABUB TRIFLE

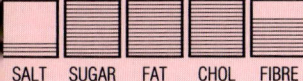

SALT	SUGAR	FAT	CHOL	FIBRE

GLUTEN-FREE★ WHOLEFOOD★
TOTAL CALORIES: ABOUT 3187

The **sugar** can be reduced to medium by adding only 2 oz (50 g) to the egg whites. (Calories lost: up to 493.) The **fat** and **cholesterol** can be reduced to low by replacing the cream with 4 oz (100 g) quark whipped with 4 oz (100 g) smetana or thick low-fat yogurt, flavouring with honey if wished. (Calories lost: up to 1192.) Macaroons are often **gluten-free**, made with rice and almonds, but check the ingredients list on the packet.

it evenly and making sure the corners are filled. Bake just above the centre of a pre-heated oven at 375°F (190°C, mark 5) for 15 minutes, or until the sponge is golden and firm to the touch.

Turn the sponge on to a wire rack and leave to cool completely, preferably overnight. Meanwhile, clean the fruit, wash and drain it thoroughly on absorbent kitchen paper. Whip the double cream until it is thick and fluffy.

Carefully cut the sponge across into two halves, with a sharp knife. Spread just over half of the whipped cream over one half. Cut an oblong out of the other half, leaving an outer, unbroken edge, 1 in (2½ cm) wide, all round.

Carefully lift this frame on to the cream-covered base and fill the box, or cavity, with the fruit, reserving a few pieces for decoration. Sprinkle the sieved icing sugar over the fruit, and cover the box with the lid set at a slight angle. Pipe the remaining cream on to the lid and decorate with the reserved fruit.

The cake will keep for 2–3 hours in a refrigerator, but it should not be assembled too far in advance, or the fruit will become mushy and stain the cream.

RHUBARB CRUMBLE

In late spring, rhubarb is larger and slightly tougher than the tender early forced rhubarb. The tart flavour is more pronounced and blends well with a topping of sweet crumble.

PREPARATION TIME: *20 min*
COOKING TIME: *40 min*
INGREDIENTS *(for 4–6):*
2 lb (900 g) rhubarb
6 oz (175 g) caster sugar
6 oz (175 g) plain flour
3 oz (75 g) unsalted butter
¼ pint (150 ml) double cream
1 piece preserved ginger
1 teaspoon ginger syrup

Wash the rhubarb stalks, top and tail them, discard any damaged pieces and remove tough strings. Chop the stalks into ½ in (1 cm) sections. Put the rhubarb in a deep baking dish, sprinkle over half the sugar and add 2 tablespoons of cold water. Sift the flour and rub the butter in until it forms a crumbly mixture; blend in the remaining sugar. Cover the rhubarb with this crumble, patting it down well. Bake in the centre of an oven pre-heated to 375°F (190°C, mark 5) for about 40 minutes or until crisp and golden on top.

Whip the cream until it stands in soft peaks; flavour with chopped ginger and the syrup.

Serve the crumble warm or cold and offer the cream in a bowl separately.

STRAWBERRY SYLLABUB TRIFLE

There is a recipe for macaroons on page 12, or you could use the ratafia recipe on page 55.

PREPARATION TIME: *30 min*
RESTING TIME: *4 hours*
INGREDIENTS *(for 6–8):*
1 lb (450 g) strawberries
½ lb (225 g) green grapes
6 oz (175 g) small macaroons
3 egg whites
6 oz (175 g) caster sugar
¼ pint (150 ml) dry white wine
Juice of half lemon
2 tablespoons brandy
½ pint (300 ml) double cream

Hull, wash and drain the strawberries, and remove the pips from the grapes (page 80). Set 6–8 strawberries aside, and arrange half the remainder together with half the grapes over the base of a glass dish. Set 8 macaroons aside, and lay half of the remainder over the fruit. Cover the macaroons with the rest of the strawberries and grapes and lay the remaining macaroons over them.

Whisk the egg whites with half the sugar until stiff, but not dry, then fold in the remaining sugar with a metal spoon. Mix the wine, lemon juice and brandy, and blend it carefully into the egg whites. Whisk the cream until it just holds its shape, set a little aside for decoration, and fold the egg-white mixture into the remaining cream.

Spoon the cream over the macaroons, smoothing it neatly, and leave in a cool place, not the refrigerator, for several hours.

Decorate the trifle with the reserved strawberries and macaroons sandwiched with cream.

STRAWBERRY SHORTCAKE

This makes a wonderful ending for a summer luncheon party.

PREPARATION TIME: *25 min*
COOKING TIME: *20 min*
INGREDIENTS:
8 oz (225 g) plain flour
1 level teaspoon cream of tartar
½ level teaspoon bicarbonate of soda
Pinch of salt
2 oz (50 g) butter or margarine
1½ oz (40 g) caster sugar
1 egg
3–4 tablespoons milk
FILLING:
½ lb (225 g) hulled strawberries
½ pint (300 ml) double cream
1 tablespoon milk
Caster sugar
Butter

Sift together the flour, cream of tartar, bicarbonate of soda and salt into a bowl. Cut the butter into small pieces and rub into the flour until the mixture resembles fine breadcrumbs. Blend in the sugar. Make a well in the centre, stir in the beaten egg and enough milk to give a soft but manageable dough. Knead lightly and roll out into a 7 in (18 cm) circle.

Place on a greased baking tray, dust lightly with flour and bake towards the top of an oven pre-heated to 425°F (220°C, mark 7) for about 20 minutes. Cool slightly on a wire rack.

For the filling, slice the strawberries thickly. Whisk together the cream and the milk, sweetened with caster sugar to taste, until it holds its shape. Cut the warm shortcake into three layers, horizontally, with a serrated knife, and lightly butter each. Spread the cream over all three circles, then top with the sliced strawberries and sandwich the cake together. Decorate the top with piped cream.

STRAWBERRY WATER ICE

Water ices are both easy and economical to make. They are refreshing at any time of day and make a perfect summer sweet after a rich main course. Turn the refrigerator to its coldest setting before freezing them.

PREPARATION TIME: *10 min*
FREEZING TIME: *minimum 3 hours*
INGREDIENTS (*for 4–6*):
½ lb (225 g) strawberries
1 oz (25 g) icing sugar
¾ pint (425 ml) lemonade
2 egg whites

Wash and hull the strawberries, drain them thoroughly in a colander, then cut them into small pieces. Rub the strawberries through a sieve and stir the sugar into the purée. (Alternatively, put the fruit and sugar in a liquidiser to purée.) Add enough lemonade to the purée to make ¾ pint (425 ml) liquid. Spoon the mixture into an ice cube tray or a plastic freezing container, cover with foil or a lid and put in the freezing compartment of the refrigerator.

When the mixture is beginning to freeze round the sides of the container, remove from the freezer. Scrape the frozen bits into the centre of the container with a fork to break up any ice crystals. Whip the egg whites until stiff, but not dry, and fold them into the strawberry mixture. Return to the freezer, either in the original container or spooned into small moulds. Cover and freeze the ice until set.

Serve the water ice spooned into glasses or in their moulds.

STRAWBERRY SHORTCAKE

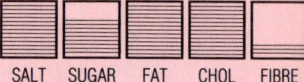

| SALT | SUGAR | FAT | CHOL | FIBRE |

GLUTEN-FREE*   WHOLEFOOD*
TOTAL CALORIES: ABOUT 3149

The high **salt** level is due to the astonishingly high level in baking soda. To avoid this, low-salt baking powder can be bought at health food stores: it is used just like conventional baking powder, replacing both soda and cream of tartar.

If no **sugar** is beaten into the cream, or only 1 tablespoon (taken from the amount in shortcake base mixture) this recipe will be low sugar, especially if it serves more than 4 people. (Calories lost: up to 99.)

The shortcake base is much lower in **fat** than a usual shortcrust pastry, and is worth using for other dishes, including savouries if sugar is omitted. The amount of fat can be reduced to 1½ oz (40 g), and vegetable margarine chosen to avoid the **cholesterol** of the butter (or a mixture used). (Calories lost: up to 78.)

The remaining high fat level comes from the cream, which can be replaced by a half-and-half mixture of 8 oz (225 g) thick low-fat yogurt with 8 oz (225 g) low-fat quark, and from the butter spread over the layers, which can be painlessly omitted. (Calories lost: up to 1196.)

These changes give a low-fat, low-cholesterol dish.

A **gluten-free** base can be made, using a mixture of wheat starch, gluten-free flour and buckwheat flour for flavour.

Freezing: ☑ up to 2 months.

STRAWBERRY WATER ICE

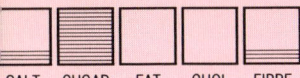

SALT	SUGAR	FAT	CHOL	FIBRE

GLUTEN-FREE WHOLEFOOD
TOTAL CALORIES: ABOUT 277

For low **sugar** use home-made lemonade, with no more than 1 oz (25 g) sugar to each pint (570 ml). (Calories lost: up to 55.)

Food processor: ✓ for the purée.
Freezing: ✓ up to 3 months.

STRAWBERRY ICE CREAM

SALT	SUGAR	FAT	CHOL	FIBRE

GLUTEN-FREE WHOLEFOOD
TOTAL CALORIES: ABOUT 1370

Less **sugar** can be used, say 1 oz (25 g), giving a low sugar level. (Calories lost: up to 197.)
The high **fat** level from the cream cannot be changed without changing the character of the ice cream. However, a mixture of 8 oz (225 g) low-fat quark blended with 8 oz (225 g) thick low-fat yogurt, or 4 oz (100 g) yogurt and 4 oz (100 g) smetana, will give a delicious but different ice, with low to moderate fat and **cholesterol**. (Calories lost: up to 699.)
The result will be harder, so thaw slightly before serving.
Wholefood: use a pale type of sugar as otherwise the flavour may overwhelm that of the strawberries.

Food Processor: ✓ for the purée.
Freezing: ✓ up to 3 months.

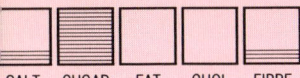

STRAWBERRY ICE CREAM

This sweet is best if prepared the day before.

PREPARATION TIME: *15–20 min*
FREEZING TIME: *12 hours*
INGREDIENTS *(for 6):*
½ lb (225 g) strawberries
3 oz (75 g) icing sugar
Squeeze lemon juice
¼ pint (150 ml) double cream
¼ pint (150 ml) single cream
GARNISH:
6–8 large strawberries

Hull and wash the strawberries in a colander, drain them thoroughly and cut them into small pieces. Put them in the liquidiser, with the sieved sugar and lemon juice (alternatively, rub the strawberries through a fine sieve and add the sugar and lemon juice to the purée). Whisk the two creams until thick, but not stiff; blend this well into the strawberry purée.

Spoon the strawberry mixture into a plastic freezing container, cover with a lid and leave to freeze for 12 hours. One or two hours before serving, remove the ice cream from the freezing compartment and thaw slightly in the refrigerator.

Scoop the ice cream into individual glasses and decorate with slices of fresh strawberries.

ICED TANGERINES

For a special dinner party, this refreshingly tangy and impressive looking ice cream is a fitting ending. Prepare the ice cream a day ahead.

PREPARATION TIME: *30 min*
COOKING TIME: *25 min*
INGREDIENTS *(for 6):*
8 medium-sized tangerines
(preferably the Wilkins variety)
6 oz (175 g) caster sugar
½ pint (300 ml) water
Juice of half lemon
1 egg yolk
½ pint (300 ml) double cream
GARNISH:
Crystallised violets
Tangerine slices
Camellia leaves
Langues de chat

Wipe the tangerines, cut off the tops and carefully scoop out the flesh from both tops and bottoms. Place six of the empty tangerine skins in a polythene bag in the refrigerator and set the remaining two aside. Squeeze ½ pint (300 ml) of juice from the tangerine pulp. Boil the sugar and water in a saucepan over a high heat for 10 minutes to make a syrup. Remove and allow to cool. Stir into the syrup the tangerine and lemon juices. Beat the egg yolk and stir into the syrup. Return to the heat and cook gently for 5 minutes, stirring continuously. Cool, pour into a freezing container, cover tightly with a lid and place in the freezing compartment of the refrigerator until lightly set, for approximately 1½–2 hours.

Grate the rind of the remaining two tangerines and beat the cream

until stiff. Break the frozen syrup into a bowl and beat vigorously with a fork until it has an even texture. Beat in the cream and tangerine rind until the colour is uniform and the rind evenly distributed. Spoon this ice cream back into the freezing container, cover with a lid and freeze for a further 2½ hours.

Turn out the mixture, break it down as before and beat until the texture is even; return to the freezer. One hour before serving, scoop the ice cream into the empty tangerine skins and fix on

the lids at an angle.

Brush the outsides of the tangerines with water and place in the freezer. Ten minutes before serving, remove the tangerines from the freezer in order to let the frost on the skins settle.

Serve on a tray decorated with well-washed camellia (or other glossy evergreen) leaves, crystallised violets and tangerine slices. A dish of langues de chat could be served separately.

ICED TANGERINES

SALT   SUGAR   FAT   CHOL   FIBRE

GLUTEN-FREE   WHOLEFOOD
TOTAL CALORIES: ABOUT 2378

This method is based on a tangerine-flavoured sugar syrup. Instead, you can sweeten 1 pint (570 ml) of juice, mixing tangerine and apple juice if wished, with about 2 oz (50 g) sugar, or honey. This reduces the **sugar** level to medium. (Calories lost: up to 408.)

To reduce the **fat** and **cholesterol** levels to low, replace the cream with 8 oz (225 g) low-fat quark mixed with 4 oz (100 g) smetana and 4 oz (100 g) low-fat yogurt, lightly sweetened with a spoonful of honey and a few drops of natural vanilla flavouring if liked. (Calories lost: up to 969.)

This dish is not **wholefood** because of the garnishes, which are likely to carry colourings, preservatives and sugar. Instead, garnish the dish with fresh fruit slices, or flowers (ideally orange blossom or scented jasmine).

An alternative treatment of this recipe would be to replace some of the juice with jasmine tea.

Freezing: ☑ up to 3 months.

TUTTI FRUTTI PUDDING WITH ORANGE FOAM SAUCE

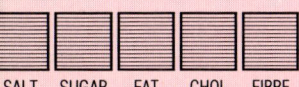

SALT	SUGAR	FAT	CHOL	FIBRE

GLUTEN-FREE*   WHOLEFOOD*
TOTAL CALORIES: ABOUT 2796

Low-salt baking powder would reduce the **salt** level to low. For low **sugar**, omit both butter and sugar from the sponge. Instead, beat 3 eggs with 3 tablespoons honey and the orange rind in a bowl over a pan of hot water until thick and fluffy. The sauce can be made with half the quantity of sugar. Coat the bottom of the pudding basin with honey instead of golden syrup. The sauce can be made with half the quantity of sugar. (Calories lost: up to 382.)

This will also give a medium **fat** level, but the **cholesterol** will remain medium to high because of the eggs. For low to moderate cholesterol, replace the foam sauce with 6 tablespoons of marmalade, made without added sugar, heated gently with the grated rind and juice of an orange and, if liked, a little lemon juice and/or apple juice concentrate. (Calories lost: up to 404.)

For a **wholefood** pudding, replace the glacé cherries and angelica with fresh cherries. If you have fresh angelica, this can be used. Commercial **gluten-free** flour makes quite a satisfactory sponge.

Pressure cooker: ☑ for the pudding.
Freezing: ☑ up to 3 months (the pudding only).
Microwave: ☑ for the pudding.

TUTTI FRUTTI PUDDING WITH ORANGE FOAM SAUCE

A steamed pudding is an ideal winter sweet especially when it is composed of a light-textured sponge and colourful fruit. It is served with a feather-light orange-flavoured sauce.

PREPARATION TIME: *40 min*
COOKING TIME: *2 hours*
INGREDIENTS *(for 6):*
2 oz (50 g) prunes
2 oz (50 g) dried apricots
2 oz (50 g) glacé cherries
1 oz (25 g) angelica
4 oz (100 g) unsalted butter
4 oz (100 g) caster sugar
Grated rind and juice of an orange
2 eggs
3 oz (75 g) self-raising flour
2 oz (50 g) fresh breadcrumbs
2 tablespoons golden syrup
6 tinned apricot halves or 6 stoned prunes
ORANGE FOAM SAUCE:
1 oz (25 g) unsalted butter
Grated rind and juice of an orange
2 level teaspoons plain flour
2 oz (50 g) caster sugar
1 egg
Lemon juice

Finely chop the dried prunes, apricots, glacé cherries and angelica. Thoroughly grease a 1½-pint (900 ml) pudding basin. Cream together the butter and sugar until light and fluffy, then add the grated orange rind. Whisk the eggs lightly and gradually beat them into the butter. Mix the sifted flour and the breadcrumbs together and lightly fold them into the pudding mixture. Add the orange juice and fold in the

chopped fruit.

Coat the bottom of the pudding basin with golden syrup and arrange the six apricot halves or soaked stoned prunes in a circle over the syrup. Spoon over the pudding mixture and cover the bowl with buttered foil or a double layer of greaseproof paper. Tie securely with string. Place the pudding basin in a steamer or in a pan with boiling water reaching two-thirds up the sides of the basin. Steam for 1¾–2 hours or until the pudding has risen and is set.

While the pudding is steaming, prepare the sauce: cream the butter with the grated orange rind and gradually beat in the flour mixed with the sugar. Separate the egg and beat the yolk into the butter and flour mixture, add the orange juice–made up with water to 5 fluid oz (150 ml). Do not worry if the mixture curdles at this stage; it will become smooth again as it cooks.

Cook the sauce in a small heavy saucepan over low heat, stirring constantly, until the sauce thickens and the flour is cooked through. Add a little extra water if necessary to keep the sauce to a pouring consistency. Remove the pan from the heat and cover with a lid to keep warm.

Just before serving, fold the stiffly beaten egg white into the sauce and sharpen with a little lemon juice.

Unmould the cooked pudding on to a hot serving dish, and serve the orange foam sauce separately.

BREAD PUDDING

The genuine Welsh bread pudding is packed with fruit, spices and peel. It is served warm as a pudding; any left-overs can be served cold at tea-time.

PREPARATION TIME: *35 min*
COOKING TIME: *2 hours*
INGREDIENTS *(for 4–6)*:
8 oz (225 g) stale bread
½ pint (300 ml) milk
2 oz (50 g) candied peel
Peel of a small orange
Peel of a lemon
4 oz (100 g) currants
2 oz (50 g) sultanas
3 oz (75 g) shredded beef suet
2 oz (50 g) demerara sugar
2 level teaspoons mixed spice
1 large egg
Milk
Butter
Grated nutmeg
Caster sugar

Cut away all the crust from the bread; break the bread into small pieces. Place in a large mixing bowl and pour over the milk; leave to soak for 20 minutes. Finely chop the candied peel, grate the orange and lemon peel, add to the bread and mix in. Add the dried fruit, suet, sugar and mixed spice; blend well. Beat the egg and stir it into the mixture which should have a dropping consistency. If necessary, add a teaspoon or two of milk.

Spoon the bread mixture into a well-greased 2 pint (1·2 litre) pie dish and grate a little nutmeg over it. Bake on the middle shelf of an oven heated to 350°F (180°C, mark 4) for 1¾–2 hours or until browned.

Serve hot or cold, liberally sprinkled with caster sugar. You can also serve custard or cream separately in a bowl to accompany the pudding.

BREAD AND BUTTER PUDDING

Slightly stale buttered bread is the basis for this traditional English nursery pudding.

PREPARATION TIME: *15 min*
COOKING TIME: *30 min*
INGREDIENTS *(for 4)*:
8 slices buttered bread
2 oz (50 g) sultanas
Grated rind of a lemon
2 eggs
3 level tablespoons caster sugar
1 pint (570 ml) vanilla-flavoured milk

Remove the crusts and cut the bread into 1 in (2½ cm) squares. Place them in a lightly buttered fireproof dish, with alternate layers of sultanas mixed with grated lemon rind.

Beat the eggs lightly with 2 tablespoons of the sugar and all the milk. Pour this custard over the bread. Sprinkle the remaining sugar over the top, and bake the pudding in a pre-heated oven, at 350°F (180°C, mark 4) for about 30 minutes.

STEAMED JAM PUDDING

The well-tried nursery puddings never lose their appeal for children and adults. Fresh breadcrumbs give this suet pudding a particularly light texture.

PREPARATION TIME: *15 min*
COOKING TIME: *2–2½ hours*
INGREDIENTS *(for 4–6)*:
6 oz (175 g) self-raising flour
1 level teaspoon baking powder
Salt★
3 oz (75 g) fresh breadcrumbs
4 oz (100 g) shredded beef suet
4 oz (100 g) caster sugar
1 egg
Milk to mix
1 tablespoon red jam
SAUCE:
2 rounded tablespoons red jam
2 oz (50 g) caster sugar

Sift the flour, baking powder and a little salt into a mixing bowl, add the breadcrumbs, suet and sugar, and mix well. Lightly beat the egg and stir into the flour, with sufficient milk to make the dough a soft dropping consistency. Blend thoroughly. Butter a 1½–2 pint (about 1 litre) pudding basin and put 1 tablespoon red jam in the bottom. Spoon in the pudding mixture until the basin is two-thirds full. Cover with a double thickness buttered greaseproof paper and fold a pleat in this to allow the pudding to expand as it cooks. Secure the paper with string.

Set the pudding in a steamer over a saucepan half-filled with simmering water, or put the basin on an upturned saucer in a saucepan and fill the pan with boiling water to come two-thirds up the side of the basin. Cover the pan with a tightly fitting lid and

BREAD PUDDING

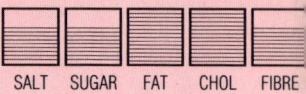

SALT	SUGAR	FAT	CHOL	FIBRE

GLUTEN-FREE★   WHOLEFOOD★
TOTAL CALORIES: ABOUT 2411

The **salt** level will be low if unsalted bread is used.
The **sugar** content is medium if the pudding serves 6 people, high if it serves 4. It can be avoided by puréeing about ⅓ of the dried fruit in the milk (you can use soya milk which is a little sweeter) and omitting the added sugar. If wished, a little brown sugar can be sprinkled on top when serving. (Calories lost: up to 197.)
For low **fat** and **cholesterol**, use skim milk (or soya milk) and only 1 oz (25 g) soft vegetable margarine instead of the suet; for very low cholesterol, use only the egg white. (Calories lost: up to 608.)
The **fibre** level is medium if the pudding serves 6, high if it serves 4. Using wholemeal bread makes it very high fibre.
Wholefood: some may like to replace the candied peel with fresh rind grated finely from a very well scrubbed orange.

Freezing: ✓ up to 2 months.

BREAD AND BUTTER PUDDING

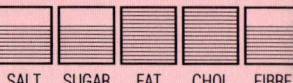

SALT	SUGAR	FAT	CHOL	FIBRE

GLUTEN-FREE★   WHOLEFOOD★
TOTAL CALORIES: ABOUT 1907

The **salt** level will be low if unsalted bread is used.
To reduce the **sugar** content to low, use only 1 tablespoon

beaten with the eggs. Sprinkle the top with extra sultanas, or add some chopped dates, instead of sugar. Soya milk is slightly sweet and could be used instead of ordinary milk. (Calories lost: up to 55.)
For low **fat** and **cholesterol**, omit the butter on the bread, use skim milk (or soya milk), and omit one egg yolk. (Calories lost: up to 662.)

STEAMED JAM PUDDING

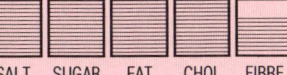

| SALT | SUGAR | FAT | CHOL | FIBRE |

GLUTEN-FREE★   WHOLEFOOD★
TOTAL CALORIES: ABOUT 2425

The high **salt** level can be reduced to low by using low-salt baking powder and breadcrumbs made from unsalted bread.
The **sugar** and **fat** level in the pudding can be reduced to 3 oz (75 g) each and the sauce made much lower in sugar by using jam made without added sugar, heated very gently. This still gives a moderately high fat and sugar level and high **cholesterol**, especially as the egg is needed for the texture. The jam in the sponge can also be the no-added-sugar variety, which has roughly half as much sugar as conventional jam but tastes perfectly sweet enough. (Calories lost: up to 367.)

Pressure cooker: ☑
Freezing: ☑ up to 3 months.
Microwave: ☑

steam for 2 to 2½ hours. Top the pan up with more boiling water if it has evaporated before steaming is finished.
About 10 minutes before the pudding is cooked, prepare the sauce: put the jam, sugar and 2 tablespoons of water into a pan, stir over low heat to dissolve the sugar, then bring to the boil. Simmer the sauce for 2–3 minutes or until thick and syrupy.

Loosen the sides of the pudding with a knife and turn out on to a hot serving dish. Pour the sauce into a bowl and serve separately.

Custards and Ices

CRÈME BRÛLÉE

This rich but delicious pudding, ideal for an important dinner party, is a traditional speciality of Trinity College, Cambridge. Be very careful when cooking the cream not to let it boil. If you keep a jar of sugar with a vanilla pod in it, use this sugar and omit the vanilla essence.

PREPARATION TIME: *20 min*
CHILLING TIME: *4 hours plus*
    2–3 hours
INGREDIENTS *(for 12)*:
2½ pints (1½ litres) single cream
12 egg yolks
2 level tablespoons caster sugar
½ teaspoon vanilla essence
4 level tablespoons Demerara sugar

Put the cream in the top half of a large double boiler or in a bowl over a pan of gently simmering water. Carefully stir the egg yolks, beaten with the caster sugar and vanilla essence, into the warm cream. Continue cooking gently until the cream has thickened enough to coat the back of the wooden spoon. Strain the cream through a fine sieve into a large soufflé dish or mould and leave to chill for at least 4 hours.

Sprinkle the sifted Demerara sugar on top of the chilled cream. Set the dish or mould on a bed of ice cubes on the grill pan and place under a hot grill until the sugar has caramelised. Remove the dish and chill in the refrigerator for 2–3 hours. Serve with fruit – any fresh fruit in season – as a foil for the richness of the dish.

ZABAGLIONE

This Italian dish is probably a more popular sweet in countries outside its homeland where it is chiefly served as a tonic. It is quickly made, but care must be taken to prevent it from curdling while cooking.

PREPARATION AND
COOKING TIME: *10 min*
INGREDIENTS *(for 4)*:
4 egg yolks
2 oz (50 g) caster sugar
4–6 tablespoons Marsala wine
GARNISH:
Sponge fingers

Put the egg yolks in a mixing bowl, together with the sugar and Marsala wine. Place the bowl over a saucepan half filled with water kept simmering. Whisk the egg mixture continuously over the heat until thick and fluffy (about 5–7 minutes). On no account must the egg mixture reach boiling point.

Remove the bowl from the heat and pour the thickened mixture into warmed serving glasses. Serve at once, garnished with sponge fingers.

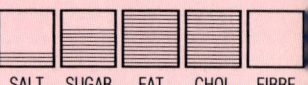
Crème brûlée is by its nature extremely high in **fat** and **cholesterol** so that apart from eating very tiny portions there is no way to reduce the levels to anything approaching moderate. There are however alternatives, which are just as good. You can make the black currant brûlée on page 20, using other soft fruits if you prefer; or you can fill half the dish with fresh peaches, nectarines or apricots before adding the custard cream – using half the quantity given will give a medium to high fat and cholesterol level. Replacing some or all of the custard cream with thick Greek yogurt gives a delicious, if rather different, result. (Calories lost: up to 3784.)

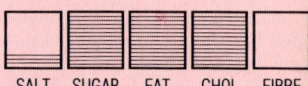
This recipe cannot be materially altered or it won't work. However, as it is quite rich, you could use only 3 egg yolks with 1½ oz (40 g) sugar among 4 people, and garnish with fingers of fresh fruit, ideally pears, rather than sponge fingers. This would give a medium to high **sugar** level and medium **fat**, but the **cholesterol** would be still quite high. (Calories lost: up to 144.)

VANILLA ICE CREAM

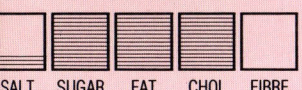

SALT	SUGAR	FAT	CHOL	FIBRE

GLUTEN-FREE WHOLEFOOD*
TOTAL CALORIES: ABOUT 2052

For medium **sugar** simply make the custard less sweet: for many people, adding 1 oz (25 g) sugar or honey would provide plenty of sweetness. (Calories lost: up to 197.)
The **fat** and **cholesterol** in this recipe can be reduced to medium by making the custard with skim milk, and thickening with 2 whole eggs rather than one egg with 2 extra yolks. Half the cream can be replaced with oz (100 g) quark, folding it in with the cream. For extra volume, fold in a stiffly beaten large egg white when the mixture is just setting. (Calories lost: up to 715.)

Freezing: ☑ up to 3 months.

BROWN BREAD ICE CREAM

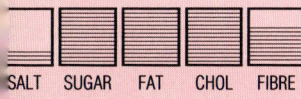

SALT	SUGAR	FAT	CHOL	FIBRE

GLUTEN-FREE* WHOLEFOOD*
TOTAL CALORIES: ABOUT 1903

For medium **sugar** add only oz (25 g) to the crumbs. (Calories lost: up to 197.)
To reduce the **fat** level, replace the double cream with 4 oz (100 g) quark, 4 oz (100 g) smetana and two egg whites, stiffly beaten and folded in when the ice cream is nearly set and crumbs are added. This will also give a low **cholesterol** level. (Calories lost: up to 1127.)

Freezing: ☑ up to 2 months.

VANILLA ICE CREAM

Delicious on its own or as an accompaniment to raspberries, strawberries or other soft fruit.

PREPARATION TIME: *25 min*
FREEZING TIME: *about 3 hours*
INGREDIENTS *(for 6):*
½ *pint (300 ml) milk*
Vanilla pod
1 whole egg
2 egg yolks
3 oz (75 g) caster sugar
½ *pint (300 ml) double cream*

Bring the milk almost to the boil with the vanilla pod, then leave to infuse off the heat for about 15 minutes. Remove the vanilla pod. Cream the whole egg, yolks and sugar until pale. Stir in the vanilla-flavoured milk and strain this mixture through a sieve into a clean pan. Heat the custard mixture slowly over gentle heat, stirring all the time, until the mixture thickens just enough to coat the back of a wooden spoon. Pour into a bowl and leave to cool.
Whip the cream lightly and fold it carefully and thoroughly into the cooled custard. Spoon into ice cube trays or a suitable freezing container, cover and set in the freezing compartment until half-frozen. Whisk the ice cream thoroughly, then freeze until firm.
Remove from the freezing compartment and put in the refrigerator for 20 minutes before serving to soften slightly.

BROWN BREAD ICE CREAM

For a picnic treat, spoon this crunchy ice cream straight into a wide-necked vacuum jar, and pack any spaces with sliced peaches or pears.

PREPARATION TIME: *20 min*
FREEZING TIME: *2–3 hours*
INGREDIENTS *(for 6):*
½ *pint (300 ml) double cream*
1 oz (25 g) vanilla sugar (page 99)
3 oz (75 g) stale, crustless brown bread
3 oz (75 g) soft dark brown sugar

An hour before preparing the ice cream turn the refrigerator to its coldest setting. Blend the cream and vanilla sugar in a bowl and whisk until fluffy. Spoon the mixture into shallow ice trays or a polythene container, cover with foil or the lid, and put into the freezing compartment of the refrigerator. When the mixture has begun to set round the edges, take it out of the freezer and stir the sides into the middle to prevent ice crystals forming. Repeat this twice during freezing.
Reduce the bread to fine crumbs and mix with the brown sugar. Spread the crumbs on a lightly oiled baking tray and put this into the centre of an oven, pre-heated to 400°F (200°C, mark 6). Leave until the sugar caramelises and the crumbs are golden brown; stir them occasionally. When cool, break up into crumbs again with a fork.
When the ice cream is nearly set, turn it into a chilled bowl, beat with an egg whisk and stir in the crumbs. Spoon the mixture into the ice trays and return them, covered, to the refrigerator. Freeze until firm.

BISCUIT TORTONI

During the 19th century, Tortoni's restaurant in Paris was famous for its buffet table, patronised by many great writers.

PREPARATION TIME: *15 min*
FREEZING TIME: *3 hours*
INGREDIENTS *(for 6–8):*
¾ pint (425 ml) double cream
¼ pint (150 ml) single cream
2 oz (50 g) icing sugar
Salt★
12 macaroons
3 fluid oz (75 ml) brown sherry
GARNISH:
Wafers or ratafia biscuits

About 1 hour before beginning preparations, turn the refrigerator to its coldest setting.

Whip the creams together with the sugar and a pinch of salt, until the mixture is firm but not stiff. Spoon into a 9 in (23 cm) loaf tin or plastic box, cover with a lid or a double layer of foil and freeze the cream until nearly solid.

Put the macaroons into a plastic or greaseproof paper bag and crush them to fine crumbs with a rolling pin. Set aside a third of the crumbs for decoration.

Break up the frozen cream mixture into a basin and blend in the sherry and remaining macaroon crumbs with a hand whisk. The mixture should stay light and bulky; add a little more sugar and sherry if necessary. Spoon the cream mixture into the washed and dried container, cover and return to the freezing compartment of the refrigerator.

When the cream has frozen quite firm again, remove it from the refrigerator and invert the container on to a serving plate. Rub the container with a cloth wrung out in very hot water until the ice cream drops out. Press the macaroon crumbs lightly into the top and sides of the ice with a broad-bladed knife.

GRANITA AL CAFFÈ

Strong, bitter black coffee, preferably a continental roast, should be used for this Italian water ice. It is sometimes served with whipped cream.

PREPARATION TIME: *10 min*
CHILLING TIME: *3–4 hours*
INGREDIENTS *(for 4):*
¾ pint (425 ml) strong black coffee
4½ level tablespoons caster sugar
¼ pint (150 ml) whipping cream

Turn the refrigerator to its coldest setting 1 hour before beginning preparations. Melt 4 tablespoons of sugar in ¼ pint (150 ml) of water over moderate heat, stirring until the sugar has completely dissolved. Bring this syrup to the boil and boil steadily for 5 minutes. Remove from the heat and leave the syrup to cool.

Stir the strained coffee into the cold syrup, and pour the mixture into ice cube trays. For the best texture, the dividers should be left in the trays so that the ice will set in cubes. Put the trays into the freezing compartment for at least 3 hours. Stir the ice occasionally with a fork to scrape the frozen crystals round the edges into the centre.

Turn the frozen cubes into a bowl and crush them lightly with a pestle or break them up with a fork. Spoon the ice into individual glasses and serve at once with a separate bowl of whipped cream, sweetened with the remaining sugar.

BISCUIT TORTONI

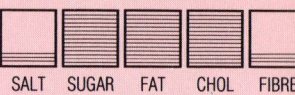

SALT	SUGAR	FAT	CHOL	FIBRE

GLUTEN-FREE   WHOLEFOOD
TOTAL CALORIES: ABOUT 3216

This alternative recipe is very low in **sugar**, **fat** and **cholesterol**.

8 oz (225 g) curd cheese (12% fat variety)
10 oz (275 g) thick low-fat yogur
2 egg whites
2 tablespoons honey
2–3 tablespoons sherry
12 macaroons

Mix the curd cheese, yogurt and honey, and freeze for abou 1 hour until mushy. Beat egg whites until stiff. Beat frozen mixture smooth, stir in the sherry, and 8 crushed macaroons, and then fold in th egg whites. Freeze and continue with recipe. Transfer to refrigerator about hour before serving to soften. drop of almond essence could be mixed with the sherry.

Freezing: ✓ up to 2 months.

GRANITA AL CAFFÈ

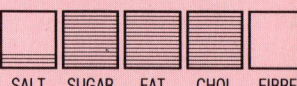

SALT	SUGAR	FAT	CHOL	FIBRE

GLUTEN-FREE   WHOLEFOOD
TOTAL CALORIES: ABOUT 783

The **sugar** level can be reduced slightly but will still be fairly high, as for most people's taste at least 3 tablespoons will be needed to sweeten the coffee. The **fat** and **cholesterol** are all in the cream, and this can be omitted completely as the granita is very good on its own. Calories lost: up to 597.)

Freezing: ☑ up to 2 months (the coffee ice only, not the cream).

CHAMPAGNE CHARLIE AND OAT BISCUITS

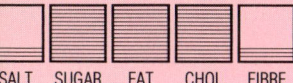

SALT	SUGAR	FAT	CHOL	FIBRE

GLUTEN-FREE* WHOLEFOOD*
TOTAL CALORIES: ABOUT 4666

The **sugar** in the ice cream can be reduced to 4 oz (100 g), still high, with 3½ fluid oz (95 ml) water, but the sugar and golden syrup in the oat biscuits can be omitted. (Calories lost: up to 650.)
About half the double cream can be replaced with quark, and 2 stiffly beaten egg whites will help make up the lost bulk, folded in when the mixture is just setting. This will give medium **fat** and **cholesterol**. (Calories lost: up to 1080.) Ratafias are usually **gluten-free**, but check ingredients list.

Freezing: ☑ up to 3 months (both ice cream and biscuits).

MIRIAM'S HONEY RATAFIAS

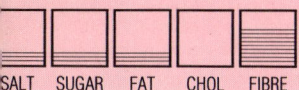

SALT	SUGAR	FAT	CHOL	FIBRE

GLUTEN-FREE WHOLEFOOD
TOTAL CALORIES: ABOUT 242

This recipe is specifically designed to conform to healthy guidelines.

CHAMPAGNE CHARLIE

George Leybourne, star of the English music hall of the 1890s, often ordered champagne for his audiences, a gesture which earned him the nickname of 'Champagne Charlie'. This ice cream, named after him, is a superb sweet for a special occasion.

PREPARATION TIME: *30 min*
COOKING TIME: *10 min*
FREEZING TIME: *5 hours*
INGREDIENTS *(for 6)*:
6 oz (175 g) caster sugar
2 oranges and 2 lemons
1 pint (570 ml) chilled champagne
1 pint (570 ml) double cream
8 tablespoons brandy
36 ratafia biscuits
GARNISH:
Langues de chat or oat biscuits
Lemon peel

One hour before beginning preparations, set the refrigerator to its coldest setting.

Put the sugar in a pan with ¼ pint (150 ml) of water. Bring to the boil and boil rapidly for 6 minutes to make a syrup. Meanwhile, grate the rind from one orange and squeeze the juice from the oranges and lemons. Add the rind and the strained juice to the syrup and leave to cool. Stir in the chilled champagne.

Pour the mixture into a plastic container, and cover with the lid or a double layer of foil. Freeze for 1½–2 hours or until frozen round the edges. Scoop the mixture into a chilled bowl and whip until smooth. In a separate bowl, beat the cream until stiff, and blend it slowly into the champagne syrup until it is smooth and uniform in colour. Blend in 2 tablespoons of brandy. Spoon the mixture into the container, cover and freeze for about 3 hours.

About 30 minutes before serving, place six ratafia biscuits in the bottom of each champagne glass. Pour 2 teaspoons of brandy over the biscuits and leave them to soak. Scoop the ice cream into the glasses. Hang a thin spiral of lemon peel from the rim of each glass and pour a teaspoon of brandy over each portion.

Serve immediately, with a separate plate of langues de chat or oat biscuits.

Oat Biscuits
PREPARATION TIME: *15 min*
COOKING TIME: *20–25 min*
INGREDIENTS *(for 24 biscuits)*:
3 oz (75 g) plain flour
½ level teaspoon bicarbonate of soda
3 oz (75 g) Demerara sugar
3 oz (75 g) rolled porridge oats
3 oz (75 g) unsalted butter
1 tablespoon rum
1 tablespoon golden syrup

Sift the flour and bicarbonate of soda into a bowl; add the sugar and the oats, blending thoroughly. Heat the butter with the syrup and the rum in a small pan until the butter has just melted. Pour into the flour mixture and blend thoroughly with a wooden spoon.

Shape the dough into balls, 1 in (2½ cm) wide, between floured hands. Set the balls well apart on greased baking trays. Bake in the centre of the oven, pre-heated to 325°F (170°C, mark 3), for 20–25 minutes or until golden brown. Allow to cool before serving.

MIRIAM'S HONEY RATAFIAS

PREPARATION TIME: *10 min*
COOKING TIME: *12–15 min*
INGREDIENTS *(for about 15 ratafias)*:
1 egg white
2 tablespoons clear honey
1½ oz (40 g) ground almonds
Few drops natural almond flavouring (optional)
Sheets of rice paper

Beat the egg white until it forms stiff, but not hard, peaks. Continue beating while drizzling in the honey, then the ground almonds and flavouring (if used). Spoon in very small heaps on rice paper, allowing only a little room for spreading. Bake in a pre-heated oven at 350°F (180°C, mark 4) for 12–15 minutes. Cool on a wire rack. They will crisp up as they cool.

Pastries

TREACLE TART

British country cooking is justly famous for its variety of sweet and savoury tarts and pastries. The popularity of this traditional lattice tart has never diminished. It is, in spite of its name, always made with golden syrup.

PREPARATION TIME: *20 min*
COOKING TIME: *25–30 min*
INGREDIENTS *(for 6):*
7 oz (200 g) plain flour
½ level teaspoon salt★
1 egg yolk
5 oz (150 g) unsalted butter
5 rounded tablespoons golden syrup
3 heaped tablespoons fresh breadcrumbs
1 level teaspoon finely grated lemon rind
1 tablespoon lemon juice

Sift the flour and salt into a mixing bowl. Cut the butter into small knobs and rub into the flour until the mixture resembles breadcrumbs. Mix in the egg yolk with a fork, and add just enough cold water to make a dough. Knead this pastry on a lightly floured surface before rolling it out, ⅛ in (¼ cm) thick. Line an 8 in (20 cm) shallow pie plate with the pastry and prick the base lightly with a fork. Mix the other ingredients together and spread over the pastry. Roll out the pastry trimmings, cut them into ½ in (1 cm) wide strips and lay them in a lattice pattern over the tart; trim the edges neatly. Bake the tart on the middle shelf of an oven preheated to 400°F (200°C, mark 6) for 25–30 minutes.

LINZERTORTE

This classic Austrian torte, or tart, named after the town of Linz, is popular both as a dessert and as an accompaniment to morning or afternoon coffee. It is traditionally served with *Schlagsahne*. This consists of sweetened whipped cream into which stiffly beaten egg white is sometimes folded just before serving.

PREPARATION TIME: *30 min*
CHILLING TIME: *1½ hours*
COOKING TIME: *1 hour*
INGREDIENTS *(for 6):*

3 oz (75 g) plain flour
½ level teaspoon ground cinnamon
3 oz (75 g) caster sugar
3 oz (75 g) unblanched ground almonds or hazel nuts
Grated rind of half lemon
4 oz (100 g) unsalted butter
2 egg yolks
¼ teaspoon vanilla essence
¾ lb (350 g) thick raspberry jam
GLAZE:
1 egg yolk
1 tablespoon double cream

Sift the flour, cinnamon and sugar into a mixing bowl. Add the ground almonds and finely grated lemon peel; blend thoroughly before rubbing in the butter until the mixture resembles breadcrumbs.

Beat the egg yolks with the vanilla essence and stir into the flour and almond mixture. Using a wooden spoon, work it into a soft dough. Wrap in greaseproof paper or foil, and chill for 1 hour in the refrigerator.

Grease a loose-bottomed flan tin 8 in (20 cm) wide by 1½ in (4 cm) deep. Knead the dough to soften it slightly, then press it

TREACLE TART

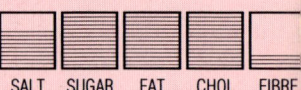

GLUTEN-FREE★
TOTAL CALORIES: ABOUT 1951

Golden syrup has a significant sodium level. The alternative is to use honey, in the same amount, giving a low **salt** dish. To reduce the **sugar** level is virtually impossible, given the character of the recipe. If wished, the amount of treacle topping could be halved, and spread over a layer of cooked fruit purée. If sweet fruit, such as dessert apples or dried apricots were used, almost no sugar would be needed for this resulting in a medium sugar dish. (Calories lost: up to 94.) To reduce the **fat** also requires a basic change to the recipe, using some other type of pastry such as a yeast or a scone dough as shortcrust pastry does not adapt to using lower fat: it just becomes hard. However, a very low fat pastry (as on page 23) is acceptable if the dish is eaten straight from the oven. (Calories lost: up to 1043.) For very low **cholesterol** use pastry made with oil or vegetable margarine.

Freezing: ☑ up to 6 months.

LINZERTORTE

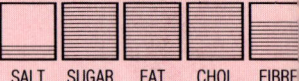

GLUTEN-FREE★   WHOLEFOOD★
TOTAL CALORIES: ABOUT 2899

For low **sugar** omit the sugar from the dough, and use jam made with no added sugar. (Calories lost: up to 772.)

Reducing the **fat** is more difficult, since it involves changing the type of pastry used, ideally to a yeast type. There is still a substantial amount of fat from almonds, which are roughly half oil. If hazel nuts are used instead, the amount of fat from the nuts will be reduced by about $\frac{1}{3}$ or to a medium level for the dish, if combined with low fat pastry. However, almonds have twice as much **fibre** as hazels. (Calories lost: up to 493.)

To reduce the **cholesterol** level almost to zero, vegetable fat can be used in the pastry and the egg yolks wholly or partly replaced by egg whites. Serve with slightly sweetened yogurt or quark in place of cream. If the above changes to the jam are made, this recipe can be considered **wholefood**.

Freezing: ✓ up to 6 months.

SHOO FLY PIE

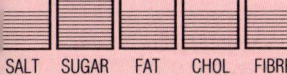

SALT	SUGAR	FAT	CHOL	FIBRE

GLUTEN-FREE*   WHOLEFOOD*
TOTAL CALORIES: ABOUT 2162

This can be low **salt** if you use a low-salt baking powder.

For low to medium **sugar** use chopped dates to mix with the raisins, and substitute ground almonds for some or all of the sugar in the topping. (Calories lost: up to 137.)

For low **fat**, use a low-fat pastry as suggested on page 10 and use only half the amount of butter in the topping; for low **cholesterol**, replace the butter with vegetable margarine. (Calories lost: up to 612.)

Freezing: ✓ up to 6 months.

with the fingers over the base of the tin and up the sides. The lining should be not more than $\frac{1}{4}$ in ($\frac{1}{2}$ cm) thick, and the surplus dough should be pushed up over the top edge and trimmed off neatly with a knife. Spread the jam evenly over the base of the flan.

Knead the pastry trimmings together and roll them out on a well-floured board to a rectangle 8 in (20 cm) by 3 in (7$\frac{1}{2}$ cm). Cut this into six strips, each $\frac{1}{2}$ in (1 cm) wide. Lift the strips, one at a time, with a palette knife, and lay them across the raspberry filling in a lattice pattern. Press the ends of the strips into the pastry lining. Run a sharp knife round the top of the tin to loosen the pastry that extends above the lattice pattern, then fold it inwards and down on to the strips to make a $\frac{1}{2}$ in (1 cm) wide border.

For the glaze, beat the egg yolk and cream together and brush it over the lattice and border. Chill the tart for 30 minutes in the refrigerator, then bake it in the centre of a pre-heated oven at 350°F (180°C, mark 4) for about 1 hour or until crisp and lightly browned.

Leave the tart to cool and shrink slightly, then loosen the edge with a knife. Place the tin on a jar and gently push down the rim of the flan tin. Slide the tart on to a serving plate, and serve it warm or cold with a bowl of *Schlagsahne*.

SHOO FLY PIE

This pie, a favourite in the deep south of the United States, takes its name from its extreme sweetness. Flies and bees are so attracted to the pie that it is necessary to shoo them away while the pie is cooling.

PREPARATION TIME: *30 min*
COOKING TIME: *35 min*
INGREDIENTS *(for 6)*:
4 oz (100 g) shortcrust pastry
   (page 85)
4 oz (100 g) stoneless raisins
2 oz (50 g) soft brown sugar
$\frac{1}{4}$ level teaspoon bicarbonate of
   soda
TOPPING:
4 oz (100 g) plain flour
$\frac{1}{2}$ level teaspoon cinnamon
$\frac{1}{4}$ level teaspoon ground nutmeg
$\frac{1}{4}$ level teaspoon ground ginger
2 oz (50 g) unsalted butter
2 oz (50 g) soft brown sugar

Prepare the shortcrust pastry and roll it out thinly on a lightly floured board. Line a 7 in (18 cm) flan tin or shallow pie plate with the pastry. Crimp the edges between finger and thumb for a decorative finish. Prick the base of the pastry all over with a fork and cover with the raisins. Mix the brown sugar with 3 tablespoons of hot water and the bicarbonate of soda; pour over the raisins.

For the topping, sift together the flour and spices. Cut the butter into small knobs and rub them into the flour until the mixture resembles fine breadcrumbs. Stir in the brown sugar and sprinkle over the filling.

Bake the pie on the shelf above the centre of a pre-heated oven, at 425°F (220°C, mark 7), until the pie begins to brown. Reduce the heat to 325°F (170°C, mark 3) and bake for a further 20 minutes, or until the topping has set.

Cut the pie into wedges and serve it warm or cold. A jug of cream may be offered although it is not traditional.

PROFITEROLES

Do not disturb these little buns while they are cooking, or the steam will escape thus causing them to collapse.

PREPARATION TIME: *1 hour*
COOKING TIME: *15 min*
INGREDIENTS (*for 20–25*):
1 portion choux pastry (page 88)
½ pint (300 ml) double or
  whipping cream
Icing sugar
¼ lb (100 g) plain dark chocolate
1 small tin evaporated milk

Make up the choux pastry and spoon it into a forcing bag fitted with a plain ½ in (1 cm) vegetable nozzle. Pipe 20–25 small bun shapes, well apart, on to greased baking trays, and bake in a pre-heated oven, in the centre or just above, at 425°F (220°C, mark 7) for about 15 minutes until well risen, puffed and crisp. If the profiteroles are not thoroughly dry after 15 minutes, reduce the heat to 350°F (180°C, mark 4) and continue baking for a further 10 minutes. Cool on a wire rack.

Split the buns not quite in half, lengthways. Fill the hollow centres with whipped cream and dust the tops with sifted icing sugar. To serve, carefully pile the profiteroles into a pyramid on a serving dish and pour a little chocolate sauce over them; serve the remainder separately.

To make the sauce, melt the chocolate, broken into pieces, in a bowl over a pan of hot water. Stir in the evaporated milk and beat thoroughly.

SOURED CREAM FLAN

This flan, whose texture is reminiscent of cheesecake, makes a good weekday dessert and may be served hot or cold. For a more elaborate sweet, a chilled apricot purée could be served with it.

PREPARATION TIME: *30 min*
COOKING TIME: *40 min*
INGREDIENTS (*for 6*):
6 oz (175 g) shortcrust pastry
  (page 85)
3 eggs
5 oz (150 g) caster sugar
8 oz (225 g) sultanas
½ level teaspoon ground cinnamon
¼ level teaspoon ground cloves
¼ level teaspoon salt*
5 oz (150 g) soured cream
Grated rind of a lemon

Roll out the prepared shortcrust pastry, ⅙ in (½ cm) thick, on a floured surface. Line a 9 in (23 cm) flan ring with the pastry. Prick the base with a fork and leave it to rest in the refrigerator.

Separate the eggs and beat the yolks thoroughly with the sugar until pale yellow and thick enough to leave a trail. Finely chop the sultanas and beat them into the eggs, together with the cinnamon, cloves, salt, soured cream and lemon rind. Beat the egg whites in a separate bowl until stiff, but not dry. Fold the egg whites carefully and evenly into the yolk mixture, and spoon it into the flan case. Bake for 15 minutes on a shelf low in the oven, pre-heated to 425°F (220°C, mark 7), then reduce the heat to 350°F (180°C, mark 4) for a further 25 minutes.

Leave the flan for about 10 minutes before removing the ring and serving the flan.

PROFITEROLES

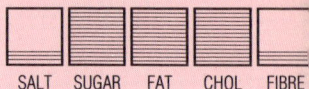

SALT	SUGAR	FAT	CHOL	FIBRE

WHOLEFOOD*
TOTAL CALORIES: ABOUT 2996

For low **sugar** use carob bars without added sugar and unsweetened evaporated milk. (Calories lost: up to 13.) The **fat** and **cholesterol** will be moderate to fairly high, if some or all of the double cream filling is replaced with quark lightly sweetened with honey. Less chocolate can also be used, and water instead of the milk-and-water mixture in the pastry. (Calories lost: up to 1250.) Choux pastry made with either commercial **gluten-free** or **wholemeal** flour is excellent.

Freezing: ✓ up to 3 months (profiteroles and sauce should be frozen separately).

SOURED CREAM FLAN

SALT	SUGAR	FAT	CHOL	FIBRE

GLUTEN-FREE*   WHOLEFOOD*
TOTAL CALORIES: ABOUT 2948

For medium **sugar** use only half. (Calories lost: up to 296.) For a low **fat** level, replace the soured cream with smetana (or for a very low-fat filling, quark) and use only 1 egg yolk with 2 oz (50 g) tofu. Use a low-fat pastry. (Calories lost: up to 415.) This, plus the use of vegetable fat in whatever pastry is used, will give low **cholesterol**.

Freezing: ✓ up to 1 month.

CHOCOLATE CREAM PIE

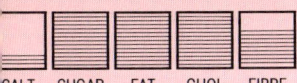

SALT	SUGAR	FAT	CHOL	FIBRE

GLUTEN-FREE* WHOLEFOOD*
TOTAL CALORIES: ABOUT 4444

For medium **sugar** use oatcakes instead of digestives, omit sugar from the filling and only a little for the dusting. (Calories lost: up to 355.)

The **fat** and **cholesterol** will be medium if you use crumbled biscuits, such as ginger nuts, which have less fat, and no binding fat. Use skim milk, together with only ½ oz (10 g) butter for the sauce, and make the topping with quark or only half the cream, into which a stiffly beaten egg white is folded just before serving. (Calories lost: up to 1721.)

Food processor: √ for the biscuit crust.

Freezing: √ up to 2 months.

PARIS-BREST

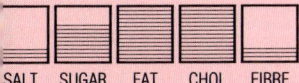

SALT	SUGAR	FAT	CHOL	FIBRE

WHOLEFOOD*
TOTAL CALORIES: ABOUT 2534

For low **sugar** omit sugar in the pastry and use 1 tablespoon honey in the filling. (Calories lost: up to 119.)

To reduce the **fat** level to low, use skim milk and replace the double cream with quark. The **cholesterol** level will remain high because of the eggs. Use thinly flaked hazel nuts instead of almonds. (Calories lost: up to 205.)

Freezing: √ up to 3 months.

CHOCOLATE CREAM PIE

The biscuit crust for this light fluffy pie should be chilled for 2 hours before filling.

PREPARATION TIME: *20 min*
CHILLING TIME: *1 hour*
INGREDIENTS *(for 6)*:
1 portion biscuit crust (page 86)
FILLING:
½ pint (300 ml) milk
1 oz (25 g) caster sugar
1 oz (25 g) plain flour
1½ level teaspoons cornflour
2 eggs
1 oz (25 g) unsalted butter
3–3½ oz (75–90 g) dark plain chocolate, grated
2 teaspoons brandy or rum
Icing sugar
TOPPING:
¼ pint (150 ml) double cream
1 tablespoon milk
Grated chocolate (optional)

Make up the biscuit crust according to the basic recipe and line an 8½ in (21½ cm) fluted flan case.

Heat the milk. Blend the sugar, flour, cornflour and beaten egg together in a bowl, then stir in the milk. Return this mixture to the pan and cook over low heat, stirring continuously, until the mixture thickens and just comes to the boil. Remove the pan from the heat and stir in the butter, cut into small pieces, the chocolate and brandy. Stir until smooth, then leave to cool slightly. Spoon the filling into the biscuit crust, and dust it with icing sugar to prevent a skin forming. Chill.

Just before serving, whip the cream with the milk until thick enough to hold its shape. Spoon this over the filling and dust with a little coarsely grated chocolate; if used.

PARIS-BREST

In the late 19th century, this sweet was created in honour of a famous bicycle race which was run on a circular route from Paris to Brest and back again. It is a concoction of choux pastry filled with Chantilly cream.

PREPARATION TIME: *30 min*
COOKING TIME: *30 min*
INGREDIENTS *(for 4)*:
1 oz (25 g) unsalted butter
1 level teaspoon caster sugar
¼ pint (150 ml) milk
4 oz (100 g) plain flour
3 eggs
1½ oz (40 g) flaked almonds
CHANTILLY CREAM:
½ pint (300 ml) double cream
3 level tablespoons icing sugar
1 egg white

For the choux pastry, put the butter, caster sugar and milk into a saucepan over moderate heat, and bring to the boil. Stir in the sifted flour, remove the pan from the heat, and beat vigorously with a wooden spoon until the dough leaves the sides of the pan clean. Beat 2 eggs, one by one, into the dough. Then add the yolk of the third egg, beating vigorously until the dough is smooth and shiny. If necessary, beat in the remaining egg white.

Spoon the dough into a forcing bag fitted with a large plain nozzle. Pipe a ring, about 1½ in (4 cm) wide and 8 in (20 cm) in diameter, on to a greased baking tray. Sprinkle the almonds over the dough and bake for 30 minutes on the middle shelf of an oven pre-heated to 425°F (220°C, mark 7) for 30 minutes, or until dark brown. Cool on a wire rack, then split in half, horizontally.

For the Chantilly cream, whip together the double cream, 2 tablespoons sifted icing sugar and an egg white until light and fluffy. Spoon the cream into the hollow bottom half of the ring. Cover with the lid, and dust with the remaining icing sugar.

AMERICAN CHEESE CAKE

This transatlantic cheese cake is not baked like the European version, but set with gelatine. It is chilled and decorated with fruit for an unusual sweet.

PREPARATION TIME: *35 min*
CHILLING TIME: *3 hours*
INGREDIENTS *(for 6)*:
8 oz (225 g) cottage cheese
4 oz (100 g) fresh cream cheese
2–3 oz (50–75 g) unsalted butter
3 oz (75 g) crushed cornflakes
4 oz (100 g) sugar
4 oz (100 g) powdered gelatine
Rind and juice of a small lemon
2 eggs
Salt★
¼ pint (150 ml) double cream
GARNISH:
Black grapes and mandarin
    orange segments

Melt the butter in a small saucepan over low heat. Remove the pan from the heat and with a fork stir in the cornflake crumbs and 1 oz (25 g) of sugar. Press this mixture over the base of an 8 in (20 cm) loose-bottomed flan or cake tin. Put the flan in the refrigerator to chill while preparing the cheese mixture.

Put 3 tablespoons of cold water in a small pan and sprinkle the gelatine evenly on the surface. Set aside to soak for 5 minutes. Meanwhile, rub the cottage cheese through a coarse sieve into a large basin and add the cream cheese. Finely grate the lemon rind and mix in well.

Separate the eggs; add 1½ oz (40 g) of sugar and a pinch of salt to the yolks and beat until creamy and light. Gently heat the pan of soaked gelatine, stirring continuously, but do not allow it to boil. Remove from the heat once the gelatine has dissolved, and add the strained lemon juice. Gradually whisk this liquid into the egg yolks, before blending it all into the cheese mixture. Whisk the egg whites until thick, then whisk in the remaining sugar and beat until stiff. Fold the beaten egg whites and the lightly whipped cream into the cheese mixture. Pour into the prepared chilled cake base and level the top. Chill in the refrigerator for 2–3 hours or until firm.

When ready to serve, loosen the sides of the cheese cake with a knife blade. Remove the cake from the tin and decorate the top with halved black grapes and mandarin orange segments.

Serve cut into wedges.

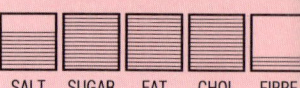
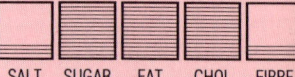

The amount of **fat** can be reduced by making what is known as a fatless sponge (see Strawberry Cream Sponge, on the next page) where the only fat comes from the eggs. This is very satisfactory if eaten the same day, or frozen. Using quark in place of cream in fillings gives a low fat content; or for medium fat, replace half the cream with quark, and fold in a beaten egg white. (Calories lost: up to 1115.)

The **cholesterol** remains high because of the eggs.

Freezing: ✓ up to 6 months.

GINGERBREAD

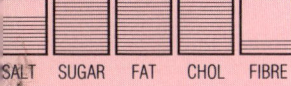

SALT	SUGAR	FAT	CHOL	FIBRE

GLUTEN-FREE*
TOTAL CALORIES: ABOUT 5014

For low **salt** use honey instead of golden syrup, unsalted butter and low-sodium baking powder. For a less rich cake use skim milk and halve the sugar, butter, treacle and syrup. If wished, 4 oz (100 g) raisins or sultanas can be liquidised in the milk to give a moist sweetness and more bulk (also more fibre). The levels of **fat**, **cholesterol** and **sugar** will of course depend on the size of the slice you cut, but will then be between medium and low. (Calories lost: up to 1428.) **Gluten-free** buckwheat flour can be used successfully. This kind of cake is excellent made with **wholemeal** flour, with a spoonful of water added to the mix before putting in the tin.

Freezing: ✓ up to 6 months.
Microwave: ✓

VICTORIA SANDWICH

In this traditional layer cake, the fat is creamed before the flour is beaten in, giving a rich cake with a close, even grain and soft crumb.

PREPARATION TIME: *15 min*
COOKING TIME: *25 min*
INGREDIENTS:
4 oz (100 g) butter or margarine
4 oz (100 g) caster sugar
2 large eggs
Vanilla essence or grated lemon or orange rind
4 oz (100 g) self-raising flour

Grease two 7 in (18 cm) straight-sided sandwich tins and line the bases with buttered greaseproof paper. In a bowl, beat the butter until soft, then add the sugar and cream until light and fluffy. Beat in the eggs, one at a time, then add a few drops of vanilla essence or finely grated lemon or orange rind. Beat in the sifted flour.

Divide this mixture equally between the two tins, and level off the surface. Bake the cakes side by side, if possible, in the centre of the oven pre-heated to 350°F (180°C, mark 4) for about 25 minutes. Cool on a wire rack.

Layer the two cakes with jam or a butter cream filling and dust the top lightly with caster or sifted icing sugar.

GINGERBREAD

This is best if made 4–7 days in advance, to give the flavour time to mellow. Cut into chunks just before serving.

PREPARATION TIME: *15 min*
COOKING TIME: *1½ hours*
INGREDIENTS:
1 lb (450 g) plain flour
3 level teaspoons ground ginger
3 level teaspoons baking powder
1 level teaspoon bicarbonate of soda
*1 level teaspoon salt**
8 oz (225 g) Demerara sugar
6 oz (175 g) butter
6 oz (175 g) black treacle
6 oz (175 g) golden syrup
½ pint (300 ml) milk
1 large egg

Grease a 9 in (23 cm) square cake tin, about 2 in (5 cm) deep, and line with buttered greaseproof paper. Sift all the dry ingredients, except the sugar, into a large bowl. Warm the sugar, butter, treacle and syrup in a pan over low heat until the butter has just melted. Stir the melted ingredients into the centre of the dry mix, together with the milk and beaten egg. Beat thoroughly with a wooden spoon. Pour the mixture into the prepared tin and bake in the centre of an oven, pre-heated to 350°F (180°C, mark 4), for about 1½ hours, or until well-risen and just firm to the touch. Leave to cool in the tin for 15 minutes, then turn out to cool on a wire rack. When cold, wrap in foil, without removing the lining paper, and store in a tin.

HUNGARIAN HAZEL NUT TORTE

Hungarian dessert cakes – or *torten* – are internationally famous, and several of them were perfected by Dobos, a 19th-century Hungarian confectioner.

This classic hazel nut cake has a chocolate cream filling and a caramel topping. It improves in flavour if kept for a day or two in a completely airtight tin.

PREPARATION TIME: *30 min*
COOKING TIME: *30–40 min*
INGREDIENTS *(for 6)*:

4 oz (100 g) unblanched hazel
   nuts
4 eggs
5 oz (150 g) caster sugar
FILLING:
2 oz (50 g) unsalted butter
2 oz (50 g) icing sguar

2 rounded teaspoons chocolate
   powder
1 rounded teaspoon instant coffee
TOPPING:
3 oz (75 g) caster sugar
12 hazel nuts

Lightly grease two round 7 in (18 cm) sandwich tins. Grind the unblanched hazel nuts finely in a liquidiser or coffee grinder. Separate the eggs and whisk the whites until stiff, but still moist. Whisk the egg yolks with the caster sugar until pale lemon in colour and the mixture trails off the whisk in ribbons.

Fold the ground nuts and whisked egg whites alternately into the egg yolks. Divide the mixture equally between the two sandwich tins and bake in the centre of an oven pre-heated to 350°F (180°C, mark 4) for 30 minutes, or until set. Test by pressing the top of the cakes with a finger – it should leave no impression. Remove the cakes from the oven, and allow them to shrink slightly before turning them out to cool on a wire rack.

Meanwhile, prepare the filling: cream the butter until fluffy and sift the icing sugar, chocolate

and coffee together; beat it gradually into the butter. When the cakes are cool, sandwich them together with the filling. Set aside while you are preparing the caramel topping.

Put 2 tablespoons of water and the caster sugar in a small, heavy-based saucepan. Stir the contents over low heat until dissolved into a clear syrup. Increase the heat and boil the syrup rapidly, without stirring, until it is a rich golden colour.

Remove the pan from the heat immediately and pour most of the caramel over the top of the cake. Spread it evenly with an oiled knife and mark the topping into portions with the same knife. Decorate the top quickly with the whole nuts before the caramel hardens. As the remaining caramel cools it can be trickled over the nuts or pulled into a spun sugar veil and arranged on top of the cake.

STRAWBERRY CREAM SPONGE

A very light cake which uses no fat, its texture depending entirely on the incorporated eggs.

PREPARATION TIME: *20 min*
COOKING TIME: *15 min*
INGREDIENTS:
3 oz (75 g) plain flour
Pinch of salt*
3 eggs
3 oz (75 g) caster sugar
Strawberry jam
¼ pint (150 ml) double or
   whipping cream
Caster or icing sugar for dusting

Butter and dust with flour and sugar two 7 in (18 cm) straight-sided sandwich tins. Sift the flour with the salt twice into a bowl. Place a deep mixing bowl over a pan of hot water, break the eggs into the bowl and gradually whisk in the sugar. Continue whisking until the mixture is pale, and thick enough to leave a trail. Carefully fold in the sifted flour and salt. Divide the mixture equally between the two tins, putting any scrapings from the bowl at the side of the tins, not in the middle. Bake just above the centre of an oven, pre-heated to 375°F (190°C, mark 5), for about 15 minutes or until pale brown and springy to the touch.

Carefully ease away the edges of the baked cakes with a palette knife, and cool on a wire rack.

When cold, spread the bases of both sponges with a thin layer of jam, cover one sponge with whipped cream and place the other cake, jam downwards, on top. Press lightly together and dust with caster or sifted icing sugar. Chill until serving.

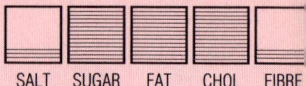
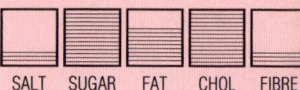

by omitting 1 or 2 egg yolks, although this will change the colour and flavour of the cake. One egg yolk plus 3 whites works well, but the cooking time is less, only 7–10 minutes. (Calories lost: up to 130.)

Freezing: ☑ up to 6 months.

DANISH LAYER CAKE

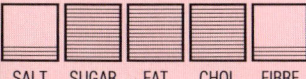

SALT SUGAR FAT CHOL FIBRE

GLUTEN-FREE* WHOLEFOOD*
TOTAL CALORIES: ABOUT 4442

The **sugar** in the cake cannot be reduced, but the amount in the filling can be halved, as the chocolate and pineapple (if using tinned, choose fruit tinned in juice, not sugar syrup) will add sweetness. If wished, the sponge recipe on the facing page can be substituted. This gives medium sugar. (Calories lost: up to 514.)

The high **fat** level can be reduced to moderate by substituting quark for the double cream. If the cream flavour is still wanted, replace only half the cream with quark, and fold in 1 large stiffly beaten egg white when the mixture is just setting. Soft cheese fillings work very well for this type of cake. (Calories lost: up to 2109.) The **cholesterol** level remains high because of the eggs.

Wholefood: if using wholemeal flour, sieve and retain the bran in the sieve. Use to 'flour' the greased cake tins, mix into the filling, or keep for another time.

Freezing: ☑ up to 3 months.

DANISH LAYER CAKE

There are numerous versions of the Danish layer cake, from a simple jam sandwich to a huge eight-layer concoction of wafer-thin sponge cakes in alternating layers of thick cream and fruit. It is served with morning coffee and afternoon tea, as an after-dinner sweet or with evening coffee.

PREPARATION TIME: *45 min*
COOKING TIME: *25 min*
CHILLING TIME: *1 hour*
INGREDIENTS (*for 6*):
4 eggs
Rind and juice of half lemon
5 oz (150 g) icing sugar
3 oz (75 g) plain flour
1 oz (25 g) cornflour
½ level teaspoon baking powder
FILLING:
½ oz (10 g) gelatine
1 pint (570 ml) double cream
4 level teaspoons vanilla sugar
 (page 100)
4 slices fresh or tinned pineapple
3 oz (75 g) dark bitter chocolate

Separate the eggs and put the yolks in a large bowl, together with the lemon rind and juice. Sift the icing sugar into the yolks and beat until fluffy and pale cream in colour. Whisk the egg whites in a separate bowl until they stand in soft peaks, then fold them carefully into the yolk mixture. Sift the two flours and baking powder together and blend into the sponge mixture.

Grease a loose-bottomed round cake tin, 8 in (20 cm) wide, and line with buttered grease-proof paper. Spoon the sponge mixture into the tin, smoothing it level round the sides. Bake in the centre of a pre-heated oven at 350°F (180°C, mark 4) for 25 minutes or until the sponge is golden and well risen.

Loosen the edges of the sponge with a sharp knife and turn the cake out on a wire rack to cool. When completely cold, cut the cake into three thin rounds.

Dissolve the gelatine in a few spoonfuls of warm water and leave to cool slightly. Whip the cream, setting one-third aside for decoration. Fold the cooled gelatine into the remaining cream and sweeten with the vanilla sugar. Peel and trim the pineapple slices (or drain thoroughly if using tinned pineapple); set one slice aside and chop the other three finely. Grate the chocolate and blend into the cream with the chopped pineapple. Leave the filling to set.

Assemble the layer cake about 2 hours before serving. Divide the filling equally over the sponge layers and spread it evenly; sandwich the layers together. Pipe the rest of the whipped cream through a narrow rosette nozzle, round the edge and down the sides of the cake. Garnish the top with the reserved pineapple, cut into small chunks.

Chill the layer cake in the refrigerator for about 1 hour and serve it cut into wedges.

Cakes and Breads

CARROT CAKE

The natural sweetness of carrots is brought out in this moist cake with its rich orange colour.

PREPARATION TIME: *25 min*
COOKING TIME: *35–40 min*
INGREDIENTS:
8 oz (225 g) butter
1 lb (450 g) sugar
1 teaspoon ground cinnamon
½ teaspoon ground mace or nutmeg
½–1 teaspoon grated orange rind
4 eggs
6 oz (175 g) carrots
3 oz (75 g) walnuts or hazel nuts
10 oz (275 g) plain flour
3 teaspoons baking powder
½ teaspoon salt★
5 tablespoons warm water

Grate the carrots or shred them finely. Toast the walnuts or hazel nuts (page 000) and chop them finely. If you are using hazel nuts, rub them in a coarse cloth after toasting them to loosen the skins, which are then easily removed.

Cream the butter and sugar together until light and fluffy. Beat in the cinnamon, mace (or nutmeg) and the grated orange rind. Add the eggs one at a time, beating well after each addition. Gradually stir in the grated carrots and chopped nuts.

Sift together the flour, baking powder and salt. Add them, with the warm water, to the creamed mixture. Do not beat it but fold in the flour to the point where it is just well moistened.

Pour the batter into a buttered 11 by 15 in (28 by 38 cm) cake tin and bake in a pre-heated oven at 350°F (180°C, mark 4) for 35–40 minutes, or until the cake springs back when it is pressed lightly in the centre.

Leave the cake for just a few minutes after removing it from the oven, then loosen it from the sides of the tin and turn it out on a rack to cool.

FARMHOUSE FRUIT CAKE

This recipe uses soft tub margarine, which cuts the preparation time, as there is no need to beat it until creamy as is the case with butter. An electric mixer can be used instead of beating with a wooden spoon; switch it off from time to time and scrape the cake mixture down into the bowl before continuing.

PREPARATION TIME: *10 min*
COOKING TIME: *about 1½ hours*
INGREDIENTS:
6 oz (175 g) soft tub margarine
6 oz (175 g) caster sugar
3 oz (75 g) sultanas
3 oz (75 g) seedless raisins
3 oz (75 g) glacé cherries, chopped
12 oz (350 g) self-raising flour
Pinch of salt★
1 level teaspoon mixed spice
3 tablespoons milk
3 eggs

Grease an 8 in (20 cm) round cake tin and line it with buttered greaseproof paper. Mix the margarine and all the dry ingredients in a bowl, then add the milk and eggs and beat with a wooden spoon until well mixed, for 2–3 minutes. Turn into the prepared tin and level the top.

Bake in the centre of the oven pre-heated to 350°F (180°C, mark 4) for about 1½ hours. When a skewer comes away clean, the cake is cooked. Leave the cake in the tin for 15 minutes before turning out on a rack to cool.

TYROL CAKE

This is an example of a plain, rubbed-in cake, the easiest type of all to make. They are best eaten within 2 or 3 days of baking.

PREPARATION TIME: *25 min*
COOKING TIME: *1¾ hours*
INGREDIENTS:
8 oz (225 g) plain flour
Pinch of salt★
1 level teaspoon ground cinnamon
3½ oz (90 g) margarine
2 oz (50 g) caster sugar
2 oz (50 g) currants
2 oz (50 g) sultanas
1 level teaspoon bicarbonate of soda
¼ pint (150 ml) milk
3 level tablespoons clear honey

Grease a 6 in (15 cm) round cake tin. Sift the flour, salt and cinnamon into a bowl, cut up the margarine and rub into the flour until the mixture resembles fine breadcrumbs. To keep the mixture cool, raise the hands high when letting the crumbs drop back into the bowl. Stir in the sugar, currants and sultanas and made a well in the centre. Dissolve the bicarbonate of soda in the milk, stir in the honey and pour this mixture into the well in the flour. Using a wooden spoon, gradually work in the dry ingredients, adding more milk if necessary to give a firm dropping consistency.

Spoon the cake mixture into the prepared tin and level the top. Bake in the centre of the oven, pre-heated to 325°F (170°C, mark 3), for 1¾–2 hours or until well risen.

Test with a fine skewer – if it comes away clean, the cake is cooked. Cool on a wire rack.

CARROT CAKE

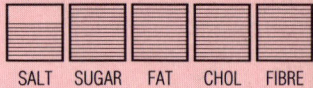

SALT   SUGAR   FAT   CHOL   FIBRE

GLUTEN-FREE★   WHOLEFOOD★
TOTAL CALORIES: ABOUT 5195

Reduce the **salt** to low by using a low-salt baking powder.
Using only 4 oz (100 g) **sugar** with the same amount each of ground almonds and (optional) chopped dates will make the cake quite sweet enough and gives an overall low to medium level. (Calories lost: up to 566.)
For moderate **fat** and **cholesterol**, use half the amount of butter and only 2 egg yolks, with an extra egg white. (Calories lost: up to 937.)

Freezing: ☑ up to 6 months.

FARMHOUSE FRUIT CAKE

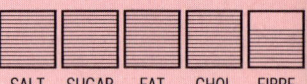

SALT   SUGAR   FAT   CHOL   FIBRE

GLUTEN-FREE★
TOTAL CALORIES: ABOUT 3986

For medium **salt** use unsalted baking powder and margarine.
To reduce **fat** to low use only 1 or 2 oz (25 or 50 g). (Calories lost: up to 639.)
For medium **sugar** reduce it by half and add an extra 4 oz (100 g) dried fruit. (Calories lost: up to 99.)
For medium **cholesterol** omit 2 yolks and add a fourth egg white plus an extra spoonful of milk, if needed.
For a **wholefood** cake, use wholemeal flour, honey in place of sugar and chopped dried apricots in place of cherries.

Freezing: ☑ up to 6 months.

TYROL CAKE

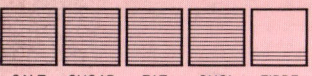

SALT	SUGAR	FAT	CHOL	FIBRE

GLUTEN-FREE★   WHOLEFOOD★
TOTAL CALORIES: ABOUT 2167

To reduce **salt** level to low, use low-sodium margarine and baking powders.
The amount of **sugar** can be halved, adding a spoonful of extra milk if needed. (Calories lost: up to 99.)
Both salt and **fat** levels can also be reduced by halving the amount of fat added. Skim milk can also be used, which with reduction of fat will produce a low-fat recipe with virtually no **cholesterol** provided the margarine is vegetable. (Calories lost: up to 376.)

Freezing: ☑ up to 6 months.

ANADAMA BREAD

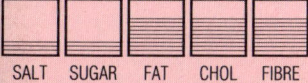

SALT	SUGAR	FAT	CHOL	FIBRE

GLUTEN-FREE★   WHOLEFOOD★
TOTAL CALORIES: ABOUT 2706

The low **salt** level assumes unsalted butter or oil is used.
The **fat** level can be reduced to very low by omitting the butter from the dough, and covering loosely with polythene when rising, rather than greasing: both measures are intended to stop surface drying from contact with air, which will stop bread rising fully. However, fat-free bread stales quickly, so 1–2 tablespoons butter or oil is worth adding, and will still give low fat and **cholesterol**. (Calories lost: up to 211.)

Freezing: ☑ up to 3 months.

ANADAMA BREAD

This is a variation, using molasses, on the cornbread that is popular in the southern United States.

PREPARATION TIME: *20 min (plus rising)*
COOKING TIME: *55 min*
INGREDIENTS *(for 2 loaves):*
10–12 oz (275–350 g) strong plain flour
4 oz (100 g) cornmeal
1 oz (25 g) fresh yeast
1 tablespoon salt
8 fluid oz (225 ml) water
2½ oz (65 g) unsalted butter
8 fluid oz (225 ml) molasses

Heat the water until it feels warm to the hand. Mix a little of it (about half a cup) with the yeast and stir until well blended. Leave for 10 or 15 minutes until frothy.

Combine 10 oz (275 g) flour, the cornmeal and salt in a large bowl. Mix the rest of the warm water with the butter and molasses. Add this to the flour mixture together with the yeast. Beat for 3 minutes with an electric mixer set at medium speed, or beat by hand – about 150 strokes with a wooden spoon. Add flour as necessary to make a stiff dough.

Turn the dough on to a floured surface and knead for about 10 minutes until it is no longer sticky. Place the dough in a buttered bowl, turning it over in the bowl 2 or 3 times until it is well greased. Set aside to rise in a warm place for 1–1½ hours, or until the dough has doubled in size.

Punch down the dough, divide it into 2 balls, and place each in a buttered 8 in (20 cm) round cake pan. Allow to rise again until doubled in size, then bake in the centre of a pre-heated oven at 375°F (190°C, mark 5) for about 55 minutes or until deep brown. The bread is done if the bottom of the bread sounds hollow when rapped with the knuckles.

SALLY LUNN

This can be baked in an ordinary cake tin, as below, or in a tube pan or plain ring mould, which looks attractive and is easy to slice.

PREPARATION TIME: *25 min (plus rising)*
COOKING TIME: *15–20 min*
INGREDIENTS *(for 2 loaves):*
1 lb (450 g) strong plain flour
2 oz (50 g) butter
¼ pint (150 ml) milk plus 4 tablespoons
1 level teaspoon caster sugar
½ oz (10 g) fresh yeast
2 eggs
1 level tablespoon salt★
SUGAR TOPPING:
1 level tablespoon caster sugar
1 tablespoon water

Melt the butter in a small pan, then add the milk and sugar. Put the yeast in a bowl, beat the eggs and add them, with the warm milk mixture, to the yeast: blend thoroughly until the yeast has dissolved.

Sift the flour and salt into a large bowl, make a well in the centre and pour in the milk mixture. Gradually incorporate the flour with the fingers of one hand and beat the dough against the bowl until it leaves the sides clean. Knead the dough on a lightly floured surface until smooth.

Divide the dough into two equal portions, knead each piece into a ball and place it in a greased 15 in (12½ cm) round cake tin. Slide each tin into an oiled polythene bag and leave in a warm place for about 1 hour or until the dough has risen almost to the top of the tins.

Remove the polythene and set the tins on baking trays. Bake just above the centre of a pre-heated oven at 450°F (230°C, mark 8) for 15–20 minutes. Meanwhile, make the sugar topping by heating the sugar and water in a small pan over low heat until the sugar has dissolved: boil rapidly for 1–2 minutes.

Turn the Sally Lunns out on to a wire rack and, while still warm, brush the tops with the sugar.

BABAS

These are traditionally flavoured with rum, but if you do not have any to hand you could use brandy instead. Although unorthodox, it is quite successful.

PREPARATION TIME: *40 min (plus rising)*
COOKING TIME: *15–20 min*
INGREDIENTS *(for 16 babas):*
8 oz (225 g) strong plain flour
1 oz (25 g) fresh yeast
6 tablespoons warm (110°F, 43°C) milk
½ level teaspoon salt★
1 oz (25 g) caster sugar
4 eggs
4 oz (100 g) butter
4 oz (100 g) currants
Lard
SYRUP:
4 tablespoons clear honey
4 tablespoons water
3 tablespoons rum (approx.)
GARNISH:
½ pint (300 ml) whipped cream

Blend the yeast, milk and 2 oz (50 g) of the measured flour together in a large bowl and beat with a wooden spoon until smooth. Leave the yeast in a warm place for about 20 minutes or until frothy. Sift the remaining flour and the salt into the yeast and blend in the sugar, the lightly beaten eggs, softened butter and the currants. Beat the mixture, which should be fairly soft, with a wooden spoon for 4 minutes.

Grease 16 small ring moulds with lard and, using a teaspoon, spoon in the dough until the moulds are half full. Set the ring moulds on baking trays and cover them with sheets of lightly oiled polythene.

Leave the babas to rise in a warm place until the dough has risen about two-thirds up the sides of the moulds.

Bake the babas just above the centre of an oven pre-heated to 400°F (200°C, mark 6) for 15–20 minutes or until golden brown.

Meanwhile, prepare the syrup: heat the honey and water in a small pan over low heat; stir in rum to taste. Leave the baked babas to cool for a few minutes in the moulds before turning them out on to a plate. While the babas are still hot, spoon the warm syrup over them until it has soaked in. Leave to cool, then transfer the rum-soaked babas to a serving dish and fill the centres with spooned or piped whipped cream.

Serve at once.

SALLY LUNN

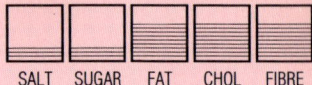

SALT   SUGAR   FAT   CHOL   FIBRE

GLUTEN-FREE★   WHOLEFOOD★
TOTAL CALORIES: ABOUT 2288

The low **salt** level assumes unsalted butter is used.
The **sugar** can be replaced by honey if wished, adding ½ tablespoon of water to make the topping. (Calories lost: up to 25.)
The **fat** and **cholesterol** levels can be reduced to low by adding only 1 oz (25 g) butter, using skim milk and 1 egg only. (Calories lost: up to 342.)
The **fibre** content depends on the flour used: it will be medium, as shown, if refined flour is used, but high if wholemeal flour is used.

Freezing: ☑ up to 3 months.

BABAS

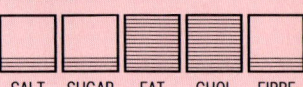

SALT   SUGAR   FAT   CHOL   FIBRE

GLUTEN-FREE★   WHOLEFOOD★
TOTAL CALORIES: ABOUT 3865

The low **salt** level depends on unsalted fat being used.
The **sugar** content will only be low if strict level spoonfuls of honey are used. If wished, use only 3 carefully measured spoonfuls and ½ in (1 cm) dough, for an overall low sugar level. (Calories lost: up to 60.)
The **fat** and **cholesterol** levels can be reduced to low by using skim milk, only 1 oz (25 g) butter and only 1 egg yolk but all the whites. (Calories lost: up to 779.)

Freezing: ☑ up to 3 months.

CHELSEA BUNS

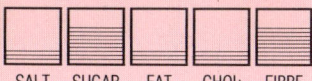

| SALT | SUGAR | FAT | CHOL: | FIBRE |

GLUTEN-FREE*   WHOLEFOOD*
TOTAL CALORIES: ABOUT 1695

The amount of **sugar** will depend on how much honey is used. To minimise, make your own chopped peel from well-scrubbed citrus rind (which will not be soaked in sugar, and will also be free from preservative), and replace the sugar with 2 oz (50 g) clear honey, which tends to give a sweeter flavour, weight for weight. Use honey for brushing sparingly, heating gently before applying to get a thinner coating. This will give a low sugar level. (Calories lost: up to 133.)

Freezing: ☑ up to 1 month.

CHELSEA BUNS

This is a not too rich version of these famous small buns. A little mixed spice – about half a teaspoon – can be added.

PREPARATION TIME: *20 min (plus rising and proving)*
COOKING TIME: *30–35 min*
INGREDIENTS *(for 9 buns):*
8 oz (225 g) strong plain flour
½ level teaspoon caster sugar
½ oz (10 g) fresh yeast
4 fluid oz (100 ml) warm (110°F, 43°C) milk
*½ level teaspoon salt**
½ oz (10 g) margarine or lard
1 egg
3 oz (75 g) dried fruit (sultanas, currants or seedless raisins)
1 oz (25 g) chopped mixed peel
2 oz (50 g) light soft brown sugar
½–1 oz (10–25 g) melted butter
Clear honey

Sift 2 oz (50 g) of the measured flour into a bowl and add the caster sugar. Crumble in the yeast and beat in the milk with a wooden spoon. Leave this yeast mixture in a warm place for about 20 minutes or until frothy. Sift together the remaining flour and the salt and rub in the margarine. Make a well in the centre, add the beaten egg and pour in the yeast mixture. Using one hand, gradually work in the flour.

Beat the dough in the bowl until it leaves the sides clean; it should be fairly soft and pliable. Turn the dough on to a lightly floured surface and knead it for 10 minutes, until smooth. Put it in a lightly oiled polythene bag and leave it to rise at room temperature for 1–1½ hours or until it has doubled in size.

Knead the risen dough on a lightly floured surface until smooth, then roll it out with a well-floured rolling pin, to a rectangle 12 by 9 in (30 by 23 cm). Mix the dried fruit, peel and soft brown sugar together, brush the dough with melted butter and spread the fruit mixture on top to within ½ in (1 cm) of the longer edges. Roll up the dough, starting with one of the long sides, and press the join to seal it.

Cut the roll into nine equal slices and lay them flat, in rows of three, in a greased 7 in (18 cm) square cake tin. Leave to rise in a polythene bag, in a warm place, for about 30 minutes.

Remove the polythene bag and bake the buns in the centre of a pre-heated oven at 375°F (190°C, mark 5) for 30–35 minutes. Turn the buns on to a wire rack and, while hot, brush with honey.

Cakes and Breads

BARN BRACK

An Irish tea bread, similar to the Welsh bara brith and the Manx bonnag. The word "barn" comes from the Irish for loaf and its resemblance to the Saxon word "barm", meaning yeast, is co-incidental. This has caused some confusion, especially since this bread would originally have been made using yeast. The word "brack" means speckled.

SOAKING TIME: *overnight*
PREPARATION TIME: *10 min*
COOKING TIME: *1¾ hours*
INGREDIENTS:
1 lb (450 g) sultanas
1 lb (450 g) stoned raisins
1 lb (450 g) soft brown sugar
1½ pints (900 ml) black tea or 1 pint (600 ml) tea and ½ pint (300 ml) Irish whiskey
1 lb (450 g) plain flour
3 eggs
3 level teaspoons baking powder
3 teaspoons mixed spice (optional)
Honey

Soak the sultanas, raisins and sugar in the tea (or tea and whiskey) overnight. The next day add, gradually, the flour and the lightly beaten eggs to the fruit and sugar mixture. Blend in the baking powder and mixed spice.

Spoon the mixture into three greased loaf tins, 8 in long by 4 in wide by 3 in deep (20 cm by 10 cm by 7½ cm). Bake in the centre of a pre-heated oven at 300°F (150°C, mark 2) for 1¾ hours.

Leave the loaves to cool on a wire rack. Glaze the tops lightly by brushing with melted honey.

POTATO CAKES

These originated in Ireland, but are also known in Scotland and parts of the north of England.

PREPARATION TIME: *15 min*
COOKING TIME: *30 min*
INGREDIENTS (*for 10–12 cakes*):
8 oz (225 g) self-raising flour
1 teaspoon salt★
3 oz (75 g) butter or margarine
6 oz (175 g) mashed potatoes
2½ fluid oz (75 ml) milk
Caraway seeds (optional)

Sift the flour with the salt and rub in the butter or margarine. Mix in the mashed potatoes, which should be warm, and add the milk to make a soft dough (you may not need quite all the milk). Roll out about ½ in (1 cm) thick and cut into 10 or 12 rounds, 3 in (7½ cm) across. If liked, sprinkle with caraway seeds. Bake on lightly floured baking trays in a pre-heated oven at 450°F (230°C, mark 8) for 20–30 minutes. Serve the potato cakes split and spread with butter.

BRIOCHES

Special brioche tins, large or small, with sloping fluted sides are available for making this delicious sweet yeast bread.

PREPARATION TIME: *25 min (plus rising and proving)*
COOKING TIME: *10 min*
INGREDIENTS (*for 12 brioches*):
8 oz (225 g) strong plain flour
½ level teaspoon salt★
1 level tablespoon caster sugar
½ oz (10 g) fresh yeast
1½ tablespoons warm water
2 eggs
2 oz (50 g) butter, melted

Sift the flour and salt into a bowl and add the sugar. Cream the yeast with the water in a small bowl, and stir it, together with the beaten eggs and the melted butter, into the flour with a wooden spoon. Beat the dough until it leaves the sides of the bowl clean, then turn it out on to a lightly floured surface and knead for 5 minutes.

Put the dough in an oiled polythene bag and leave it to rise at room temperature for 1–1½ hours or until it has doubled in

BARN BRACK

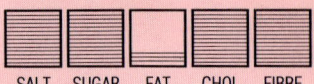

| SALT | SUGAR | FAT | CHOL | FIBRE |

GLUTEN-FREE★ WHOLEFOOD★
TOTAL CALORIES: ABOUT 6636

To reduce the **salt** level to low, use low-sodium baking powder.
The high added **sugar** level can be replaced with about 4 tablespoons honey, or by liquidising 8 oz (225 g) of the dried fruit in the tea. (Calories lost: up to 1210.)
The high **cholesterol** level can be reduced to low by using only 1 egg yolk with all the whites. The mixed spice is advisable here, as the removal of the yolks also diminishes flavour. (Calories lost: up to 130.)

Freezing: ✓ up to 6 months.

POTATO CAKES

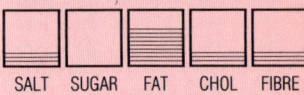

| SALT | SUGAR | FAT | CHOL | FIBRE |

GLUTEN-FREE★ WHOLEFOOD★
TOTAL CALORIES: ABOUT 1575

For a low **fat** level, reduce the amount of butter or margarine to 2 oz (50 g) and use skim milk to mix. If vegetable margarine is used, the **cholesterol** will be almost nil. Serve spread with cottage or low-fat curd cheese instead of butter. (Calories lost: up to 209.)

Freezing: ✓ up to 3 months.

BRIOCHES

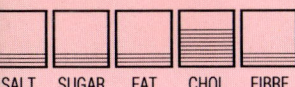

| SALT | SUGAR | FAT | CHOL | FIBRE |

WHOLEFOOD*
TOTAL CALORIES: ABOUT 1372

The **fat** level can be further lowered, and the **cholesterol** level reduced to low, by using only 1 egg, and either reducing butter to 1 oz (25 g) or replacing with 1 oz (25 g) vegetable margarine. (Calories lost: up to 275.)

Freezing: ✓ up to 1 month.

DANISH PASTRIES

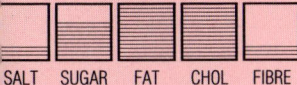

| SALT | SUGAR | FAT | CHOL | FIBRE |

GLUTEN-FREE* WHOLEFOOD*
TOTAL CALORIES: ABOUT 3654

To keep **sugar** level to the low level given by the amount in the pastries themselves, brush with jam made with no added sugar, lightly warmed, in place of icing. Decorate with almond flakes if wished. (Calories lost: up to 565.)
To reduce the **fat** level, use only 2 oz (50 g) unsalted butter, and omit lard from dough. In filling, replace almond paste with sultanas or stewed whole dried apricots, or thick apple purée. The low fat level will give a less 'flaky' texture to the pastries, but they can still be delicious.
For low **cholesterol**, use less butter, as above, and egg whites only, both in the mixture and for the glaze. (Calories lost: up to 1093.)

Freezing: ✓ up to 1 month.

size. Turn the risen dough on to a lightly floured surface and knead it until smooth. Shape the dough into a sausage and divide it into 12 equal pieces.

Brush 3 in (7½ cm) fluted patty pans with oil and shape three-quarters of each piece of dough into a ball; place it in a patty pan. Using a floured finger, press a hole in the centre of the dough as far as the base of the tin. Shape the remaining piece of dough into a knob and insert it in the hole. Press lightly with the fingertip to unite the two pieces of dough. When all 12 brioches have been shaped, set the patty pans on a baking tray and cover them with oiled polythene. Leave to rise (prove) until the dough is puffy and just below the tops of the tins.

Remove the polythene and bake the brioches in the centre of a pre-heated oven at 450°F (230°C, mark 8) for 10 minutes or until golden brown.

DANISH PASTRIES

These can be made in a variety of shapes, including squares, crescents and pinwheels.

PREPARATION TIME: *45 min (plus rising)*
RESTING TIME: *50 min*
COOKING TIME: *10 min*
INGREDIENTS:
8 oz (225 g) plain flour
*Pinch of salt**
1 oz (25 g) lard
1 level tablespoon caster sugar
½ oz (10 g) fresh yeast
5 tablespoons cold water
2 eggs
5 oz (150 g) unsalted butter
FILLINGS:
Almond paste
1 oz (25 g) butter

1 oz (15 g) caster sugar
1 level teaspoon cinnamon
Currants and chopped mixed peel
GARNISH:
Glacé icing

Sift the flour and salt into a large bowl. Cut up the lard and rub it into the flour with the fingertips; add the sugar and make a well in the centre of the flour. Blend the yeast with the water in a small bowl until creamy and smooth, then add it to the flour together with 1 lightly beaten egg. Gradually work in the flour, then beat the soft dough until it leaves the sides of the bowl clean.

Turn the dough out on to a lightly floured surface and knead it until smooth. Put it inside a lightly oiled polythene bag and chill for 10 minutes.

Beat the butter with a wooden spoon until soft but not oily, then shape it into a rectangle about 5 in by 9½ in (13 by 24 cm). On a floured board, roll out the dough to a 10–11 in (26–27 cm) square and place the butter in the centre. Fold the two unbuttered sides over so that they just overlap the butter. Seal the open sides with the rolling pin, then roll the dough into an oblong strip, about three times as long as it is wide; fold in three.

Place the dough in a lightly oiled polythene bag and leave in the refrigerator for 10 minutes. Remove the polythene and roll out the dough, in the opposite direction, to an oblong strip and fold in three. Repeat the resting, rolling and folding twice more. Finally, rest the dough for 10 minutes in the refrigerator before rolling it out to any of the traditional shapes.

Almond Squares Roll out half

the dough to a 10 in (25½ cm) square, then cut it into four equal pieces. Fold two corners of each square to meet in the centre, envelope style, and repeat with the other two corners. Press down firmly to seal. Place a small round of almond paste in the centre.

Crescents Roll out the dough as for almond squares, and cut each square diagonally in half. Place a small piece of almond paste at the base of each triangle, then roll it up from the base and curve into a crescent shape.

Pinwheels Roll out half a portion of pastry dough to a rectangle 12 in by 8 in (30 by 20 cm). Cream the butter with the sugar and cinnamon and spread over the dough to within ¼ in (½ cm) of the edges. Scatter a few currants and a little mixed peel over the butter. Cut the dough in half, lengthways, and roll each piece, from the shorter end, into a thick roll. Cut this into 1 in (2½ cm) thick slices.

Alternatively, make cuts, 1 in (2½ cm) apart, through three-quarters of the depth of the rolls. Ease the near-cut pinwheels apart so that they overlap each other slightly; bake for about 30 minutes.

Set the pastry shapes well apart on greased baking trays and cover with sheets of oiled polythene. Leave the pastries to rise in a warm place for 20 minutes. Remove the polythene and brush the pastries with lightly beaten egg. Bake near the top of a pre-heated oven, at 425°F (220°C, mark 7), for about 10 minutes or until golden. Leave on a wire rack and, while still warm, brush almond squares, crescents and pinwheels with glacé icing. Leave to set before serving.

OVEN SCONES

If you like fruited scones, you can add about 2 oz (50 g) dried fruit – raisins, currants or sultanas – to the mixture.

PREPARATION TIME: *15 min*
COOKING TIME: *10 min*
INGREDIENTS (*for 10–12 scones*):
8 oz (225 g) plain flour
Pinch of salt★
½ level teaspoon bicarbonate of soda
1 level teaspoon cream of tartar
1½ oz (40 g) firm margarine
About 4 tablespoons each milk and water mixed
Milk for glazing

Sift together the flour, salt, bicarbonate of soda and cream of tartar into a wide bowl. Cut up the margarine and rub it into the flour. Gradually add the milk and water and mix with a round-bladed knife to give a soft but manageable dough.

Knead the dough quickly on a lightly floured surface, to remove all cracks. Roll the dough out ½ in (1 cm) thick, and cut out 2 in (5 cm) rounds with a plain or fluted pastry cutter. Knead the trimmings together, roll them out and cut out as many scones as possible. Set the scones on a heated, ungreased baking tray, brush them with milk and bake them near the top of a pre-heated oven at 450°F (230°C, mark 8) for about 10 minutes, until well risen and light golden brown.

SODA BREAD

Another Irish speciality, soda bread does not keep well and should be eaten on the day it is made.

PREPARATION TIME: *15 min*
COOKING TIME: *30 min*

INGREDIENTS:
1 lb (450 g) plain flour
2 level teaspoons bicarbonate of soda
2 level teaspoons cream of tartar
1 level teaspoon salt★
1 oz (25 g) lard
1–2 level teaspoons caster sugar (optional)
½ pint (300 ml) soured milk, or 9 fluid oz (250 ml) buttermilk made up to ½ pint (300 ml) with milk

Sift the flour, bicarbonate of soda, cream of tartar and salt into a bowl. Cut up the lard and rub it into the flour with the fingertips until the mixture resembles fine breadcrumbs. Mix in the sugar if used. Make a well in the centre of the flour, add the milk (soured with 1 tablespoon of lemon juice) or the buttermilk, and mix to a soft but manageable dough, working the ingredients with a round-bladed knife. Add more milk if necessary.

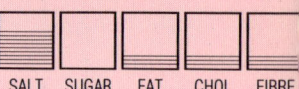
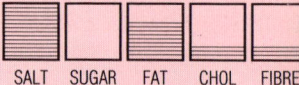

DROP SCONES

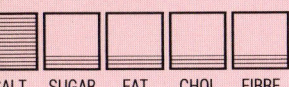

‌SALT	SUGAR	FAT	CHOL	FIBRE

GLUTEN-FREE*   WHOLEFOOD*
TOTAL CALORIES: ABOUT 809

The **salt** level can be reduced to low by using low-sodium baking powder with plain flour. Use skim milk and the minimum of oil for cooking to keep the **fat** and **cholesterol** levels very low. For an even lower cholesterol level, use the egg white only. (Calories lost: up to 225.)

Freezing: ✓ up to 6 months.

APRICOT AND WALNUT LOAF

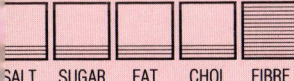

‌SALT	SUGAR	FAT	CHOL	FIBRE

GLUTEN-FREE*   WHOLEFOOD*
TOTAL CALORIES: ABOUT 1739

Sugar in the topping can be replaced with fruit sugar if wished.

To reduce the **fat** level even more, use fewer walnuts, or replace with hazel nuts which have less oil; use only ½ oz (5–10 g) fat in topping. (Calories lost: up to 184.). If you use vegetable margarine, here and in the dough in place of lard, the **cholesterol** content will be zero.

The high **fibre** content comes as much from the apricots and walnuts as from the use of brown flour.

Freezing: ✓ up to 1 month.

Turn the dough on to a floured surface, knead it lightly and shape it into a 7 in (18 cm) round; flatten it slightly. Mark the round into four with the back of a knife, set it on a floured baking tray and bake in the centre of a pre-heated oven at 400°F (200°C, mark 6) for about 30 minutes.

Cool on a wire rack and serve.

DROP SCONES

Although traditionally these are made on an iron griddle, a heavy frying pan works very well.

PREPARATION TIME: *5 min*
COOKING TIME: *3–5 min per batch*
INGREDIENTS *(for 15–18 scones):*
4 oz (100 g) self-raising flour
Pinch of salt*
1 level tablespoon caster sugar
1 egg
About ¼ pint (150 ml) milk
Lard for cooking

Set a griddle or heavy frying pan over heat. While it is warming, sift the flour and salt into a bowl and stir in the sugar. Make a well in the centre and drop in the egg; gradually add the milk, working in the flour with a spoon until a smooth batter is formed.

Grease the heated surface lightly with a little lard. When a slight haze appears, pour on small rounds of batter, well apart, either from a jug or with a spoon to give perfect rounds. As soon as the scones are puffed, bubbling on the surface and golden on the undersides, turn them over with a palette knife to brown on the other side. Serve at once, or place the scones between folds in a clean tea towel until serving time.

APRICOT AND WALNUT LOAF

A simple way of turning a basic loaf into a fruity tea bread which keeps well.

PREPARATION TIME: *30 min (plus rising)*
COOKING TIME: *40–45 min*
INGREDIENTS *(for one 1 lb, 450 g, loaf):*
Half portion quick wheatmeal dough (page 92)
4 oz (100 g) dried apricots
1 oz (25 g) caster sugar
2 oz (50 g) chopped walnuts
TOPPING:
1 oz (25 g) butter or firm margarine
1 oz (25 g) caster sugar
1½ oz (40 g) plain flour

Cut the dried apricots roughly with scissors and put them in a bowl or on a floured board, with the risen dough, the sugar and walnuts. Work the mixture together until no streaks can be seen. Line the bottom of a 1 lb (450 g) loaf tin with buttered greaseproof paper and grease the sides of the tin. Put the dough in the tin and set in a lightly oiled polythene bag; leave in a warm place for about 1 hour or until the dough has risen to within ½ in (1 cm) of the rim of the tin.

Meanwhile, make the topping. Rub together the butter, sugar and flour in a small bowl until the mixture resembles coarse breadcrumbs. Cover the risen dough evenly with the crumb mixture, and set the tin on a baking tray. Bake in the centre of a pre-heated oven at 400°F (200°C, mark 6) for 40–45 minutes. Leave the baked loaf in the tin for 10 minutes, then turn it out to cool on a wire rack.

Cakes and Breads

YORKSHIRE TEA CAKES

These are similar to the recipe for floury baps, but are sweeter and contain dried fruit.

PREPARATION TIME: *20 min*
(plus rising and proving)
COOKING TIME: *20 min*
INGREDIENTS *(for 5 cakes)*:
1 lb (450 g) strong plain flour
1 level teaspoon salt
1 oz (25 g) caster sugar
1 oz (25 g) lard
2 oz (50 g) currants
½ oz (10 g) fresh yeast
½ pint (300 ml) warm (110°F, 43°C) milk

Sift the flour and salt together into a large bowl, add the sugar and rub in the lard until evenly blended. Stir in the currants, then make a well in the centre. In a small bowl, blend the yeast with the milk until smooth and creamy. Pour this liquid into the well, mix the ingredients together, beating the dough against the bowl until it leaves the sides clean (add a little extra flour if you think it is necessary).

Turn the dough out on to a lightly floured surface and knead for about 10 minutes. Put the dough in a lightly oiled polythene bag and set aside to rise at room temperature for about 1½ hours or until it has doubled in size. Remove the polythene, place the risen dough on a lightly floured surface and knead well. Divide the dough into five equal portions and shape each portion into a round; roll each of these into a 6½ in (16 cm) wide, flat cake.

Set the cakes well apart on lightly greased baking trays and brush the tops with milk. Cover the trays with sheets of oiled polythene. Leave the cakes to rise (prove) in a warm place for 45 minutes or until doubled in size.

Bake the cakes at or just above the centre of the oven, pre-heated to 400°F (200°C, mark 6), for about 20 minutes. Cool on a wire rack and serve the cakes split in half, either cold or toasted, and with plenty of butter.

BRAN TEABREAD

A good bread to make if you have time to spare, as it keeps well and can be made in advance.

PREPARATION TIME: *10 min*
RESTING TIME: *8 hours*
COOKING TIME: *1¼–1½ hours*
INGREDIENTS:
3 oz (75 g) All Bran
8 oz (225 g) sultanas
8 oz (225 g) light soft brown sugar
½ pint (300 ml) milk
6 oz (175 g) self-raising flour
1 level teaspoon baking powder

Mix the All Bran, sultanas, sugar and milk in a bowl and leave to stand overnight, covered with a cloth.

Grease and line a loaf tin measuring 9 by 5 in (23 by 13 cm) at the top. Sift the flour and baking powder into the soaked ingredients, blend thoroughly and spoon into the prepared tin. Level the top of the mixture and bake in the centre of a pre-heated oven, at 375°F (190°C, mark 5) for about 1¼ hours until the bread is well risen and just firm to the touch. If the loaf browns too quickly, cover it with a double sheet of greaseproof paper.

Turn out the loaf, remove the paper and cool on a wire rack. Serve the loaf sliced and buttered. It is best left for a day or two to mature before serving, and will keep for 1 week in a tin.

YORKSHIRE TEA CAKES

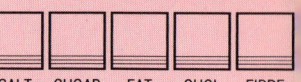

| SALT | SUGAR | FAT | CHOL | FIBRE |

GLUTEN-FREE* WHOLEFOOD*
TOTAL CALORIES: ABOUT 2161

This recipe needs no adaptation.

Freezing: √ up to 6 months.

BRAN TEABREAD

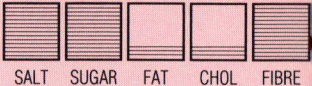

| SALT | SUGAR | FAT | CHOL | FIBRE |

GLUTEN-FREE*
TOTAL CALORIES: ABOUT 2443

All Bran is the highest of all breakfast cereals in **salt**. To reduce the salt level, use low-sodium baking powder and replace the All Bran with an unsweetened bran muesli containing pieces of compressed bran.

The high **sugar** level will also be reduced in this way (All Bran is 15% sugar). To reduce it further, omit the sugar entirely, increasing the amount of sultanas (or other dried fruit) to 1 lb (450 g), and liquidising half of this in the milk before mixing. (Calories lost: up to 253.)

To give a very low **fat** content, use skim milk. (Calories lost: up to 96.)

Using another cereal will give a lower **fibre** content, but adding extra dried fruit and using wholemeal flour will still give a high-fibre tealoaf.

Freezing: √ up to 6 months.

FLOURY BAPS

SALT	SUGAR	FAT	CHOL	FIBRE

GLUTEN-FREE★   WHOLEFOOD★
TOTAL CALORIES: ABOUT 2066

The **fat** and **cholesterol** levels are low because each of the baps will be large enough for 2 portions. The level can be reduced further by using skim milk and only 1 oz (25 g) fat, replacing lard with other fats if wished. (Calories lost: up to 171.)

Freezing: √ up to 1 month.

FLOURY BAPS

Split in half and toasted in front of a fire, these are most comforting on a dreary winter day.

PREPARATION TIME: *15 min (plus rising and proving)*
COOKING TIME: *25 min*
INGREDIENTS *(for 4 baps):*
1 lb (450 g) strong plain flour
½ oz (10 g) fresh yeast
½ pint (300 ml) milk and water, mixed
1 level teaspoon salt★
2 oz (50 g) lard

Blend the yeast with all the liquid until smooth; sift the flour and salt into a wide bowl and rub in the cut-up lard. Stir in the yeast liquid and work the dough until firm, adding a little extra flour if needed. Turn the dough out on to a lightly floured surface and knead for about 5 minutes. Place in an oiled polythene bag and leave to rise at room temperature for 1½ hours or until the dough springs back when lightly pressed with a finger.

Divide the risen dough into four, shape into balls and roll out to flat rounds, ½–¾ in (about 1½ cm) thick. Set the rounds on a well-floured baking tray, dredge the tops with more flour and cover with polythene. Leave to rise (prove) at room temperature until doubled in size, about 45 minutes.

Press each bap lightly in the centre with the knuckles. Bake just above the centre of a pre-heated oven, at 400°F (200°C, mark 6) for 25 minutes. Cool on a rack.

Fruit

Fresh fruit makes delicious eating on its own, in fruit salads and with cheese. Fruit is also used for jams and jellies, pickles and chutneys.

With crop-spraying so widespread in modern fruit farming, it is essential that all fruit should be washed in running water before serving, especially if it is to be eaten fresh. Apart from soft fruits such as blackberries, most fruit will keep in good condition for up to a week if stored in a refrigerator.

Top fruit, the term used by fruit growers for all tree fruits, includes apples and pears, and also stone fruits such as cherries, nectarines, plums, peaches and nuts. Buy only enough to last a few days, as fruit does not keep for long at room temperature. Apples and pears will store for a couple of weeks if they can be kept in a cool airy cellar or larder, but all stone fruit, with the exception of plums and nuts, are best eaten on the day of purchase.

Strawberries, raspberries and currants are all soft fruits which are best used on the day of purchase. All soft fruit, with the exception of gooseberries, leave stains on the bottom of the containers in which they are sold; avoid any badly stained containers as the fruits are bound to be mushy and often mouldy. As soon as possible after buying, tip berries carefully on to a plate, pick out any mouldy berries and set the remainder well apart on a tray until serving.

Citrus fruits, which include grapefruit, lemons, limes and oranges, are grown mainly in the Mediterranean countries, South Africa, the West Indies, Florida and California. Although citrus fruits are much used in cooking, they are at their best when served fresh, with the exception of lemons and limes which are too acid.

As all citrus fruits have a fairly thick skin, it is sometimes difficult to tell the state of the fruit. In general, all fruits should have bright, taut and slightly moist skins with a definite aroma. Many greengrocers display fruits cut in half to enable customers to gauge the condition of flesh and juice content and the thickness of the skin. When buying citrus fruit, avoid any that is dry-looking or has soft indentations and blemishes to the skin.

Citrus fruits store fairly well. Lemons and grapefruit can be kept in the vegetable box of the refrigerator for 1–2 weeks, and other types can be stored in a cool larder for about 1 week. They must, however, be used before the skins shrivel. Before cutting or serving the fruits, they should be rolled between the palms or on a flat surface to get an even distribution of juice within the fruit.

Other fruits range from the well-known bananas, grapes and melons to the more exotic mango, pawpaw and passion fruit, and include dates, figs, kiwi fruit, litchis or lychees and pineapples. Most of these are eaten fresh, but dates and figs are also used dried.

Apples

These are probably the most popular fruit. Apples are divided into dessert (or eating) and cooking apples. Look for apples with smooth skins and avoid any with brownish bruises.

Dessert apples are available all year round.

Favourite varieties include: *Worcester Pearmain*, thick skin of pale green-yellow, heavily suffused with crimson, and tough, white, sweet flesh; *Laxton's Superb*, yellow-green to pale lemon skin, marked with dull red, and with firm and juicy flesh; *Egremont Russet*, reddish-brown skin and crisp firm flesh; and *Cox's Orange Pippin*, the favourite English dessert apple, with yellow-green to golden-yellow skin, flushed and streaked with orange or red, and firm, crisp, juicy and aromatic flesh. Other varieties include: *Golden Delicious*, smooth green skin which turns yellow during storage; *Granny Smith*, bright green skin, hard and crunchy flesh with sharp flavour; *Red Delicious* and *Jonathan*.

Cooking varieties include, *Bramley's Seedling* and *Newton Wonder*.

While cooking apples can only be used for culinary purposes, many dessert apples, especially if firm, are also excellent for cooking. They can be baked, stewed, made into purées or used as fillings for pastry, baked and steamed puddings, cream-based foods and mousses. Dip sliced apples for decoration in lemon juice to prevent discoloration.

For a purée, wash, peel and core 1 lb (450 g) of apples. Cook them over gentle heat, with a piece of lemon peel and 2–3 tablespoons of water, until soft. Liquidise the apple pulp or rub it through a sieve; sweeten to taste with sugar. This makes ½ pint (300 ml).

Apricots

Small stone fruits with yellow, juicy and sweet flesh. Buy firm fruits, avoiding any with bruised or squashy, brown skins.

Perfect ripe fruit are excellent served as a dessert fruit. They can also be poached or used in pie fillings.

Bananas

These are normally picked and shipped green, then stored and sold in varying stages of ripeness. The mealy flesh becomes sweeter as it matures. Choose bananas from a bunch rather than buying them loose. Preferably they should be golden-yellow, flecked with brown.

Avoid any with black spots or patches, and damaged and squashy fruit. For cooking purposes, choose underripe green bananas, as they slice better and can be kept in a cool larder for up to one week.

Slice bananas as close to serving time as possible, or leave them in fresh or tinned grapefruit juice or lemon, lime or orange juice to prevent discoloration.

Blackberries

The large cultivated berries are purple to black, juicy and sweet. Being extremely soft, they deteriorate quickly and must be used as fresh dessert berries as soon as possible after purchase. Avoid containers with too many red and unripe berries.

These berries go well with apples, and are used as pie fillings, in apple snow, fruit puddings, jams and jellies. Hull the berries before use.

Blueberries

Originally a wild fruit of heaths and woodlands, like their close relatives bilberries or whortleberries, blueberries are now grown commercially. They grow in clusters. Generally blueberries are sold ribbed or still on their stalks.

Blueberries are delicious eaten raw as a breakfast fruit or added to pancakes, waffles, biscuits, and muffins. They also make good pies, cobblers, puddings, jams, sauces and jellies.

Look for berries that are dark blue and have a silvery bloom. This is the best sign of quality. The bloom is natural waxy protective coating. Choose berries that are uniform in size and free from stems and leaves. Avoid damp containers; the fruit at the bottom may be mouldy.

Cherries

Both sweet and acid cherries are available over a short summer season. Buy firm and dry cherries and avoid containers with a high percentage of leaves to berries.

Dessert varieties are either white (or pink) and black. The berries have juicy flesh which varies from white-yellow to dark red. Among the many varieties are: *Napoleon Bigarreau*; *Frogmore Early* and *Merton Heart*.

For cooking in puddings, pies, compôtes and jams, choose Morello cherries.

Cranberries

Small American fruit similar to bilberries. The skins are lustrous, varying in colour from pink to red. The berries, which have a sharp, slightly bitter flavour and are used for preserves and sauces, should be firm and smooth.

Currants

These may be black, red or white. Black currants are usually sold stripped from their stalks. Look for containers with large berries

and no more than 15 per cent dark red and 5 per cent green berries turning red. Black currants are used as fillings for pies and sponge puddings, and make excellent jams, jellies, ice creams and sorbets. The berries are dark, almost black, with fairly tough skin and juicy, slightly acid flesh.

Red currants are always sold on their stalks, and must be stripped before being served fresh as a dessert. Avoid punnets with wet berries and with a high proportion of leaves. These bright red, glossy berries are also suitable for compôtes, fruit salads, pastries, jams and jellies. White currants, an albino strain of red currant, are usually eaten fresh.

Dates

Fresh dates are plump and shiny, yellow-red to golden brown and with smooth skins. The pulpy flesh has a sweet sugary flavour. Serve them as a dessert fruit or use in fresh fruit salads. Squeeze the stem end to remove the date from its slightly tough skin.

Dried dates should be plump, 1–2 in (2½–5 cm) long and shiny; avoid any with a shrivelled look or with sugary crystals.

Figs

Fresh or green figs are imported from the Mediterranean countries. The squat, pear-shaped fruits are soft to the touch when ripe, and the skin, which is either white, red or purple, has a bloom to it. The juicy pulp is sweet, deep

red and heavily seeded. These dessert fruits are served fresh; cut them open with a knife and fork and eat only the soft red flesh inside. Cream may be served with them.

Dried figs should come easily out of the box and not be too sticky.

Gooseberries

Dessert varieties are served on their own, but acid gooseberries are usually cooked. They may be served as a sauce with meat and fish, and they are used for favourite desserts such as gooseberry fool and in pies, puddings and tarts, and for jam and jelly-making. Avoid squashy berries or any with splits and blemishes to the skin.

Culinary varieties include *May Duke*, which has round berries with downy skin; *Keepsake*, oval, green, slightly hairy berries ripening to whitish-green; *Careless*, large, oval green berries turning milky white, dessert and culinary; *Lancer*, round, pale green, with a yellow tinge, dessert and culinary; *Howard's Leveller*, large oval and green, almost hairless, berries, excellent flavour as dessert or cooking berries; and *Whinham's Industry*, one of the most popular gooseberries, which ripens to a dark red skin with sweet juicy flesh.

Grapes

These delicious fruits are served plain or as a good addition to fresh fruit salads. They are not cooked, except for the classic garnish known as à la Véronique. The juicy, thin-skinned grapes should have a distinct bloom to them. When possible, buy in bunches and avoid any with shrivelled, split or squashed berries, or those which show mould near the stems. They are available as blue, black, red, amber and green grapes.

Grapefruit

The largest of the citrus fruits, it is a squat, round fruit with pale yellow skin which varies in thickness; the juicy flesh is pale yellow. A spongy soft skin is often an indication of thick peel and a lack of fruit juice and flesh. Grapefruit contain few or no pips, and where they are present they are so large that they can be easily seen and removed. Grapefruit is usually served fresh as a breakfast dish or a starter; it is also used in marmalade making. It is grown in Brazil, Cyprus, Israel, Jamaica, Morocco, South Africa, Spain and Trinidad. Pink-tinged grapefruit, with sweet pale pink flesh, are grown in the United States.

Kiwi fruit (Chinese gooseberries)

Egg-shaped or oblong, with brownish-red, hairy skins, these have soft, juicy, sweet, green flesh, pitted with seeds. Avoid any with shrivelled skins. Peel before eating. They are especially attractive as part of a fruit salad, with the pattern of black seeds

against the pale green; or cut them in half across and scoop out the juicy flesh with a teaspoon. They can also be used for jams and jellies.

Kumquats

A small, oval, orange-like fruit with bright yellow skin and juicy, slightly bitter flesh. It may be served fresh, when it is eaten whole, including the skin, or used for marmalades, bottled and preserved in sugar syrup. It is also used fresh as a garnish for duck. Originally the kumquat was a Japanese fruit, but it now often comes from Morocco.

Lemons

Lemons are large or small with smooth and thin or thick and knobbly skin.

Generally, plump lemons, heavy for their size and with smoothy oily skins, have less peel and more juice than large, knobbly skinned lemons. Chiefly grown in France, Spain, Italy, Israel and California, they are available all year round.

Lemon is one of the most useful fruits in the kitchen and both the rind and juice are used in a large number of dishes. It makes an attractive garnish for food and long drinks. Rub sugar lumps over the skin of a lemon until they are well coloured and use the lumps whole or crushed in iced drinks.

Lemon juice can be substituted for vinegar in any recipe, except pickling, and can be used to sour fresh or evaporated milk or fresh cream: add 1 tablespoon juice to $\frac{1}{4}$ pint (150 ml).

Lemons can be stored in the refrigerator, but if they are cut wrap them in plastic film.

Limes

These are small fruit, similar to lemons but rounder, and with green-yellow thin skin and tart yellow flesh. The flavour is very distinctive. They are used in a similar way to lemons, and lime juice is particularly good squeezed over melon and paw-paw wedges. It also gives a fresh tangy flavour to salad dressings. Limes are much used in curry dishes, but are more expensive than lemons. Grown mainly in South Africa and the West Indies.

Litchis, lychees

Of Chinese origin, these stone fruits are the size of large cherries, with hard, scaly skins, turning through pink to brown. The white pulpy flesh is firm, juicy and slippery. Buy when skin is red, but avoid any with shrivelled dry skins.

Litchis are served as a dessert fruit on their own or added to fruit salad. Pinch the parchment-like outer skin to crack it and then peel it off.

Loganberries

These tangy juicy fruits have the shape of blackberries, but the colour of raspberries. They are

tapering and seedless. Usually sold with the hulls or centres in; avoid containers with heavy fruit stains and mouldy berries.

Loquats

These stone fruits, also known as Japanese medlars, are similar in shape and size to plums, with smooth, golden-yellow, orange or red-brown skins. The juicy cream-coloured flesh is slightly tart. Choose firm fruit.

Mangoes

These large tropical stone fruits come in different shapes and sizes; some are round, others long and narrow, kidney or pear-shaped. The largest fruits may weigh up to 3 lb ($1\frac{1}{2}$ kg), and the smallest are the size of an average peach. The tough hard skins range in colour from green to yellow, orange and red, flushed with pink. The orange-yellow, juicy flesh has a delicate fragrance and spicy taste. Fresh mangoes are served as dessert fruits; avoid mushy-looking fruits with blemishes. Mangoes are also made into chutney and served as a side dish with curries.

Melons

These refreshing juicy fruits come in different sizes and shapes. When buying melons, always insist on touching them to check for ripeness; a ripe melon will yield to pressure applied gently at the stalk end. Melons are generally available throughout the year, with the exception of watermelons which are available throughout the summer.

The Cantaloup melon has a slightly flattened shape, with green to yellow rough skin. The flesh is heavily scented, succulent and orange-yellow.

Charentais melon is perfectly round and small. The yellow-green, slightly rough skin is marked with downward indentations, and the deep orange flesh is faintly scented.

Honeydew melon is the most widely available. It is shaped like a rugby ball and has green, yellow or white wrinkled skin. The sweet flesh is pale green to pink.

Ogen melon has yellow to orange skin marked with faint green stripes. The pale yellow flesh is very sweet and juicy.

Watermelon is the largest of all melons. Glossy dark skin surrounds the scarlet and juicy, almost watery, flesh and prominent black seeds.

Cool ripe melon is served as a first or last course, with sugar, finely chopped stem ginger or a squeeze of fresh lemon or lime juice. Refrigerate melon only long enough to chill it, or the delicate flavour will be lost.

Nuts

Almonds Small, oval, flat nuts in light brown pitted shells. They are available bitter and sweet, shelled and unshelled, and are best bought with the thin brown skin on.

Brazil nuts Hard, dark brown, three-edged shells enclose firm, slightly oily nuts of coconut and hazel nut flavour. They are sold unshelled and shelled. Avoid any which feel light or rattle in the shells.

Chestnuts The shiny brown fruits of the sweet chestnut are enclosed in a fleshy outer covering which breaks open when the nuts are ripe. Avoid any that look dry and shrivelled. The large French chestnuts, 'marrons', are sold tinned or preserved.

Coconuts These large nuts have a hard, dark brown outer shell closely covered with tough fibres. At the top of each nut are three small indentations which must be punctured so that the colourless liquid can be shaken out. This is served chilled as a drink. Crack the tough shell by hitting it with a cleaver about one-third of the way down from the top. Prise the shells open, and cut out the tough flesh with a small sharp knife. To test a whole coconut for freshness, shake it to make sure it contains liquid.

Hazel or cob nuts The small, grey-brown nuts are partly covered with leafy husks. Ripe, fresh nuts should have firm, not shrivelled, husks.

Filbert nuts These are a variety of hazel nut, but the fruits are flask-shaped and should be completely covered by firm husks.

Peanuts The two major types are the Virginia and the Spanish. The former has a longer shell, larger nut, and more pronounced flavour. Available shelled, plain or roasted; or unshelled.

Pecans These nuts, related to walnuts and native to North America, are grown in the south-eastern United States as far north as Indiana, as far west as Texas, and in northern Mexico. Available in the shell. Shelled, they are sold roasted, dry-roasted, salted or plain.

Walnuts The brown shells should have a faint damp sheen. Avoid any which rattle, as they will be dry and shrivelled. Green or under-ripe walnuts are sometimes seen in early autumn. They may be eaten fresh, but are more often used for pickling.

Oranges

The most widely available citrus fruits, oranges can be both bitter and sweet.

The most popular bitter orange is the Seville orange, or bigarade, a thin-skinned, orange-red fruit with an acid, deep yellow flesh and numerous pips. The flesh is too acid for dessert use, but it is excellent and almost exclusively used for making marmalade. Seville oranges are imported from Spain and are only available for a few weeks in January and February.

The shape and flavour of sweet dessert oranges varies according to their origins. Israel exports the world-famous Jaffa oranges. Shamouti oranges, which are a variety of Jaffa orange, are large, oval and thick-skinned. They are almost seedless, with very juicy and sweet flesh.

Navel oranges have thin, smooth skins and are distinguished by the raised embryo growth at one end; they have juicy flesh with few pips.

Blood or Malta oranges are small, with slightly rough skin flushed with red, and have sweet juicy flesh, flecked with red, usually with a number of pips.

Valencias are thin-skinned oranges, rounded in shape, with sweet, very juicy and practically pipless flesh.

Oranges are served fresh on their own and in fruit salad. They are much used in cooking, especially in sauces and stuffings.

Ortaniques

This cross between an orange and tangerine has orange-yellow thin skin and sweet, juicy, orange-coloured flesh. Use flesh as a dessert fruit. It is also good for marmalade.

Passion fruit

These tropical fruits are similar in shape and size to large plums. The tough skin is purple and

77

deeply wrinkled when ripe. The aromatic orange pulp is sweet and juicy, and deeply pitted with small black seeds which are eaten with the flesh.

The sharp tangy juice is used to flavour cocktails, punches or fresh fruit cups, as well as fruit pies. It may also be served as a dessert fruit and the flesh eaten with a little sugar.

Pawpaws, papayas

Large tropical fruits, pawpaws have smooth skins which ripen through green to yellow or orange. The sweet juice is orange-pink and melon-like in texture; the brown-black seeds lie in the centre. Avoid fruits with dry or blemished skins.

Peaches and Nectarines

Free-stone peaches have juicy soft flesh which comes easily away from the stone. Cling stone peaches have firmer flesh adhering tightly to the stone. Free-stone peaches are considered to have a better flavour but are seldom seen in the shops. Avoid any which have split or those with bruised skins and brown or soft spots.

Nectarines are a smooth-skinned variety of peach, and are served as a dessert fruit. Nectarines are usually expensive, and sold when fully ripe and perfect; use on the day of purchase.

Peaches are usually served whole as a dessert, but are also excellent in fruit salads, flans and pies. Peach purée can be used as a base for ice creams, soufflés and other sweet recipes.

Nectarines need no peeling. Serve with dessert knives and forks, cut the fruits in half and slip out the stones.

Pears

Like apples, pears are divided into dessert and cooking varieties. Pears bruise easily and should be handled with care; they are best bought before fully ripe and left in the airing cupboard for 2–3 days. Ripe pears will yield when gently pressed at the stalk end.

The following are varieties of dessert pears and can also be served poached or lightly stewed: *Conference*, a tapering dark green pear, heavily spotted with russet, with creamy-pink, juicy and sweet flesh; *Doyenné du Comice*, large, oval-shaped pear with pale yellow skin, occasionally flushed with red or russet and pale yellow, very juicy, cinnamon-flavoured flesh; *William's Bon Chrétien*, medium tapering pear with pale green skin turning yellow, with juicy sweet flesh.

Cooking pears include *Pitmaston Duchess*, nearly round and with tough yellow to green skin, irregularly spotted with russet. The cream-yellow flesh is soft and juicy.

Really ripe dessert pears can be eaten on their own or served in fruit salads. They may also be poached and served chilled with a raspberry or hot chocolate sauce. To prepare pears for poaching, cut them in half lengthways with a sharp knife. Fresh pears discolour quickly and stainless steel or silver tools should be used in the preparation. Scoop out the core and pips with a pointed spoon. Poach the pears at once before they turn brown.

Persimmons

These tropical fruits look like large tomatoes with their leathery skins which turn from yellow to bright red. The orange-yellow juicy and soft flesh has a sharp flavour and may be astringent even when ripe. Fruits with pitted or cracked skins should be avoided.

For serving fresh, wash and lightly chill the fruits and serve with a pointed spoon, to dig the juicy flesh out of the skin. A squeeze of lemon or lime may be added, and the skin can be marked in quarters and peeled back for an attractive presentation. The pulp may be used as a basis for ice creams, milk drinks, jellies and sauces.

Pineapples

Large oval fruits with hard, knobbly top skin, which varies from deep yellow to almost orange-brown. The firm, yellow to cream flesh is sweet and juicy. Look for fruits with stiff leaves.

Plums, Greengages, Damsons

Plums include both dessert and culinary varieties. Gages are a type of plum, round and green to yellow in colour. Damsons, too, are plums with dark blue to black skin; they are oval in shape and smaller than gages, and should only be used cooked and for jam-making. Dessert plums should be firm to the touch, with a bloom on the skin; they are often sold slightly under-ripe and can be kept in a cool larder for 1–3 days before serving. Varieties include: *Czar*, large, dark blue, culinary or dessert plum with golden flesh and red juice; *Pershore*, tapering dessert plum, with yellow, faintly red-tinted skin and sometimes mealy flesh; *Victoria*, large oval plum, yellow flushed with scarlet, sweet and juicy flesh, suitable for dessert and bottling; *Kirke's Blue*, a large, purple-black plum with a distinct bloom and juicy dark flesh. All types are also suitable for pies, fruit salads, flans, baked and steamed puddings, jams, chutneys and pickles.

Among the varieties of gages are: *Ouillin's Golden Gage* and *Cambridge Gage*. Ripe greengages are served fresh and are also delicious halved and stoned as pie fillings.

Pomegranates

These are the size of oranges with thin but tough rind. In prime fruits, the rind is pink or bright red, and the juicy flesh crimson. The pulp is packed with seeds, and the flesh is sucked from the seeds. These fruits are served fresh as a dessert. Serve them with the top sliced off and dislodge the large seeds with a nut pick or spoon.

Quinces

These are sometimes available in the shops during the autumn. They have tough golden skin when ripe, and the firm acid flesh is highly aromatic. Indigestible if eaten raw, they make excellent jams and jellies, or are used to flavour pies.

Raspberries

Like other soft fruit, ripe raspberries should be used as soon as possible after picking. If it is necessary to wash them, put them in a colander and let water flow gently through them. Drain and use at once. They are less juicy than most other soft fruit, and are often sold hulled. Avoid berries which show cracks or pits near the top and any that are squashy and mouldy. Raspberries are usually served fresh as a dessert, with cream; they may also be used for jams.

There are two types of raspberries: summer crop and autumn berries. Summer fruits include *Lloyd George* which has large, bright red and juicy berries. Summer varieties, including *Glen Clova*, are particularly recommended for freezing.

To make raspberry purée, rub the fruit through a nylon sieve, pressing it with a wooden spoon, or use an electric liquidiser and sieve the purée to remove the seeds – 1 lb (450 g) fresh raspberries will give $\frac{1}{2}$ pint (300 ml) purée.

Rhubarb

Although in fact a vegetable, rhubarb is used as a fruit. It is extremely acid and must be stewed or poached before eating. The leaves are highly poisonous. Early or forced rhubarb has tender, pink and delicately flavoured stalks which do not require peeling. Maincrop rhubarb has a stronger flavour and tough brittle stalks. Avoid limp and split stalks.

Particularly suited for pie fillings, in baked puddings, fools and jams, rhubarb blends well with many other flavours, such as grated orange rind, ginger and cinnamon. Forced tender rhubard needs little preparation apart from cutting off the root ends and the leaves. Older rhubarb is somewhat coarser, and tough strings of skin must be peeled off. Wash and drain thoroughly before use.

Satsumas

Similar to tangerine, this round and squat orange has smooth, fairly thick skin and pale orange-yellow flesh without pips. Use fresh as a dessert fruit or for marmalades. Grown in Spain and Morocco.

Strawberries

The most popular and eagerly awaited fruit of the berry season. Fresh strawberries are served with cream and sugar, used fresh in cakes and tarts, eaten with ice cream and water ices and used for jams. The sweet and juicy red berries should be used on the day they are bought. Choose berries with fresh-looking leaves and avoid over-ripe and under-ripe fruit and those with grey mould.

One of the best-known varieties is *Cambridge Vigour*, which has conical light red-scarlet, fairly juicy, moderately sweet berries. *Royal Sovereign*, the favourite English strawberry, is bright pinkish-orange to scarlet, juicy and very sweet-flavoured. *Talisman*, smaller and deeper red than *Royal Sovereign*, is exceptionally juicy and sweet. *Redgauntlet*, with large, scarlet berries turning dark crimson, is grown chiefly in Scotland. *Grandee* is the largest strawberry, almost round in shape and scarlet-crimson in colour. It is a juicy, sweet berry.

Like raspberries, these soft fruits must be eaten soon after picking. Serve whole or sliced (use a stainless-steel knife to prevent discoloration). Strawberry purée is made in the same way as raspberry purée and yields the same amount.

Tangerines

A small type of sweet orange distinguished by its loose, bright-orange to red skin and small, juicy segments. It contains numerous pips, but is a delicious dessert fruit and can be successfully used for marmalades.

Ugli Fruit

Also known as tangelo, this cross between a tangerine and a grapefruit is approximately the size of a large grapefruit. The ugli fruit has a thick knobbly and greenish yellow skin; the juicy yellow flesh is sweeter than that of grapefruit and has only a few pips. It is mainly grown in Jamaica.

Ugli fruit may be prepared and served as grapefruit halves; as they are sweet, they do not need any sugar.

Preparation of fruit

This section gives some hints, with illustrations, of how to prepare fruit for eating raw or for cooking.

Apricots

Stone apricots by cutting them in half with a sharp knife, following the slight indentation line. Twist the two halves in opposite directions to separate them; remove the stone.

CUTTING APRICOTS IN HALF

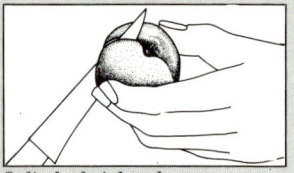

Split the fruit lengthways

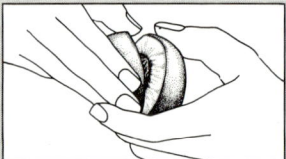

Separate the two halves

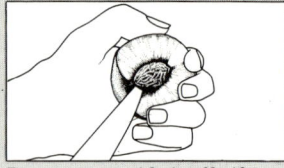

Remove stone with tip of knife

Cherries

Before cooking cherries, strip them of the stalks and ideally push out the stones with the tool known as a cherry stoner.

Currants

Before cooking, strip currants off the stalks by running a fork down the length of the stalk.

Gooseberries

Top and tail gooseberries with a knife or with scissors.

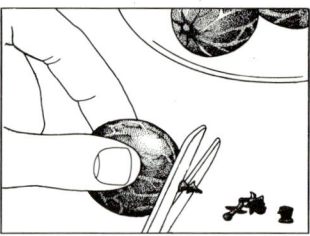

Top and tail gooseberries by snipping off stalk and flower ends

Grapefruit

To prepare a grapefruit, cut the fruit in half across and use ideally a curved saw-edged grapefruit knife to cut round inside the skin to loosen the flesh. Make deep cuts between the grapefruit pieces close to the membranes dividing them. Flip out any pips with the point of the knife. The central core may be cut away, but this is not essential. Serve with or without sugar.

Empty half grapefruit shells look attractive used as serving 'dishes'. Use kitchen scissors to cut out a series of small V's round the edge of the half shells (known as vandyking). Florida cocktail – half orange and half grapefruit segments with a mint-leaf garnish – is usually served in this way.

To peel and segment a whole grapefruit, hold the fruit firmly with the tips of the fingers and cut a thin slice from the stem end of

PREPARING GRAPEFRUIT

Loosen flesh from skin

Cut between individual segments

PEELING WHOLE GRAPEFRUIT

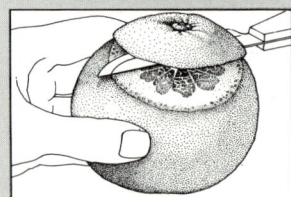

Cut off slice from stalk end

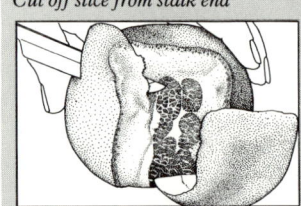

Remove strips of pith and peel

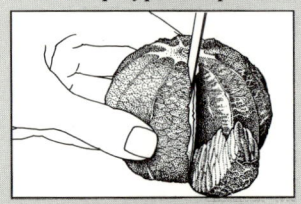

Cut out the segments

the fruit until the flesh just shows. Place the grapefruit, cut side down, on a plate and with a sawing action carefully cut the peel and pith off in strips to reveal the flesh.

Trim off any remaining pith. Carefully cut out each segment of fruit by placing the knife close to the membrane and cutting through to the centre: work the knife under the segment and up against the next membrane to release the segment.

Grapes

Most grapes are easily peeled, away from the stem end using the fingernails. If the skins are difficult to remove dip a few grapes at a time in boiling water for 30 seconds, then plunge them immediately into cold water.

Remove the pips from whole grapes by digging the rounded end of a clean hair grip into

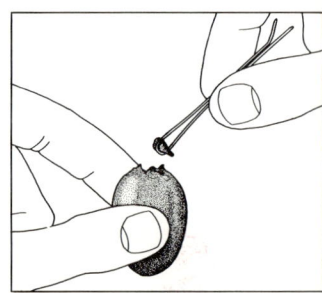

Remove pips from grapes by inserting a hair grip from the stalk end

the stem end of the grape; scoop out the pips. Alternatively, make a shallow cut down the length of the grape, and ease out the pips with the tip of the knife.

Mangoes

These tropical fruits should not be cut until just before serving. Cut the fruit lengthways, into three slices, above and below the stone. However, in this way the aroma escapes and ideally

SERVING MANGOES

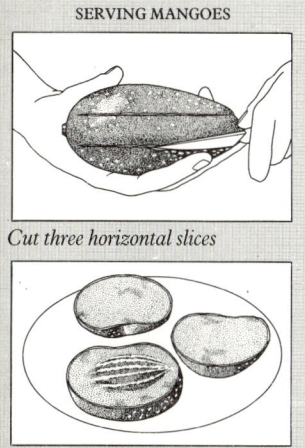

Cut three horizontal slices

Serve the slices unpeeled

fresh mango should be served whole with only the skin cut. Peel the skin back with a knife and scoop out the pulp with a spoon.

Melons

To prepare a large melon, such as honeydew, cut it in half length-ways with a sharp knife. Cut each half lengthways into segments and scoop out the pips with a spoon or fork. A fully ripe melon segment may be served with the skin attached or the skin may be loosened by running the knife blade between flesh and skin. Leave the skin underneath the melon segment.

A small melon, such as Charentais or Ogen, usually only serves two people. Cut it in half across and scoop out the pips with a teaspoon.

PREPARING MELON

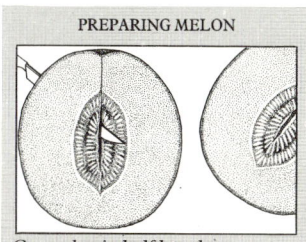

Cut melon in half lengthways

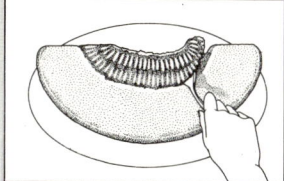

Remove pips from melon segments

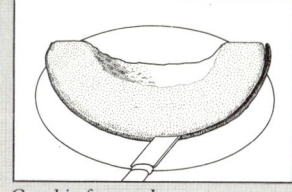

Cut skin from melon

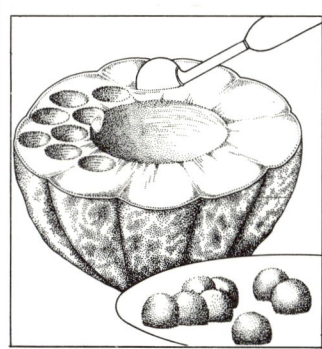

To make melon balls, use a small semicircular scoop

Oranges

Peel and cut oranges as described under grapefruit. Alternatively, peel oranges in round strips, remove all pith and cut into slices across the grain. If oranges do not peel easily, chill them in the refrigerator for 1 hour or cover them with boiling water and leave for a few minutes.

Pawpaws

Prepare ripe fruits like melon, cutting them in half and removing the black seeds. Serve with lime (or lemon) juice as a dessert or breakfast fruit, or diced and mixed into a fruit salad.

Peaches

To peel fresh peaches, dip them in a bowl of boiling water, count up to ten, then drain and put the peaches at once in a bowl of cold water. Peel off the skin with a small knife.

Pineapple

A ripe pineapple is best served as a dessert fruit. Slice off the leaf and the stem ends, and cut the pineapple across into $\frac{1}{2}$ in (1 cm) thick slices. Using a sharp knife cut off the skin and the woody 'eyes' in the flesh of each slice. Remove the tough centre core with a small plain pastry cutter or an apple corer. Arrange the slices on a flat dish; sprinkle with caster sugar and 2 tablespoons of liqueur. Leave to marinate for about 2 hours before serving.

For a spectacular party sweet, slice off the leaf end only and, without splitting the skin, cut round the edge of the pineapple between the flesh and skin, loosening it at the base as well. Extract the pineapple flesh, remove the core and cut the flesh into wedge-shaped pieces. Set the pineapple shell on a serving dish, replace the wedges and cover with the pineapple top. Pineapple shells also make at attractive containers for fruit salads, pineapple sorbets, other water ices and ice creams.

PREPARING PINEAPPLE

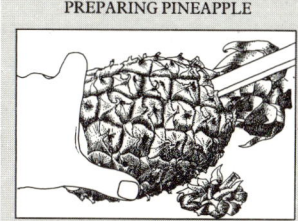

Slice off leaf top

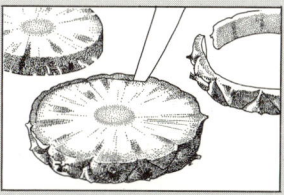

Remove skin from pineapple slices

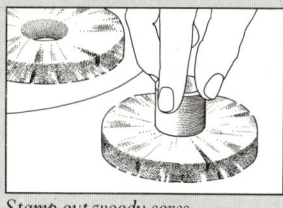

Stamp out woody cores

Strawberries

The calyxes at the stalk ends are sometimes left on the berries for decoration, but strawberries are usually hulled.

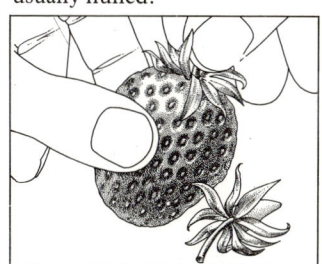

To hull strawberries, remove the green leaves and soft centre stalk

Sweets and Puddings

Desserts are often served before cheese, although gourmets maintain that desserts should follow the cheese. Family favourites include sweet pies, tarts and flans (see pastry), as well as steamed puddings and custards. For party occasions, jellies, mousses and home-made ice creams are ideal desserts.

STEAMED, BOILED AND BAKED PUDDINGS

Puddings can be steamed in a special decker steamer or in a large saucepan. Stand the pudding on a trivet or on skewers so as to raise it. Pour water into the pan until it reaches halfway up the basin. Keep at least a 1 in (2½ cm) space around the basin.

Whichever steaming method is used, the water in the steamer or pan must be kept gently boiling throughout cooking. Top up with boiling water at intervals.

Preparing a pudding basin
Butter the basin lightly and cut and butter a disc of greaseproof paper to fit the base; this prevents the pudding from sticking when it is turned out. Fill the basin no more than two-thirds with pudding mixture. Butter a piece of greaseproof paper thoroughly and make a 1 in (2½ cm) pleat in the centre to allow for the pudding to rise. Lay the paper over the top of the basin and cover it with a piece of pleated foil. Tie the paper and foil covering securely with string below the lip of the basin. Make a string handle which will help to lift the pudding out.

Many traditional and regional suet puddings are boiled rather than steamed. The pudding basin is covered tightly with a pudding

STEAMED PUDDINGS

Place pudding cloth over colander

Spoon in mixture and tie up cloth

The pudding, ready for steaming

cloth and immersed completely in a pan of boiling water. More usually, however, the pudding mixture is placed inside a scalded and flour-dusted pudding cloth. This is easiest done by laying the cloth over a colander, spooning in the pudding mixture and tying the corners tightly to shape the pudding. The two knots help to lift the pudding.

Turning out a pudding
Lift the pudding from the steamer or pan and remove the covering. Leave to cool and shrink slightly, then loosen the pudding at one side of the basin to let in the air. Place a dish over the basin, and turn it upside down.

Baked puddings
Apart from steaming and boiling, puddings can also be baked in the oven. The pudding mixture should be a little softer than for steamed puddings to give a crisp surface. To prevent jam-based puddings from caramelising, set the dish in a shallow tin of water. Bake in the centre of a pre-heated oven, at 350–375°F (180–190°C, mark 4–5).

JELLIES, MOULDS AND MOUSSES

These cold desserts are all made with gelatine, an extract from animal bones, tendons and skin. Gelatine is available in powder and leaf form, and while powdered gelatine is easier to use, some cooks consider that leaf gelatine gives a more sparkling finish to a fruit jelly.

Some fresh fruit – pineapple, for example – contains enzymes which prevent the gelling action taking place. However, these enzymes are destroyed if either tinned or cooked fruit is used in jellies.

Setting gelatine
Jellied mixtures left to set in a refrigerator need less gelatine than those set at normal room temperature. In hot weather, and without refrigeration, increase the amount of gelatine by one-third, or reduce the amount of liquid. Desserts made in individual glasses need less gelatine than a dessert made in a mould for turning out later. Jellied mixtures tend to toughen if kept too long, especially in a refrigerator. They are best eaten on the day of making.

Directions for making powdered gelatine are given on the packets. In general, one packet (3 level teaspoons) will set one pint (570 ml) of liquid for moulding in a refrigerator; and 2 level teaspoons will set the same amount of liquid spooned into serving glasses. Fruit purées and ingredients of a similar consistency, such as moulds and mousses, need 1 level teaspoon gelatine to gell ½ pint (300 ml) for setting in glasses.

For coating and glazing with jelly, for whisked jellies and for setting fruit decorations, use the jelly when it has set to the consistency of unbeaten egg white.

Leaf gelatine
Thin leaf gelatine must be washed in cold water and then soaked in a basin of cold water until soft, after 15–20 minutes. Squeeze the

softened gelatine lightly to extract surplus water, and place it in a bowl with the measured amount of liquid used in the recipe. Place the bowl in a pan of hot water and heat, without boiling, over low heat until dissolved. Six sheets of leaf gelatine equal 1 oz (25 g) of powdered gelatine.

SYLLABUBS AND TRIFLES

Syllabubs, which date back to Elizabethan times, were originally a drink, consisting of a bubbling wine, Sill or Sille, mixed with frothing cream. They later developed into a rich sweet with the addition of brandy and sherry, cream and sugar. The trifle, developed from the syllabub in the 18th century, became a little more substantial by the addition of sponge cake and jam.

Both syllabubs and trifles are ideal for dinner parties, as they can be made well in advance. The basis is still wine or liqueur or both, with eggs and cream.

EGG CUSTARDS

There are two types of custard: baked or steamed, and the softer pouring custard which is used as a sauce.

Egg whites set a baked custard, and the yolks give it the creamy consistency. However, as the yolks thicken at a higher temperature than the egg whites, it is important to cook custards at the correct heat. Too much heat, especially direct heat, will cause an egg custard to curdle. Use a double saucepan for making a pouring custard and stand a set custard in a shallow container with a little cold water. If a double saucepan is not available, use an ordinary saucepan over very gentle heat.

For baked custards, 2 whole eggs plus 2 egg yolks will set 1 pint (570 ml) of milk. For a pouring custard use 4 egg yolks to every pint (570 ml) of milk.

MERINGUES

Meringue, with its crisp outer texture and aerated inside, forms the basis for many desserts: shells and baskets can be filled with cream or fresh fruit. Meringue is also a favourite topping for sweet pies and flans.

Meringue is quite easy to make provided a few points are observed – the whisk and bowl must be absolutely clean and dry, and the eggs quite free from yolk. Ideally, use eggs that are 2–3 days old. The shapes of whisk and bowl also influence a good meringue; a balloon whisk gives greater volume but takes longer to whisk the whites than a rotary whisk. An electric mixer is the quickest, but gives the least volume. Choose a wide bowl when using a balloon whisk, and a narrow deep bowl for a rotary hand whisk.

The sugar for a meringue must be fine. Caster sugar is generally used, but equal quantities of caster and icing sugar produce a meringue of pure white colour and crisp melting texture. Do not use granulated sugar, as the coarse crystals break down the egg albumen, thus reducing the volume. If you use brown sugar, grind it finely first. A coffee grinder is excellent for grinding it to the consistency of caster or icing sugar; a food processor is useful if you are doing large quantities at a time.

Basic Meringue

INGREDIENTS:
2 egg whites
4 oz (100 g) caster sugar

Put the egg whites in a bowl and whisk them until they are fairly stiff and have the appearance of cottonwool. Tip in half the sugar and continue whisking the stiff whites until the texture is smooth and close, and stands in stiff peaks when the whisk is lifted. Lightly but evenly fold in the remaining sugar with a metal spoon.

ICE CREAM AND SORBETS

Home-made cream ices and water ices (or sorbets) are quite different in both texture and flavour to the commercial varieties. It is as easy to make these at home as it is to make an egg custard or sugar syrup. Indeed, a basic ice cream is more often than not based on a custard enriched with double cream. The basis of a water ice is a sugar syrup flavoured with fruit juice or purée.

Pointers to success

1. The amount of sugar in the mixture is important – if too much, the ice cream will not freeze, and if too little it will be hard and tasteless. Freezing does, however, take the edge off the sweetness and this must be borne in mind when tasting. In sorbets or water ices it is even more important to have the correct amount of sugar, as the soft yet firm consistency depends on the sugar content.
2. Some recipes recommend milk instead of cream, especially for strong-flavoured ice cream. The milk must be evaporated, not fresh dairy milk.
3. Use maximum freezing power. Whichever method is used for freezing the cream, it has a better texture if frozen quickly. Chill the equipment as well as the ingredients before starting.
4. Once the ice cream is frozen, it should be transferred to a shelf in the refrigerator for a little while before serving. Rock-hard ices are never pleasant and lose much of their flavour.
5. Ice cream may be stored in the freezing compartment of the refrigerator for the length of time indicated by the star rating.

Making ice cream in a refrigerator

Set the dial of the refrigerator at the coldest setting about 1 hour before the ice cream mixture is ready to freeze.

Make up the mixture according to the recipe. Remove the dividers and pour the mixture into ice trays or any other suitable freezing container, such as refrigerator boxes, loaf tins and stainless-steel dishes. Cover the trays or containers with foil or

MAKING ICE CREAM

Whisking the egg yolks

Breaking up ice crystals

lids and place in the freezing compartment.

To obtain a smooth texture, the ice crystals must be broken down as they form and the ice cream mixture whisked at intervals until part frozen and slushy. Remove the tray from the freezing compartment and scrape the ice crystals, which have formed on the sides and base, towards the centre. Whisk the mixture with a fork until smooth, and return the tray, covered, to the freezing compartment. Thereafter, leave the ice cream undisturbed until it is firm, after 2–3 hours.

Freezing time varies with different refrigerators, but several hours are necessary in every case.

Making ice cream in a home freezer

Set the dial to 'quick-freeze' about 1 hour before the ice cream is ready to be frozen.

Prepare the ice cream mixture according to the recipe, place it in a mixing bowl in the freezer and leave it until mushy.

Remove the bowl from the freezer and whisk the mixture thoroughly with a rotary beater. Pour the ice cream into empty ice-cube trays or rigid polythene containers, and freeze until firm. Set the dial of the freezer to its normal temperature. If the ice cream is to be stored for any length of time the container should be sealed and labelled.

BATTERS

Batters provide the basis for a large number of dishes from simple lemon pancakes to Russian blini, French crêpes Suzette and American waffles.

Batter is a mixture of flour, salt, egg, milk or other liquid. The proportions vary, depending on the consistency required. Pancakes, for instance, need a thin, cream-like batter, while fritters need a thick coating batter. For crisp coating batters, 1 tablespoon of oil may be used with ¼ pint (150 ml) of water, or the liquid may be half milk and half water.

Batters do not, as some people think, need to stand for a while before being cooked, although this may be done for practical reasons. Batter may be left, covered, at room temperature for any time up to 4 hours, or up to 24 hours in a refrigerator. It may be necessary to add a little more liquid to restore the batter to its original consistency.

Basic Pancake Batter

PREPARATION TIME: *10 min*
INGREDIENTS (*for 8–10 pancakes*):
4 oz (100 g) plain or self-raising flour
Pinch of salt★
1 egg
½ pint (300 ml) milk

Sift the flour and salt into a large bowl. Using a wooden spoon make a hollow in the centre of the flour and drop in the lightly beaten egg. Slowly pour half the milk into the flour, gradually working the flour into the milk. When all the flour is incorporated, beat the mixture with a wooden spoon, whisk, or rotary beater, until it becomes smooth and free of lumps. Allow it to stand for a few minutes. Then add the remainder of the milk, beating continuously until the batter is bubbly and has the consistency of single cream.

To make pancakes, use a 7 in (18 cm) heavy-based shallow frying pan with sloping sides. Add just enough lard to gloss the pan to prevent the batter sticking. Fierce heat is necessary, and the pan should be really hot before the batter is poured in.

Pour in just enough batter to flow in a thin film over the base – tilting the pan to spread it. Use a jug or ladle for pouring in the batter. The heat is right if the underside of the pancake becomes golden in 1 minute; adjust the heat to achieve this. Flip the pancake over with a palette knife or spatula, or toss by flicking the wrist and lifting the pan away from the body. The other side of the pancake should also be done in about 1 minute.

To store pancakes: if they are to be kept for a short time, stack them in a pile and cover with a clean tea cloth. If they are to be stored for one or two days, put oiled greaseproof paper between each pancake, stack them and wrap the whole pile in kitchen foil and store in the refrigerator.

To re-heat pancakes: if pancakes are to be served with lemon and sugar, wrap three or four pancakes in foil and heat through in the oven at 300°F (160°C, mark 2). Alternatively, brush a flat tin with melted butter, arrange overlapping pancakes on it, brush with butter and put into a hot oven for 4–5 minutes, or heat the pancakes in a frying pan in an orange sauce as for crêpes Suzette.

COOKING PANCAKES

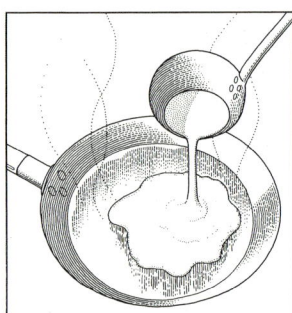

1. *Pour batter into greased pan*

3. *Straighten pancake with knife*

2. *Flip over the half-cooked pancake*

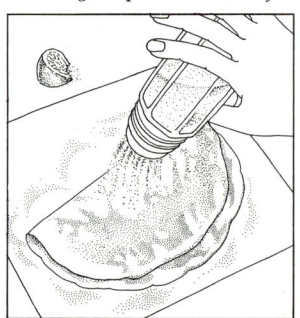

4. *Sprinkle with sugar and lemon*

Pastry

Although much mystique surrounds pastry-making, there are no great secrets to guarantee instant success, for pastry-making is an art which is mastered by care, patience and practice. There are, however, a few essentials which must be observed before good results can be achieved. The kitchen, working surface and utensils should be cool, and the recipe must always be strictly adhered to, especially in regard to measurements. Pastry should be made as quickly as possible, and handling kept to a minimum. Many pastries are best rested in a cool place before they are cooked.

SHORTCRUST PASTRY

This popular and versatile pastry is used for savoury and sweet pies, tarts, flans and tartlets. It is usually made by the 'rubbing-in' method, but there are several other ways of making shortcrust. Plain flour is recommended; self-raising flour may be used, but the pastry will be more crumbly. The fat should be lard or a white vegetable fat; ideally, use equal amounts of lard and firm margarine. Margarine alone produces a yellow, firm pastry.

The standard recipe is for 8 oz (225 g) shortcrust which always means 8 oz (225 g) flour to 4 oz (100 g) fat. The amount of flour may be doubled or halved, but proportions should remain the same: half the fat to the amount of flour.

The standard recipe yields enough pastry to cover a 2 pint (1·2 litre) dish, or a 9 in (23 cm) flan ring, or to line and cover a 7 in (18 cm) pie plate.

The following basic shortcrust pastries may be used for both savoury and sweet pies. Enriched shortcrust pastry, however, is mainly used for flans. Shortcrust pastries are usually baked in the centre of a pre-heated oven, at 400°F (200°C, mark 6).

Traditional Shortcrust
PREPARATION TIME: *15 min*
INGREDIENTS:
8 oz (225 g) plain flour
½ level teaspoon salt★
2 oz (50 g) lard
2 oz (50 g) margarine or butter
2–3 tablespoons cold water

Sift the flour and salt into a wide bowl. Cut up the firm fats and rub them into the flour, using the tips of the fingers, until the mixture resembles fine breadcrumbs. Lift the dry mixture well out of the bowl and let it trickle back through the fingers to keep the pastry cool and light. Add the water, sprinkle it evenly over the surface (uneven addition of the water may cause blistering when the pastry is cooked). Mix the dough lightly with a round-bladed knife until it forms large lumps.

Gather the dough together with the fingers until it leaves the sides of the bowl clean. Form it into one piece and knead it lightly on a floured surface until firm and free from cracks. Chill for 30 minutes before use.

Roll out as required, using short, light strokes and rotating the pastry regularly to keep it an even shape.

Shortcrust Pastry with Oil
This pastry produces a tender, flaky crumb. It must be mixed quickly and used at once – if left for any length of time, or chilled, it dries out and cannot be rolled.

PREPARATION TIME: *15 min*
INGREDIENTS:
5 tablespoons corn oil
2½ fluid oz (75 ml) cold water
8 oz (225 g) plain flour
¼ level teaspoon salt★

Whisk the oil and water together in a large bowl, using a fork. Continue whisking until they are evenly blended. Sift the flour and salt together and gradually add it to the oil. Use two knives to incorporate the flour to a dough, then turn it on to a floured surface. Knead the pastry lightly and quickly until smooth and shiny. Roll out as above.

PREPARING TRADITIONAL SHORTCRUST PASTRY

1. *Rubbing fat into flour*

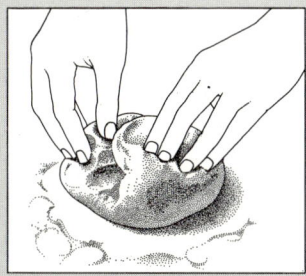
3. *Kneading dough lightly*

2. *Mixing water into dough*

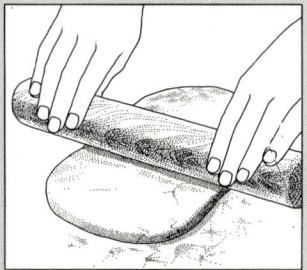
4. *Rolling out the pastry*

For shortcrust pastry with oil, use two knives to mix the flour and oil

Enriched Shortcrust Pastry

PREPARATION TIME: *10 min*
INGREDIENTS:
5 oz (150 g) plain flour
Pinch salt★
3 oz (75 g) unsalted butter or
margarine
1 egg yolk
1½ level teaspoons caster sugar
3–4 teaspoons water

Sift the flour and salt into a wide bowl. Cut up the fat and rub it into the flour with the fingertips until the mixture resembles bread-crumbs. Beat the egg yolk, sugar and 2 teaspoons of water in a separate bowl and pour it into the flour mixture. Stir with a round-bladed knife, adding more water as necessary until the mixture begins to form a dough. Gather this into a ball and turn it on to a floured surface. Knead lightly.

PÂTE SUCRÉE

This pastry is the French equivalent of British enriched short-crust pastry. It is thin and crisp, yet melting in texture, and neither shrinks nor spreads during baking. Pâte sucrée is usually baked blind (see next page).

PREPARATION TIME: *15 min*
RESTING TIME: *1 hour*
INGREDIENTS:
4 oz (100 g) plain flour
Pinch salt★
2 oz (50 g) caster sugar
2 oz (50 g) butter
2 egg yolks

Sift together the flour and salt on to a cool working surface. Make a well in the centre of the flour and put in the sugar, soft butter and the egg yolks. Using the finger-tips, pinch and work the sugar,

butter and egg yolks together until well blended. Gradually work in all the flour from the sides and knead the pastry lightly until smooth. Leave the pastry in a cool place for at least 1 hour before rolling it out. Bake in the centre of a pre-heated oven, at 350–400°F (180–200°C, mark 4–6).

AMERICAN STIRRED PASTRY

This rather sticky pastry is particularly suited to double crust fruit pies. The texture is like shortbread.

PREPARATION TIME: *10–15 min*
INGREDIENTS:
5 oz (150 g) table margarine
1½ oz (40 g) butter
8 oz (225 g) self-raising flour
½ level teaspoon salt★
3 tablespoons cold water

Beat the margarine and butter in a bowl until soft and well blended. Gradually add the sifted flour and salt, working it in with a wooden spoon. Finally add the water, blending well. The mixture will be sticky and difficult to work. Chill for at least 30 minutes.
　Roll out on a well-floured surface or between sheets of non-stick paper, dredged with flour.

BISCUIT CRUST

This is ideal for flan cases with fluffy chiffon-type fillings.

PREPARATION TIME: *15 min*
CHILLING TIME: *2 hours*
INGREDIENTS:
8 oz (225 g) digestive, wheatmeal,
rich tea or gingernut biscuits
5 oz (150 g) butter
1–2 oz (25–50 g) sugar (optional)

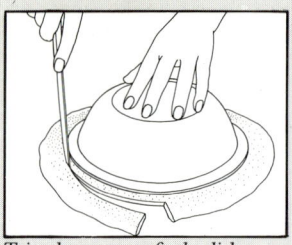
Trim the pastry to fit the dish

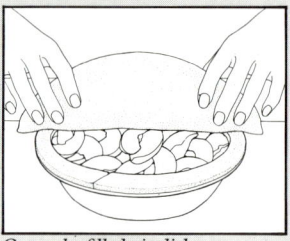
Cover the filled pie dish

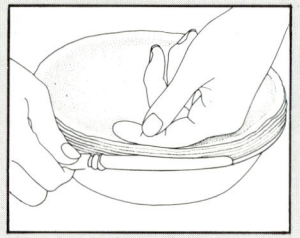
'Knock up' pastry edges

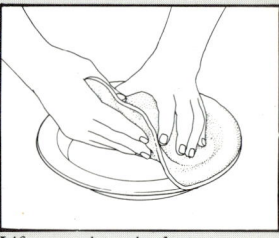
Lift pastry into pie plate

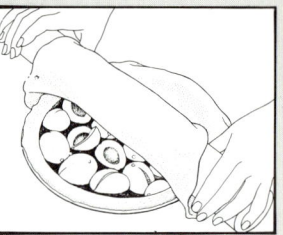
Place pastry lid in position

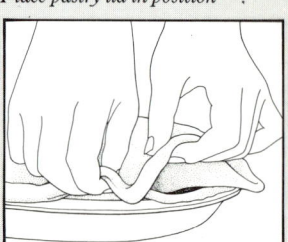
Fold surplus pastry under

Crush the biscuits, a few at a time, with a rolling pin between two sheets of greaseproof paper or in a plastic bag. For a fine crumb, break up the biscuits roughly and put them in a liquidiser. Turn the crumbs into a deep bowl. Melt the butter in a small saucepan over low heat. Add the sugar, if used, to the crumbs and mix with the melted butter, stirring until evenly combined.
　Spread the crumbly mixture into a 7–8 in (18–20 cm) wide shallow pie plate or flan dish; alternatively, use a flan ring placed on a flat serving dish or a

loose-bottomed flan tin. With the back of a spoon, press the crumbs over the base and up the sides to form a shell. Chill the flan case in the refrigerator for 2 hours before filling it.

Covering a pie dish

Roll out the pastry to the required thickness (no more than ¼ in – ½ cm – thick) and 2 in (5 cm) wider than the pie dish, using the inverted dish as a guide. Cut a 1 in (2½ cm) wide strip from the outer edge of the pastry and place it on the moistened rim of the pie dish. Seal the strip with water where it joins and brush the whole strip with water.

Fill the dish and set a pie funnel in the centre; lift the remaining pastry on the rolling pin and lay it over the dish. Press the pastry strip and lid firmly together with the fingers. Trim excess pastry with a knife blade held at a slight angle to the dish.

To seal the pastry edges firmly so that they do not come apart during baking, hold the knife blade horizontally towards the pie dish and make a series of shallow cuts in the pastry edges – this is known as 'knocking up'. Use the pastry trimmings to cut decorative shapes for the top of the pie. Cut a slit into the centre of the pastry for the steam to escape, and decorate the edges.

Preparing a double crust pie
Divide the pastry into two portions, one slightly larger than the other. Shape the larger portion into a ball and roll it out on a lightly floured surface, to the thickness of a coin. Rotate the pastry between rolls to keep the edge round; if the edge begins to break pinch it together with the fingers. Roll out the pastry about 1 in (2½ cm) wider than the inverted pie plate.

Fold the pastry in half and lift it on to the pie plate; unfold and loosely ease the pastry into position, being careful not to stretch the pastry. Put the cold filling over the pastry base, keeping it slightly domed in the centre. Roll out the remaining pastry for the lid, allowing about ½ in (1 cm) beyond the rim. Brush the edge of the pastry lining with water, then lift the lid on the rolling pin and place in position over the filling.

Seal the edges by either folding the surplus edge of the lid firmly over the rim of the lining, or by trimming the edges almost level with the plate and knocking them up with a knife. Cut a slit in the centre of the pastry lid for the steam to escape.

Lining a pie plate
For an open pie, roll out the pastry ⅙ in (½ cm) thick and about 1 in (2½ cm) wider than the pie plate. Lift the pastry into the plate and ease it loosely over the base and sides. Trim the pastry with scissors to ½ in (1 cm) from the plate edge, then fold the pastry under the rim of the plate. Flute the edge so that the points protrude over the plate rim, thus allowing for any shrinkage that may occur during baking.

Lining a flan ring
Flans are baked in plain or fluted rings set on baking trays or in a French fluted flan tin with a loose base. Roll the pastry out as thinly as possible to a circle 2 in (5 cm) wider than the ring. With the rolling pin, lift the pastry and lower it into the flan ring. Lift the edges carefully and press the pastry gently into shape with the fingers, taking care that no air pockets are left between the ring and the pastry. Trim the pastry in a plain ring with a knife or scissors, just above the rim, and knock up the edges. On a fluted flan ring, press the pastry against the inner fluted ring edges then use the rolling pin to cut the pastry level with the rim.

Baking Blind
Sometimes pastry, especially flan cases and individual tartlets, has to be baked before the filling is put in. This is known as baking blind.

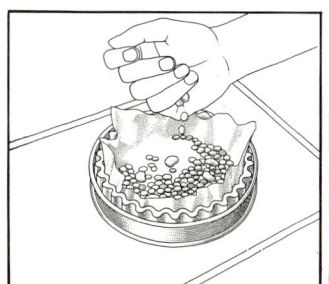

To bake blind, cover pastry with paper and weigh down with beans

Line the pastry case with foil or greaseproof paper cut to shape and weigh it down with dried beans (if kept specially for this purpose, the beans can be used again and again). Bake the pastry case in the centre of a pre-heated oven at 400°F (200°C, mark 6) for 15 minutes. Remove the beans and foil and bake for a further 5–10 minutes or until the pastry is dry and lightly browned.

Alternatively, and especially for tartlets, prick the base and sides of the pastry with a fork before lining it with foil. Dried beans are not necessary if the pastry is pricked.

Flan cases and tartlet moulds should be left on a wire rack to cool and shrink slightly before being eased out of their moulds.

Finishing and Decorations
The two edges of a covered pie can be finished in a number of decorative ways. To make a scalloped or fluted pattern on savoury pies, use the thumb or the back of a spoon handle to press the edges together. Alternatively, press the edges between thumb and index finger, at intervals of ½–¾ in (1–2 cm); draw a knife between the indentations towards the centre of the pie.

Sweet pies are usually finished with a twisted or ridged edge. Twist and slightly turn the edges together between thumb and index finger, at ½ in (1 cm) intervals. Alternatively, seal the edges with the tines of a fork.

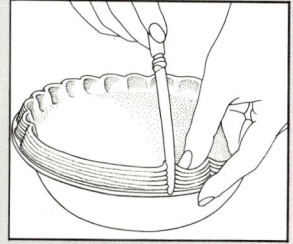

DECORATING PIE EDGES

Making a scalloped pattern

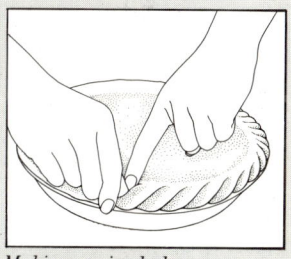

Making a twisted edge

The top of a covered pie may be decorated with the pastry trimmings. Roll the pastry out thinly and cut into small shapes.

To make leaves, cut the pastry into 1–1½ in (2–4 cm) wide strips and cut these into diamond shapes. With the back of a knife, trace the ribs.

For a tassel, cut a 1 in (2½ cm) wide pastry slice about 6 in (15 cm) long. Make cuts, ¾ in (2 cm) long, at intervals of ¼ in (½ cm), then roll up the strip, place it on the pie and open out.

Finish the edges of open flans and tarts by fluting or crimping. A simple method, using a pair of scissors, is to make cuts just over

Pastry leaf shapes

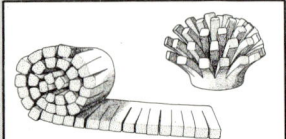

Pastry tassel

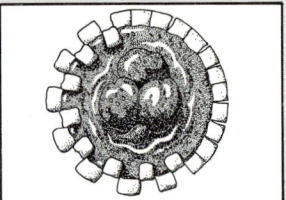

Cut edges on a flan

$\frac{1}{4}$ in ($\frac{1}{2}$ cm) deep and a little over $\frac{1}{4}$ in ($\frac{1}{2}$ cm) apart around the pastry edge. Fold alternate pieces of pastry inwards and bend the remaining pieces outwards. Or the edges can be decorated with thin pastry strips that have been twisted or braided. Moisten the pastry edge with water first.

A lattice pattern is a traditional decoration for many open flans. Cut the rolled-out pastry trimmings into strips $\frac{1}{2}$ in (1 cm) wide (a pastry wheel gives an attractive edge) and long enough to cover the flan. Moisten the flan edges, then lay half the strips over the filling, 1 in (2$\frac{1}{2}$ cm) apart, and lay the remaining strips criss-crossing the first. Trim the strips to shape at the outer edge, or fold the pastry lining down over them for a neater finish. For a really professional touch, the pastry strips should be interwoven by laying them over the filling 1 in (2$\frac{1}{2}$ cm)

apart, and a strip of pastry at a right angle across the centre. Lift alternate lengths of the first strips of pastry on one half of the tart and place a strip at right angles. Replace the top strips and repeat with the other side of the tart to complete the interwoven effect.

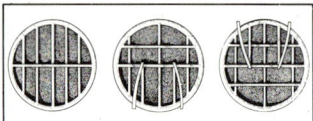

Lattice pattern: lay pastry strips over flan top; interweave crossing strips

Pies can be decorated with pastry flowers. Simple flowers are made by rolling a small piece of pastry to the size and shape of an acorn. Cut out two diamond shapes and pinch the edges to round them to a petal shape. Dampen the base of the petals and wrap around the wide base of the acorn shape. Pinch the pastry to seal the pieces together, then bend the tip of each petal slightly outwards.

More ornate flowers can be made by making a cross with a knife on a small, flattened round of pastry. Set the round on a square of dampened pastry; set this in turn on another square of dampened pastry, similar in size, to form a star pattern. Shape the corners of the squares to resemble petals. Pinch and shape each point of the central round of pastry into a petal to complete the flower.

Glazing

Brush the decorated pie or flan before baking to give a shiny golden look. Brush savoury pies with beaten whole egg or with egg yolk diluted with a little water or milk, and a pinch of salt. Glaze sweet pies with milk or egg white and dust with caster sugar.

CHOUX PASTRY

This pastry is a French speciality and is used for cream buns, chocolate éclairs and profiteroles. During cooking, the pastry should treble itself in size through the natural lift of air. The featherlight pastry surrounds a large cavity which can be filled with cream or confectioners' custard.

PREPARATION TIME: *20 min*
INGREDIENTS:
2$\frac{1}{2}$ oz (65 g) plain flour
2 oz (50 g) butter
Pinch of salt★
$\frac{1}{4}$ pint (150 ml) milk and water mixed (half of each)
2 beaten eggs

Sift the flour and salt on to a sheet of greaseproof paper. Put the butter and the liquid in a heavy-based pan and cook over low heat until the butter melts, then raise the heat and rapidly bring the mixture to the boil. Draw the pan off the heat and pour in all the flour. Stir quickly with a wooden spoon until the flour has been absorbed by the liquid, then beat until the dough is smooth and comes away from the sides of the pan. Do not overheat or the fat may leak out.

Cool pastry slightly, then beat in the beaten eggs, a little at a time. The pastry should be shiny and be thick enough to hold its shape, but not stiff. If the pastry is not going to be used immediately, cover the saucepan closely with greaseproof paper and the lid to keep the dough pliable.

MAKING CHOUX PASTRY

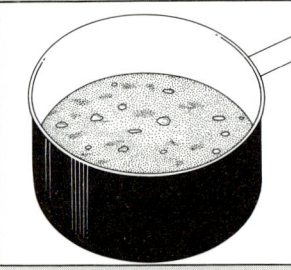

1. Heat butter and liquid

2. Pour flour into melted butter

3. Beat dough until smooth

4. Gradually add beaten egg

PUFF PASTRY

This is regarded as the finest and most professional pastry. It is time-consuming but well worth making if a large quantity is required. Uncooked puff pastry may also be stored in the home freezer for up to 3–4 months. When only small amounts of pastry are needed, commercially frozen and chilled puff pastry are particularly useful. Puff pastry, which is used for savoury pie crusts, as wrappings for meat and poultry, for vol-au-vents, cream horns, mille feuilles and palmiers, must be rolled out six times.

Vol-au-vents, patties and pastry crusts, which need the greatest rise and flakiness, should always be shaped from the first rolling of the finished dough. Second rolling, including trimmings from the first rolling, can be used for small items such as palmiers and crescents.

Prepared uncooked puff pastry can be stored for two or three days in the refrigerator.

PREPARATION TIME: *30–45 min*
RESTING TIME: *2½ hours*
INGREDIENTS:
1 lb (450 g) plain flour
2 level teaspoons salt★
1 lb (450 g) butter
½ pint (300 ml) iced water
1 teaspoon lemon juice

Sift the flour and salt into a large bowl. Cut 4 oz (100 g) of the butter into small pieces and rub it into the flour with the fingertips. Add the water and lemon juice and using a round-bladed knife, mix the ingredients to a firm but pliable dough. Turn the dough on to a lightly floured surface and lightly knead it until smooth. Shape the pastry into a thick round and cut down with a wet knife through half its depth in the form of a cross.

Open out the four flaps and roll them out until the centre is four times as thick as the flaps. Shape the remaining firm butter to fit the centre of the dough, leaving a clear ½ in (1 cm) all round. Fold the flaps over the butter, envelope style, and press the edges gently together with a rolling pin. Roll the dough into a rectangle 16 in (40 cm) × 8 in (20 cm) using quick short strokes. Roll lightly but firmly, back and forth, so as not to squeeze out the butter. Brush off any surplus flour between rollings.

Fold the dough into three and press the edges together with the edge of the little finger. Wrap the pastry in a cloth or greaseproof paper, cover with polythene and leave in a cool place (not the refrigerator) for 20 minutes.

Roll out the pastry, raw edge pointed to the left, to a rectangle as before. Fold and leave to rest for 20 minutes. Repeat rolling, folding and resting four times, giving the dough a half-turn every time. Leave the dough to rest for 30 minutes in the refrigerator before shaping it. Puff pastry, properly made, should rise about six times in height and should generally be baked in the centre or just above, of a pre-heated oven, at 450°F (230°C, mark 8).

MAKING PUFF PASTRY

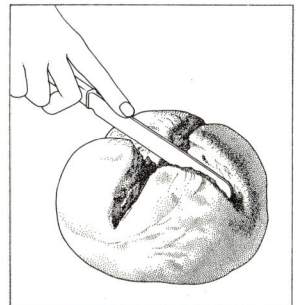
Cut a cross in rounded dough

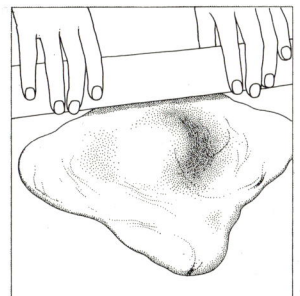
Roll out the flaps

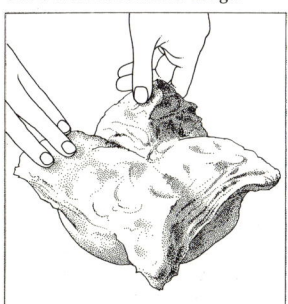
Fold out the four flaps

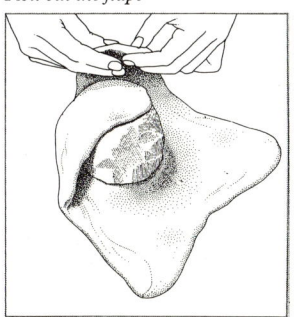
Place remaining butter in centre

COMMON FAULTS IN PASTRY MAKING

SHORTCRUST

Hard and/or tough pastry: due to too much liquid, too little fat, over-handling or insufficient rubbing in.

Soft and crumbly pastry: too little water; too much fat, or self-raising flour used instead of plain.

Shrunk pastry: excess stretching during rolling out.

Soggy pastry: filling too moist or sugar in a sweet pie in contact with pastry.

Sunken pie: oven temperature too low; cold pastry put over hot filling; too much liquid in filling, or too little filling.

Speckled pastry: undissolved sugar grains in enriched pastry crust.

CHOUX PASTRY

Mixture too soft: insufficient cooling of the flour before adding eggs; eggs added too quickly.

Pastry did not rise: self-raising flour used; oven too cold; too short baking time.

Sinking after removal from oven: insufficient baking; further period of baking sometimes remedies this defect.

PUFF PASTRY

Too few layers: insufficient resting and chilling; heavy rolling causing fat to break through and intermingle with the pastry; fat too soft.

Fat running out during baking: oven too cool.

Hard and tough pastry: too much water; over-kneading.

Shrinking pastry: insufficient resting; over-stretching during rolling.

Baking with Yeast

Home-baked bread has a strikingly different taste and texture from commercially baked loaves. Our daily bread is composed of such basic ingredients as flour, yeast, salt and liquid; enriched dough mixtures for buns and tea breads – such as babas and Sally Lunns – also include butter and spices, dried fruits and nuts.

Flour is the most important factor in bread-making, and the so-called 'strong' flours are essential for well-made loaves. A 'strong' flour has a high gluten content (from which protein is formed) of 10–15 per cent and aids rising in combination with yeast; it absorbs liquids easily and produces bread of light and open texture.

Flour
Brown flour produces a yeast dough of closer texture and with less rise than a white dough. It does not store well and should be bought as required. Wholemeal flour contains 100 per cent wheat, and wheatmeal flour has 80–90 per cent wheat including all the germ and some bran. Both these types of flour give the characteristic mealy taste to bread.

Yeast
Fresh or dried yeast may be used in bread-making. Many small private bakers will supply fresh yeast, and some supermarkets and health stores also stock it. Dried yeast is more concentrated than fresh yeast: $\frac{1}{2}$ oz (10–15 g) or 4 level teaspoons of dried yeast is the equivalent of 1 oz (25 g) of fresh yeast.

Fresh yeast should have a creamy-beige colour, and a firm consistency which crumbles easily when broken up. It can be stored in a loosely tied polythene bag in a cool place for up to 5 days, in a refrigerator for up to a month, or in the home freezer for up to a year.

Fresh yeast is added to flour in three different ways: it is rubbed in, blended with liquid or added as a batter. Rubbing in is suitable for soft doughs, quick-breads and sweet doughs. Blending with liquid is the basic way and is suitable for all bread recipes. The batter method is best suited for rich yeast doughs, and works equally well with fresh and dried yeast. It is not advisable to cream fresh yeast with sugar, as this results in the breakdown of some of the living yeast cells.

Rubbing-in method Crumble the yeast into the sifted flour and salt with the tips of the fingers. Add the specified amount of liquid to the flour and yeast mixture to make a soft dough. Work the dough with the fingertips to distribute the yeast evenly.

Blending with liquid Blend the yeast with part of the measured liquid; add this mixture to the flour and salt, together with the remaining liquid.

Batter method Mix one-third of the measured flour with the yeast, blended with all the liquid and 1 level teaspoon of sugar. Leave in a warm place until frothy, about 20 minutes, then add the rest of the flour, the salt and any other ingredients that are specified.

Dried yeast
This can be stored in a tightly lidded container for up to 6 months. Dried yeast is reconstituted in some warm water (110°F, 43°C). This water should be taken from the amount to be used in the recipe, first dissolved in the proportion of 1 level teaspoon sugar to $\frac{1}{2}$ pint (300 ml) water. Sprinkle the yeast over the water and leave in a warm place until frothy – after about 15 minutes.

Salt
Apart from improving the flavour of bread, salt also affects the gluten in the flour. If salt is omitted, the dough rises too quickly. If there is too much salt, this kills the yeast and gives the bread a heavy or uneven texture.

Liquid
This may be milk, water or a mixture of both. The amount varies from recipe to recipe, depending on the absorbency of the flour. Milk adds food value and strengthens doughs, improves the keeping quality and the colour of the crust. For plain bread, however, water alone gives a better texture.

Fat
This is used in enriched yeast doughs for buns, croissants and tea breads which have a soft outer crust. Fat makes a dough soft and also slows down yeast action so that the dough rises less than plain bread dough.

Sugar
Too much sugar added to a dough mixture delays fermentation of the yeast cells; always follow the given quantities.

Although many recipes specify sugar, it is not at all necessary for fermenting yeast and may be omitted unless of course you want a sweet dough.

Pour the liquid into the flour

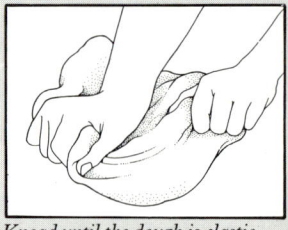
Knead until the dough is elastic

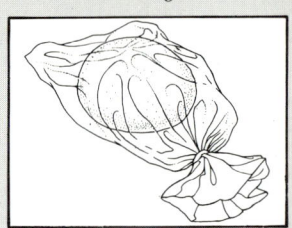
Leave to rise in polythene bag

MAKING BREAD DOUGH

Making the dough
Sift the flour and the salt into a mixing bowl, make a well in the centre and add all the liquid at once. Mix it in with one hand until thoroughly incorporated. Add

more flour if necessary, and beat the dough against the sides of the bowl until it comes away cleanly. Knead the dough on a lightly floured surface.

Kneading is most important, as it strengthens and develops the dough and enables it to rise. Gather the dough into a ball with the tips of the fingers, then fold the dough towards the body. Press down on the dough and away from the body with the palm of the hand. Give the dough a quarter-turn and repeat the kneading.

Knead the dough for about 10 minutes until it feels firm and elastic and no longer sticks to the fingers – it is better to knead the dough too much rather than too little. Bread dough may be kneaded in an electric mixer.

Rising

After kneading, the dough must be set aside for rising and proving (second rising) until it has doubled in size. A large polythene bag is useful for the rising process. Pour a few drops of corn oil into the bag and swirl it round to distribute it evenly in a thin film. Put the dough in the bag, tie it loosely and leave the dough until it has doubled in size and springs back when lightly pressed with a finger. The time the dough takes to rise depends on the temperature. Ideally allow 12 hours in a cool room, and about 2 hours at normal room temperature. Dough left to rise in a refrigerator will need 24 hours.

If time is short, the dough can be made to rise in 45–60 minutes in a warm place, for example over a pan of warm water. Be careful, however, as too much heat may kill the yeast.

PREPARING LOAVES FOR BAKING

Shape or roll up risen and proven dough to fit greased loaf tins

TRADITIONAL BREAD SHAPES

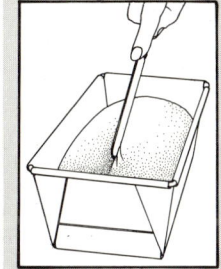 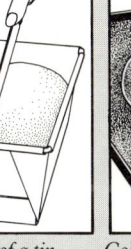 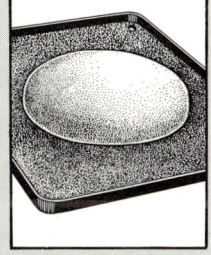 

Score the top of a tin loaf with a knife *Cob loaf is a lightly flattened ball of dough* *Arrange dough in a round tin for a crown loaf*

Knocking back and proving

After the initial rising the dough has to be knocked back, or kneaded again, to knock out the air bubbles and to ensure a good rise and even texture. Shape the kneaded dough as required and put it into tins or on to baking trays. Slip the tins or trays into oiled polythene bags and leave the loaves to rise a second time, or prove, at room temperature until double their size.

Baking

Remove the tins or baking trays from the polythene bags and bake at 400–450°F (200–230°C, mark 6–8), according to the individual recipes. A bowl of hot water placed in the bottom of the oven creates steam, which improves the bread texture.

Storing

Place the baked and cooled loaves in clean polythene bags, leaving the end open. To refresh a crusty loaf, wrap it in kitchen foil and put in the oven at 450°F (°230C, mark 8) for about 10 minutes. Leave it to cool in the foil.

Wholemeal Bread

PREPARATION TIME: *20 min (plus rising and proving)*
COOKING TIME: *30–40 min*
INGREDIENTS *(for two 2 lb (900 g) or four 1 lb (450 g) loaves):*
3 lb (1½ kg) plain wholemeal flour
1 level tablespoon caster sugar
3–4 level teaspoons salt★
1 oz (25 g) lard
2 oz (50 g) fresh yeast
1½ pints (900 ml) lukewarm water

Sift the flour, sugar and salt into a large bowl. Cut up the lard and rub it into the flour with the fingertips until the mixture resembles fine breadcrumbs. Blend the yeast, in a small bowl, with ½ pint (300 ml) of the measured water and pour it into a well in the centre of the flour; add the remaining water. Using one hand, work the mixture together and beat it until the dough leaves the bowl clean. Knead the dough on a lightly floured surface for 10 minutes.

Shape the dough into a large ball and leave it to rise in a lightly oiled polythene bag until it has doubled in size. Turn the dough on to a lightly floured surface and knead again until firm. Divide the dough into two or four equal pieces and flatten each piece firmly with the knuckles to knock out any air bubbles. Stretch and roll each piece of dough into an oblong the same length as the tin; fold it into three or roll it up like a Swiss roll. Lift the dough into the greased tins, brush the top with lightly salted water and place each tin inside an oiled polythene bag. Tie the bag loosely and leave to rise until the dough reaches the top of the tins.

Remove the tins from the bags, set them on baking trays and bake in the centre of a pre-heated oven at 450°F (230°C, mark 8) for about 30 minutes or until the loaves shrink from the sides of the tins. Cool the loaves on a wire rack and test by tapping them. If they sound hollow they are done.

For a fancy wholemeal loaf divide a quarter of the dough into four equal pieces; shape them into rolls the width of a greased 1 lb (450 g) loaf tin and fit them into the tin. Finish as before.

Quick Wheatmeal Loaves

PREPARATION TIME: *20 min* (*plus rising*)

COOKING TIME: *15–20 min*

INGREDIENTS (*for one 1 lb (450 g) loaf and 8 rolls, or two 1 lb (450 g) loaves*):
½ lb (225 g) plain brown flour
½ lb (225 g) strong plain white flour
2 level teaspoons salt★
2 level teaspoons caster sugar
¼ oz (5–10 g) lard
½ oz (10–15 g) fresh yeast
½ pint (300 ml) warm water
2–3 tablespoons cracked wheat or crushed cornflakes

Sift the two flours, the salt and sugar into a bowl. Cut up the lard and rub it into the flour with the fingertips. Blend the yeast with all the warm water until the yeast has dissolved. Make a well in the centre of the flour and pour in the yeast liquid. Mix to a soft, scone-like dough, beating until it leaves the side of the bowl clean (if necessary, add a little more flour).

Divide the dough into two equal portions. Shape each piece to half fill a greased loaf tin and brush the top of the dough with lightly salted water; sprinkle with cracked wheat or crushed corn-flakes. Place the tins on a baking tray in a lightly oiled polythene bag, tie loosely and leave in a warm place until the dough has doubled in size. Remove the polythene and bake the loaves in the centre of a pre-heated oven at 450°F (230°C, mark 8) for about 40 minutes. Test by tapping the loaves; if they sound hollow, they are baked. Cool on a wire rack.

Rolls Divide the whole, risen dough after re-kneading into 8 equal pieces. Roll each into a round on an unfloured surface, using the palm of one hand. Shake a little flour on to the palm of the hand, and press the dough down, hard at first, easing up until the rounds have the shape of a roll. Set the rolls well apart on floured baking trays, put them into oiled polythene bags and leave in a warm place to double in size.

Remove the polythene and bake the rolls just above the centre of the oven, pre-heated to 450°F (230°C, mark 8), for 15–20 minutes. Cool on a wire rack.

For soft rolls, set the shaped rolls ¾ in (2 cm) apart on the baking trays and sprinkle gener-ously with flour. The rolls will bake into contact with each other along the sides and the flour on top will give a soft surface.

Flowerpot Loaves Wheat-meal bread may also be baked in flowerpots. Use clay pots – never plastic – grease them thoroughly inside and bake them empty in a hot oven several times to seal the inner surface and prevent the dough sticking. A clay flowerpot 4–5 in (10–13 cm) wide will hold half a portion of wheatmeal dough. Finish and bake the loaf as already described.

Cob Loaf Roll each piece of dough into a ball, flatten it and set on a floured baking tray.

Crown Loaf Divide a quarter of the risen dough into five or six balls. Set these in a greased, 5 in (13 cm) wide cake tin or a deep sandwich tin.

Poppy-seed Plaits Divide the dough into three, and roll each into a 12 in (30 cm) long strand. Set the three strands side by side on a flat surface, and pass the left strand over the centre strand, then the right strand over the centre strand. Continue like this

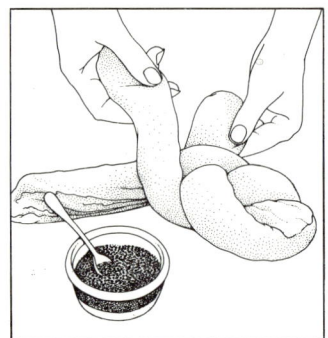

Plaited loaf: for a three-strand plait, begin crossing the dough near the top

until the whole length is plaited. Finally join the short ends neatly together and tuck them under.

Place the plaits on a lightly greased baking tray. Beat an egg with a teaspoon of caster sugar and a tablespoon of water to make the glaze. Brush the plaits evenly and sprinkle with poppy seeds. Put the plaits on the tray inside a lightly oiled polythene bag and set aside to rise (prove) again until the dough has doubled in size. Remove the polythene bag and bake the loaves in the centre of a pre-heated oven at 375°F (190°C, mark 5) for 35–40 minutes. Tap the bottom of the loaves with the knuckles – if they sound hollow they are done. Cool the loaves on a wire rack.

Fancy Rolls Enriched white dough is ideal for light, dinner-type rolls which can be shaped in a variety of ways. Use about 2 oz (50 g) of risen dough for each roll. Roll a piece of dough out, about 4 in (10 cm) long, cut it in half lengthways and, holding each strip at both ends, twist it three times. Alternatively, roll each strip into a strand and tie it into a knot in the centre.

Shape 2 oz (50 g) pieces of dough into oblong miniature loaves and score the surface with five or six marks, at even inter-vals. With a scissor-point, make triangular cuts between the score marks, through the dough, so that the points are slightly raised.

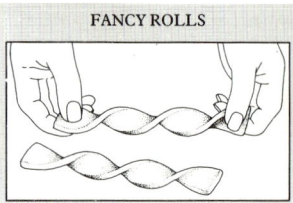

FANCY ROLLS

Twisting strips of dough

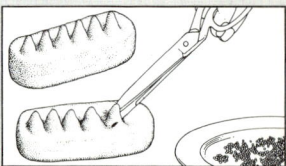

Snipping small cuts in rolls

Setting rolls on baking tray

Divide a 2 oz (50 g) piece of dough into three, shape into balls and set them on a baking tray in such a way that all three balls touch each other.

Alternatively, roll a 2 in (5 cm) piece of dough into a thick strand and shape into a snail or 'S' form.

Brush the rolls with egg glaze and set them aside to rise (prove) until doubled in size. Bake the rolls just above the centre of a pre-heated oven, at 375°F (190°C, mark 5), for 10–15 minutes or until golden.

Cake-making

The key to successful cake-making lies in following the recipe in detail, and in understanding the reaction of the various ingredients to each other. The basic ingredients are fat, flour, raising agents, eggs, sugar and often fruit. Using the right size tins, correct oven position and temperature are also important factors.

Basically cakes fall into two categories: those made with fat, and the sponge types made without fat.

In fat-type cakes, the fat is either rubbed in, creamed or melted. Rubbed-in mixtures are generally used for plain, everyday cakes, such as Tyrol cake, while creamed cakes are rich and soft with a fairly close, even grain and soft crumb as in a Victoria sandwich.

In melted cakes, e.g. gingerbread, the fat, often with liquid, sugar, syrup or treacle added, is poured into the dry ingredients to give a batter-like consistency. Mix cakes by hand or use an electric mixer after incorporating the flour with fat and eggs.

Preparations

Always use the right size tin. Bigger, smaller or shallower tins than those called for can cause a cake to fail. If the tin is of incorrect size, fill to only half its depth so that the cake will rise to, but not above, the top. Test frequently to see if the cakes are cooked. Prepare the tin either by lining or by greasing with butter and sprinkling with flour. Set the oven to the correct temperature if the cake is to be baked at once after mixing, and assemble the necessary ingredients – eggs, butter and firm margarine should be at room temperature.

Fats

Butter, margarine, whipped-up white fat, lard and corn oil are all used in cakes. However, they are not always interchangeable.

Butter gives the best flavour and improves the keeping quality of cakes, but firm margarine can be used in place of butter in most recipes, with only a slight difference in flavour. Soft table margarine, sold in tubs, is composed of blended oils; it is particularly suitable for cakes where all the ingredients are mixed in one operation.

Whipped-up white fat is light and easy to blend with other ingredients. Like lard, this fat contains little or no salt and is almost 100 per cent fat; both can be used interchangeably in recipes.

Corn oil is suitable for most recipes using melted fat, but it is advisable to follow the manufacturer's instructions, as the characteristics of oils vary. It is easy to mix in and gives a soft texture, but cakes made with it do not keep quite so well.

Flour

Plain or self-raising flour or a mixture of both are used for cakes. Whichever type of flour is used, it should always be sifted with a pinch of salt. Salt is added not only for flavour, but because of its chemical action which in effect toughens up the soft mixture of fat and sugar.

Self-raising flour is popular, as it eliminates errors in calculating the exact amount of raising agents, which are already evenly blended throughout the flour.

A mixture of plain and self-raising flour is ideal for rich cakes which would rise too much if self-raising flour only were used. Other cakes, and in particular whisked cakes such as sponges, should be made only with plain flour, as they have their own natural raising agent – air.

In some melted cakes plain flour is mixed with bicarbonate of soda. These cakes contain treacle, which on its own is slightly acid and must be offset by an alkali to act as a raising agent.

Raising agents

Baking powder is a ready-made blend of soda and cream of tartar, and these together form carbon dioxide. The rubbery substance in flour – known as gluten – is capable, when wet, of suspending carbon dioxide in the form of tiny bubbles.

Since all gases expand when heated, these bubbles become larger during baking, and thus cause a cake to rise.

However, cake mixtures can hold only a certain amount of gas, and if too much raising agent is used the cake will rise well at first, but later collapse, and this results in a heavy, close texture. A combination of cream of tartar and bicarbonate of soda is sometimes used as an alternative to baking powder, in the proportion of 2:1.

Eggs

These give lightness to cake mixtures, as they expand on heating and trap the air beaten into the mixture. When whisked egg is used in a cake mixture, air instead of carbon dioxide causes it to rise.

Cakes with a high proportion of egg, such as sponge cakes, need little if any raising agent.

In creamed mixtures, the eggs are beaten in, not whisked, and a little additional raising agent is required. In plain cakes, where beaten egg is added with the liquid, the egg helps to bind the mixture but does not act as the main raising agent.

Sugar

Granulated sugar is the least expensive white sugar; it can be used in rubbed-in cakes, but as it is coarse it may give a spotted appearance to the cake crust. Caster sugar, being finer, creams more easily with fats and gives a finer, softer cake.

You can easily grind your own granulated sugar, whether white or brown, to the desired degree of fineness.

Demerara sugar should only be used in recipes for melted cakes, where sugar is dissolved, unless otherwise recommended.

Soft brown sugar, medium or light brown in colour, is good for rubbed-in, melted and fruit cakes. The colour and flavour add richness and the soft, moist quality helps to keep certain cakes in good condition longer.

Barbados sugar, very dark brown, full-flavoured and moist,

is used in rich fruit mixtures for wedding and birthday cakes. Syrup, honey and treacle, often combined with sugar, are used to sweeten, colour and flavour cakes such as gingerbread. They give a close, moist texture.

Fruit and peel
Always choose good-quality dried fruit. Stored sultanas sometimes become hard, but they can be plumped up in hot water, and thoroughly drained and dried.

Sultanas can be bought ready-washed or unwashed. Unwashed are cheaper, but the fruit should be washed well, drained and left to dry thoroughly before use. Alternatively, clean sultanas by rubbing in a sieve with a little flour to remove the stalks.

Seedless raisins are similar in size to sultanas, but ready-prepared seeded or stoned raisins are large and juicy. To remove the stones from a raisin, work it between the fingertips to ease out the stones, occasionally dipping the fingers in water. Wash any syrup from the glacé cherries and dry them thoroughly.

Peel can be bought ready-chopped, but make sure that it looks soft and moist. Coarsely chopped, thin cut peel sometimes needs more chopping to make it finer. 'Caps' of candied orange, lemon, grapefruit and citron peel should be stripped of sugar before being shredded, grated, minced or chopped.

Preparing cake tins
All cakes should be baked in tins that have been greased, greased and floured, sugared or lined with paper.

The appearance of a finished cake depends largely on the expert preparation of the cake tin.

Sandwich tins and cake tins for rubbed-in mixtures are often greased only by brushing melted white fat evenly over the inside. But as an extra precaution against sticking and for ease of turning out, a paper liner of greased greaseproof paper fitted into the base is a good idea. The paper does not necessarily have to reach the edge of the tin but the centre must be covered.

For fatless sponges, flour the greased tin to give an extra crisp crust, or dust it with flour, blended with an equal amount of sugar. Shake the dusting mixture round the tin until evenly coated, and remove any excess by gently tapping the inverted tin.

For baking small cakes or buns, fluted paper cups set in patty tins are by far the easiest to use; otherwise grease the patty pans thoroughly.

Non-stick paper can be used instead of greaseproof paper to line both round and rectangular tins. Tins with a non-stick surface need no greasing or lining, but a paper lining helps to protect against a solid crust, especially during long baking. If the cakes are to be baked in non-stick tins, the baking time should be reduced by a few minutes as these tins brown the contents more quickly.

Lining a round cake tin
Cut a strip of greaseproof paper as long as the circumference of the tin and 2 in (5 cm) wider than the depth of the tin. Make a fold about 1 in (2½ cm) deep along one of the long edges, and cut this at ½ in (1 cm) intervals up to the fold, at a slight angle.

Curve the strip round and slip

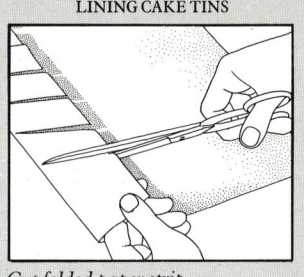
Cut folded paper strip

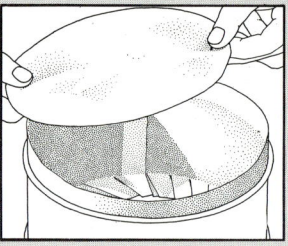
Cut a circle to fit base of tin

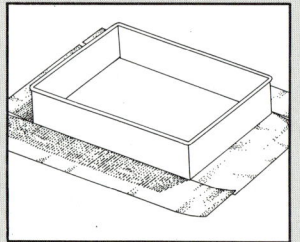
Centre rectangular tin over paper

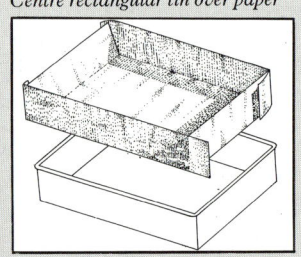
Cut and fold paper to fit tin

it around the sides of the greased tin, nicked fold downwards so that this lies flat against the base of the tin

Cut a circle of paper slightly smaller than the bottom of the tin and drop it in over the nicked paper. Then brush the paper with melted fat. For rich cakes with long cooking times, line the tin with a double thickness of the greaseproof paper.

Lining a rectangular tin
Measure the length and width of the tin and add twice the tin's depth to each of these measurements.

Cut a rectangle of greaseproof paper to this size and place the tin squarely in the centre. At each corner, make a cut from the angle of the paper as far as the corner of the tin.

Grease the inside of the tin and put in the paper so that it fits closely overlapping at the corners. Brush the paper with melted fat.

Oven positions
In gas cookers, the hottest shelf is at the top, but in electric cookers the heat is more evenly distributed. A cake is generally baked in the centre of the oven.

When baking two cakes, place them side by side but do not let them touch the side of the oven or each other. If the tins are too large, bake the cakes on two oven shelves but avoid placing the tins directly over each other, and switch the tins over when the cake mixture has set.

Small cakes are usually baked above the centre, but not at the top of the oven. Place the tins or patty pans on baking trays before putting them in the oven.

Cooling cakes
With only a few exceptions, all cakes should be thoroughly cooled before being cut, frosted or stored. After baking, most

cakes are best left to settle in their tins for 5–10 minutes before being turned out. Large cakes and rich fruit cakes are often left to get lukewarm before turning them out.

Run a spatula, small palette knife or round-bladed knife around the edge of the cake (do not use metal tools on non-stick tins). Place a wire rack over the cake and invert both the cake and rack, then lift the tin carefully. The lining paper may be peeled off or left on. Turn the cake with the aid of a second rack or the hand so that the top is uppermost. Leave the cake to cool completely on the wire rack. To prevent the wire mesh marking the surface of a soft-textured cake, first place a tea towel over the rack.

Storing cakes
Storage time depends on the type of cake. Generally, iced cakes stay fresh longer than un-iced cakes, and the more fat in the cake mixture the longer it keeps. Fatless sponges should preferably be eaten on the day of baking.

Store both plain and iced cakes in airtight cake tins or similar containers. Cream-filled cakes are best kept in the refrigerator. Wrap fruit cakes with the lining paper left on in kitchen foil before storing. If slightly warm when wrapped they retain the moisture better. Most cakes freeze well.

RUBBED-IN CAKES

These plain cakes are the easiest of all to make. As the proportion of fat to flour is half or less, rubbed-in mixtures are best eaten when fresh or within 2–3 days of baking. Rubbing in consists of blending flour and fat to a crumb-like mixture, using the fingertips.

To keep the mixture cool, raise the hands high when letting the crumbs drop back into the bowl. Shake the bowl occasionally to bring bigger crumbs to the surface. Make sure the texture is even, but do not handle more than necessary, or the crumbs will toughen and the fat become soft and oily.

The amount of liquid added can be critical: too much results in a doughy texture, whereas too little gives a crumbly cake which quickly dries out. For a large cake, the mixture should only just drop off the spoon when gently tapped. An example is the Tyrol cake on page 64.

CREAMED CAKES

These are all made from the basic method of blending fat with sugar. Put the cut up butter or margarine into a bowl large enough to allow the fat – and sugar – to be beaten vigorously without overflowing. With a wooden spoon, beat the fat against the sides of the bowl until soft; add the sugar and beat or cream the mixture until fluffy and pale yellow. After 7–10 minutes the volume should have increased greatly and the mixture should drop easily from the spoon. Eggs may be added whole or beaten.

If an electric mixer is used, set the dial at the speed suggested in the manufacturer's instructions, and allow 3–4 minutes for beating. Switch off the mixer from time to time and scrape the cake mixture down into the bowl. An example is the Victoria sandwich on page 61, or the farmhouse fruit cake on page 64.

CREAMED CAKE MIXTURE

Beat butter and sugar until fluffy

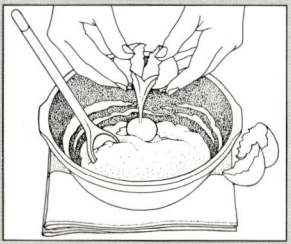
Break egg into mixture and stir

Alternatively, add beaten egg

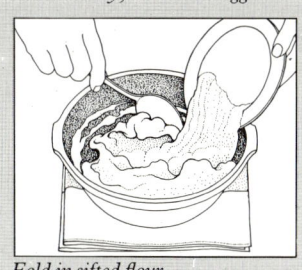
Fold in sifted flour

WHISKED CAKES

These are the lightest of all cake mixtures, their texture depending entirely on the incorporated eggs. The fatless cake mixture is used for sponges, which should be baked as soon as mixed.

Use a hand-operated, rotary or balloon whisk and to stabilise the mixture, place the deep bowl of eggs and sugar over hot, not boiling, water. Do not let the mixture become too hot or the sponge will have a tough texture. For a maximum rise, the mixture should be thick enough to leave a trail when the whisk is lifted. If an electric mixer is used, it is unnecessary to heat the bowl.

Blending in the flour is another important step. Sift the flour two or three times, the last time over the whisked egg mixture, then fold it carefully into the mixture without flattening the bulk. Use a metal spoon or plastic spatula in a figure-of-eight movement. An example is the strawberry cream sponge on page 62.

ENRICHED BUTTER SPONGE CAKES

When butter is added to a whisked sponge mixture, it is known as Genoese sponge, a richer variety than fatless sponges and one which needs slightly longer baking, but keeps better. Genoese sponge mixtures are used for gâteaux, layered with cream and fruit, or baked and cut into small individual cakes before being iced and decorated.

MELTED CAKES

These have a dense, slightly tacky texture and a consistency similar to a thick batter. Treacle or syrup is a major ingredient, with baking powder as the main raising agent together with bicarbonate of soda. An example is the gingerbread on page 61.

Freezing

FREEZING PRE-COOKED FOOD

For successful freezing follow these pointers:

1. Working surroundings must be scrupulously clean, as freezing does not destroy germs in food.
2. Use top-quality ingredients and season lightly; more seasoning can always be added later.
3. Always slightly undercook dishes which are to be frozen, allowing for the time the food will be in the oven to heat through.
4. When recipes call for the addition of cream or egg yolks, omit these before freezing and add them when the dishes are being re-heated. Do not freeze dishes with custard.
5. Cool all cooked and baked dishes thoroughly before packing and freezing.
6. Garnish re-heated food before serving, not before freezing.

FREEZING FRESH FRUIT

Top-quality fruit in peak condition is suitable for freezing whole; slightly over-ripe fruit is better made into purées.

To prepare fruit for freezing, wash it in chilled water, drain and dry thoroughly. Soft berries should be washed only if absolutely necessary.

Keep fruit in a cool place or in the refrigerator until it is prepared for freezing. Stoned fruit may be frozen whole, halved or sliced. There are three ways of freezing: dry-freezing, sugar-freezing and syrup-freezing.

Dry-freezing is particularly suitable for small whole berry fruits. Spread the cleaned and dry fruit in a single layer on paper-lined trays. Place in the freezer until firm and pack in rigid containers or heavy-duty bags.

Sugar-freezing is recommended for soft fruits such as blackberries, raspberries, and strawberries. Pick over the fruit, but do not wash. Layer the fruit with caster sugar in rigid containers or mix the two together, allowing 4 oz (100 g) sugar to 1 lb (450 g) prepared fruit.

Syrup-freezing is the best method for non-juicy fruits and those which discolour during preparation and storage. The strength of the syrup varies according to the fruit (see chart). Pack the fruit in rigid containers, leaving $\frac{1}{2}$ in (1 cm) headspace.

Label all packages with the name of the fruit, the weight, the amount of sugar added and the date of freezing.

Whole and sliced frozen fruit will store for up to one year, fruit purées for 6–8 months, and fruit juices for 4–6 months.

All frozen fruit should be thawed slowly in their unopened containers. To serve fruits as a dessert thaw in the refrigerator for 6 hours or at room temperature for 2–3 hours. Serve chilled.

Dessert fruits frozen in syrups should have the lid removed from the container and a piece of waxed paper pressed over the fruit to keep them immersed.

Frozen fruit to be stewed can be cooked without thawing, but fruit for pies and puddings should first be thawed.

FREEZING PRE-COOKED DISHES

Food (storage time in brackets)	Method
Biscuits *unbaked* (6 months)	Shape dough into cylinders about 2 in (5 cm) wide and wrap in f polythene. Shape soft mixtures on to a paper-lined tray, freeze, pack carefully in rigid containers, separating layers with paper
baked	Pack as for shaped soft biscuits before freezing
Bread (4 weeks)	Wrap in polythene bags
bought part-baked bread and rolls (4 months)	Freeze immediately after buying; leave loaves in own wrapper, p rolls in polythene bags or foil
Cakes (6 months – iced cakes lose quality after 2 months)	Use less essence and spice than usual. Fill cakes with cream, bu jam, before freezing. Wrap unfilled layer cakes separately or sep with waxed paper or cellophane; pack in foil or polythene. Freez cakes unwrapped until icing has set, then wrap in foil or celloph pack in boxes to protect icing
Croissants and Danish pastries *unbaked* (6 weeks)	Prepare dough to the stage when all fat has been absorbed, but d give final rolling. Wrap tightly in polythene bag
baked (Croissants 2 months, Danish pastries 1 month)	Wrap in polythene bags or foil, or in rigid foil containers
Ice cream (home-made 3 months, commercial 1 month)	Wrap bought ice cream in moisture-proof bags; freeze home-ma cream in moulds or waxed containers, and overwrap with polyth
Mousses, cold soufflés (2 months)	Freeze in special toughened glassware, or line dishes or moulds foil, freeze, then remove from container and wrap in polythene store
Pancakes *unfilled* (2 months)	Stack pancakes between layers of greaseproof paper or cellophan conveniently sized stacks in foil or polythene
Pastry, *uncooked* (3 months)	Make as usual and roll out to size required. Line foil plates or pi dishes, freeze unwrapped, remove from pie dishes, and wrap in polythene. Roll out pastry lids and separate with waxed paper b wrapping in polythene. Stack, separating the layers with two sh waxed paper, place on cardboard and wrap. Single or double crust fruit pies may be frozen uncooked with th in place, ready for baking. Do not make slits in the top crust bef freezing. Wrap in foil or polythene bags when frozen solid
cooked (pastry cases and fruit pies 6 months)	Bake pies in foil containers and cool quickly. Wrap in foil or pol Tops may be protected with an inverted foil dish before wrappin
Scones and teabreads (6 months)	Wrap in polythene bags in convenient quantities

awing and serving

htly thaw rolls of uncooked dough, slice and
e. Shaped biscuits can be cooked from
en state but will need 7–10 minutes more
king time

sp in a warm oven after thawing

aw in wrapper at room temperature (3 hours
1½ lb, 700 g) or overnight in refrigerator.
y be thawed in oven at 300°F (160°C, mark
or about 30 min, but this causes it to go stale
ckly.

cook, place frozen unwrapped loaf in oven
25°F (220°C, mark 7) for about 40 min. Cool
ore cutting. Bake unwrapped rolls at 400°F
)°C, mark 6) for 15 min.

am-filled cakes are best sliced while frozen.
wrap iced cakes before thawing so that paper
s not stick to icing. Thaw at room
perature: allow 1–2 hours for plain layer
es and small cakes, 4 hours for iced cakes

ve in polythene bag but unseal it and re-tie
sely to allow dough to rise. Thaw overnight
efrigerator or for about 5 hours at room
perature. Complete rolling and shaping
ore baking

aw in wrapping at room temperature for
ut 1 hour. If wished, heat in oven,
wrapped, at 350°F (180°C, mark 4) for 5 min.

ce in refrigerator for 1–1½ hours to soften

aw in refrigerator for 6–8 hours, or at room
perature for 2–3 hours

aw in wrapping at room temperature for 2–3
rs, or overnight in refrigerator. To thaw
ckly, unwrap, spread out pancakes and thaw
oom temperature for about 20 minutes. Heat
ividual pancakes in a lightly greased frying
for 30 seconds each side. Or heat stack of
cakes wrapped in foil in oven at 375°F
)°C, mark 5) for 20–30 min

urn pie shells to original dishes. Thaw
ry lids at room temperature before fitting on
d pies. Pie cases can be baked frozen
enproof glassware should be left to stand at
n temperature for 10 min. before baking).
15 min. to baking time.
ce unwrapped fruit pies in oven at 425°F
)°C, mark 7) for 40–60 min. Slit tops of
sts when beginning to thaw

aw at room temperature; pies for 2–4 hours.
heat in oven

aw scones for 30–60 min. at room
perature; warm in oven if wished. Thaw
breads in wrapping for 2–3 hours, at room
perature, or place frozen in oven at 400°F
)°C, mark 6) for 10 min.

FREEZING FRESH FRUIT

Fruit	Preparation and Packaging
Apples	Peel, core and slice, dropping slices into cold acidulated water. Blanch for 1–2 min, cool in iced water. Drain well. Dry or sugar freeze. Pack in polythene bags or rigid containers, leaving ½ in (1 cm) headspace *Purée:* Prepare as for slices. Stew in the minimum of water, add sugar to taste. Cook until soft and beat to a smooth pulp. Cool before packing in rigid containers, leaving ½ in (1 cm) headspace
Apricots	Plunge into boiling water for 30 seconds and peel. Remove stones and halve or slice. Freeze in syrup made from 1 lb (450 g) sugar to 2 pints (1·2 litres) water and add 500 mg. ascorbic acid to each pint (600 ml) of syrup. Pack in rigid containers, leaving ½ in (1 cm) headspace
Blackberries, loganberries, raspberries and strawberries	Dry or sugar freeze, then pack in bags or rigid containers. *Purée:* press through a nylon sieve and sweeten to taste with caster sugar. Pack in rigid containers. Use for fools and mousses
Cherries	Remove stalks, wash and dry cherries and dry freeze. Alternatively, remove stones, and sugar freeze until firm. Pack in rigid containers, leaving ½ in (1 cm) headspace. Stoned cherries may also be frozen in syrup made with 8 oz (225 g) sugar to 1 pint (570 ml) water; add ½ teaspoon ascorbic acid to every 2 pints (1·2 litres) syrup. Pack in rigid containers, leaving ½ in (1 cm) headspace
Currants	Wash, dry and remove from stalks unless wanted for decoration. Dry or sugar freeze until firm, then pack in rigid containers. Black currants may be puréed. Cook with the minimum of water, and sugar to taste. Cool and pack in rigid containers. Use for drinks, ices and puddings
Damsons	Best frozen as purées. Wash, cook gently in the minimum of water, sweetening to taste; pass through a nylon sieve. Cool and pack in rigid containers
Gooseberries	Wash, dry, top and tail. Dry freeze or pack in syrup (made with 1 lb (450 g) sugar to 1 pint (570 ml) water); store in rigid containers, leaving ½ in (1 cm) headspace *Purée:* stew in the minimum of water, pass through a nylon sieve and sweeten to taste. Cool and pack in rigid containers. Use for sauces and fools
Grapefruit	Peel, removing all pith. Divide into segments and sugar freeze using 8 oz (225 g) caster sugar to 1 lb (450 g) prepared fruit; when juice starts to run, pack segments in rigid containers. Alternatively, freeze in syrup made with equal quantities of sugar and water; pack in rigid containers, leaving ½ in (1 cm) headspace
Greengages	Wash in cold water, halve and remove stones. Pack as for apricots
Lemons	Squeeze out juice, strain and freeze in ice cube trays; pack frozen cubes in polythene. Remove all pith from the peel, cut into fine strips, blanch for 1 min, cool and pack in small quantities in polythene bags. Or freeze grated peel
Melons	Cut in half and remove seeds. Cut flesh into cubes or balls. Freeze in syrup made with 8 oz (225 g) sugar to 1 pint (570 ml) water. Pack in rigid containers, leaving ½ in (1 cm) headspace
Oranges	Freeze and pack segments as for grapefruit; freeze juice and rind as for lemon. Seville oranges can be frozen whole in polythene bags. Use thawed for marmalade, allowing extra fruit to counterbalance loss of pectin during freezing
Peaches	Peel and stone peaches, cut in half or slice; brush immediately with lemon juice to prevent discoloration. Freeze and pack in syrup as for apricots. Alternatively, purée peeled and stoned peaches, add 1 tablespoon lemon juice and 4 oz (100 g) sugar to each 1 lb (450 g) prepared fruit. Pack in rigid containers
Pineapple	Peel and cut into slices or chunks. Pack them in rigid containers, separating with non-stick paper or double thickness of cellophane. Or freeze in syrup made with 8 oz (225 g) sugar to 1 pint (570 ml) water, including any pineapple juice from the preparation. Pack in rigid containers, leaving ½ in (1 cm) headspace. Mix crushed pineapple with sugar, allowing 4 oz (100 g) sugar to ¾ lb (350 g) prepared fruit; pack in rigid containers
Plums	Wash, halve and remove stones. Freeze as for apricots
Rhubarb	Wash, trim and cut into 1 in (2½ cm) lengths. Blanch for 1 min, drain, cool. Do not use aluminium containers for packing. Sugar freeze and pack in polythene bags. Alternatively, freeze in syrup made with equal quantities of sugar and water; pack in rigid containers and leave ½ in (1 cm) headspace. *Purée:* stew in a little water, sweeten to taste and press through a nylon sieve; cool and pack in rigid containers, leaving ½ in (1 cm) headspace

Pastry

Although much mystique surrounds pastry-making, there are no great secrets to guarantee instant success, for pastry-making is an art which is mastered by care, patience and practice. There are, however, a few essentials which must be observed before good results can be achieved. The kitchen, working surface and utensils should be cool, and the recipe must always be strictly adhered to, especially in regard to measurements. Pastry should be made as quickly as possible, and handling kept to a minimum. Many pastries are best rested in a cool place before they are cooked.

SHORTCRUST PASTRY

This popular and versatile pastry is used for savoury and sweet pies, tarts, flans and tartlets. It is usually made by the 'rubbing-in' method, but there are several other ways of making shortcrust. Plain flour is recommended; self-raising flour may be used, but the pastry will be more crumbly. The fat should be lard or a white vegetable fat; ideally, use equal amounts of lard and firm margarine. Margarine alone produces a yellow, firm pastry. Soft table margarine can be used for a pastry with a smooth appearance and soft crumb.

The standard recipe is for 8 oz (225 g) shortcrust which always means 8 oz (225 g) flour to 4 oz (100 g) fat. The amount of flour may be doubled or halved, but proportions should remain the same: half the fat to the amount of flour.

The standard recipe yields enough pastry to cover a 2 pint (1·2 litre) dish, or a 9 in (23 cm) flan ring, or to line and cover a 7 in (18 cm) pie plate.

The following basic shortcrust pastries may be used for both savoury and sweet pies. Enriched shortcrust pastry, however, is mainly used for flans. Shortcrust pastries are usually baked in the centre of a pre-heated oven, at 400°F (200°C, mark 6).

Traditional Shortcrust
PREPARATION TIME: *15 min*
INGREDIENTS:
8 oz (225 g) plain flour
½ level teaspoon salt★
2 oz (50 g) lard
2 oz (50 g) margarine or butter
2–3 tablespoons cold water

Sift the flour and salt into a wide bowl. Cut up the firm fats and rub them into the flour, using the tips of the fingers, until the mixture resembles fine breadcrumbs. Lift the dry mixture well out of the bowl and let it trickle back through the fingers to keep the pastry cool and light. Add the water, sprinkling it evenly (this is important) over the surface. Mix the dough lightly with a round-bladed knife until it forms large lumps.

Gather the dough together with the fingers until it leaves the sides of the bowl clean. Form it into one piece and knead it lightly on a floured surface until firm and free from cracks. Chill for 30 minutes before use.

Roll the pastry out as required, using short, light strokes and rotate the pastry regularly to keep it an even shape.

Shortcrust Pastry with Oil
This pastry produces a tender, flaky crumb. It must be mixed quickly and used at once – if left for any length of time, or chilled, it dries out and cannot be rolled.
PREPARATION TIME: *15 min*
INGREDIENTS:
5 tablespoons corn oil
2½ fluid oz (75 ml) cold water
8 oz (225 g) plain flour
¼ level teaspoon salt★

Whisk the oil and water together in a large bowl, using a fork. Continue whisking until they are evenly blended. Sift the flour and salt together and gradually add it to the oil. Use two knives to incorporate the flour to a dough, then turn it on to a floured surface. Knead the pastry lightly and quickly until smooth and shiny. Roll out and bake as traditional shortcrust.

PREPARING TRADITIONAL SHORTCRUST PASTRY

1. Rubbing fat into flour

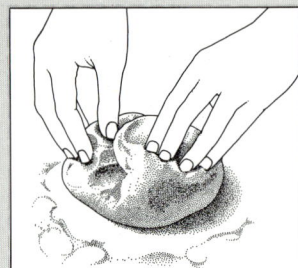

3. Kneading dough lightly

2. Mixing water into dough

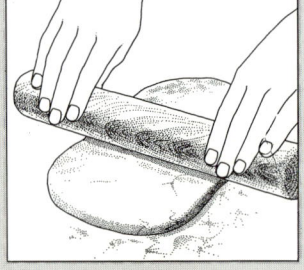

4. Rolling out the pastry

For shortcrust pastry with oil, use two knives to mix the flour and oil

A to Z of Cookery Terms

A

acidulated water Water with added lemon juice or vinegar, which prevents discoloration of some fruits and vegetables. To every ½ pint (300 ml) of cold water, add 1 teaspoon of lemon juice or vinegar

arrowroot Starch made by grinding the root of an American plant of the same name. Used for thickening sauces

B

bain marie A large pan of hot water, or 'bath', in which a smaller pan is placed for cooking the contents or to keep foods warm; a double saucepan

beating Mixing food to introduce air, to make it lighter and fluffier, using a wooden spoon, hand whisk or electric mixer

binding Adding eggs, cream or fat to a dry mixture to hold it together

blanching Boiling briefly 1. To loosen the skin from nuts, fruit and vegetables. 2. To set the colour of food and to kill enzymes prior to freezing. 3. To remove strong or bitter flavours

blending Combining ingredients with a spoon, beater or liquidiser to achieve a uniform mixture

boiling Cooking in liquid at a temperature of 212°F (100°C)

brioche Soft bread made of rich yeast dough, slightly sweetened

brûlé(e) Applied to dishes such as cream custards finished with caramelised sugar glaze

C

charlotte 1. Hot, moulded fruit pudding made of buttered slices of bread and filled with fruit cooked with apricot jam. 2. Cold, moulded dessert consisting of sponge fingers and filled with cream and fruit, or a cream custard set with gelatine

charlotte mould A plain mould for charlottes and other desserts, sometimes used for moulded salads

chilling Cooling food, without freezing it, in the refrigerator

clarified butter Butter cleared of water and impurities by slow melting and filtering

cocotte Small ovenproof, earthenware, porcelain or metal dish, used for baking individual egg dishes, mousses or soufflés

colander Perforated metal or plastic basket used for draining away liquids

compôte Dessert of fresh or dried fruit, cooked in syrup and served cold

conserve Whole fruit preserved by boiling with sugar and used like jam

corn starch Finely ground flour from maize, which is used for thickening sauces, puddings, etc.

crème Applied to fresh cream, butter and custard creams

crème brûlée Cream custard with caramelised topping

crème caramel Cold moulded egg custard with caramel topping

crème fraiche Cream that has been allowed to mature but not to go sour

crêpe Thin pancake

crêpes suzette Pancakes cooked in orange sauce and flamed in liqueur

crimping Making a decorative border to pie crusts

croûtes 1. Pastry covering meat, fish and vegetables. 2. Slices of bread or brioche, spread with butter or sauce, and baked until crisp

curd Semi-solid part of milk, produced by souring

curdle 1. To cause fresh milk or a sauce to separate into solids and liquids by overheating or by adding acid. 2. To cause creamed butter and sugar in a cake recipe to separate by adding the eggs too rapidly

D

dariole Small, cup-shaped mould used for making puddings, sweet and savoury jellies, and creams

dice Cut into small cubes

dough Mixture of flour, water, milk and/or egg, sometimes enriched with fat, which is firm enough to knead, roll and shape

dredging Sprinkling food with flour or sugar

dusting Sprinkling lightly with flour, sugar, spice or seasoning

E

éclair Light, oblong choux pastry split and filled with cream, usually topped with chocolate icing

en croûte Encased in pastry

entremêt Sweet or pudding

F

farina Fine flour made from wheat, nuts and potatoes

flambé Flamed; e.g. food tossed in a pan to which burning brandy or other alcohol has been added

folding in Enveloping one ingredient or mixture in another, using a large metal spoon or spatula

fool Cold dessert consisting of fruit purée and whipped cream

freezing Solidifying or preserving food by chilling and storing it at 32°F (0°C)

G

garnishing Enhancing a dish with edible decorations

gelatine Transparent protein, made from animal bones and tissue, which melts in hot liquid and forms a jelly when cold. Used for sweet and savoury dishes

génoise A rich sponge cake consisting of eggs, sugar, flour and melted butter; baked in a flat tin

glacé Glazed, frozen or iced

glaze A glossy finish given to food by brushing with beaten egg, milk, sugar syrup or jelly after cooking

granita Water ice

griddle Flat metal plate used to bake breads and cakes on the top of the stove

H

hard sauce Sweet butter sauce flavoured with brandy, rum or whisky, which is chilled until hard, and melts when served on hot puddings

hulling Removing green calyx from strawberries and raspberries, etc.

I

icing Sweet coating for cakes

L

langue de chat Flat, finger-shaped biscuit served with cold desserts

leaven Substance, such as yeast, which causes dough or batter to rise

M

macédoine Mixture of prepared fruit or vegetables

macerate To soften food by soaking it in liquid

meringue Whisked egg white blended with sugar

mirabelle 1. Small yellow plum, used as tart filling. 2. A liqueur made from this fruit

mousse Light sweet or savoury cold dish made with cream, whipped egg white and gelatine

P

par-boiling Boiling for a short time to cook food partially

parfait Frozen dessert made of whipped cream and fruit purée

pastry Dough made with flour, butter and water and baked or deep-fried until crisp

pastry wheel Small, serrated wooden or metal wheel for cutting and fluting pastry

pectin Substance extracted from fruit and vegetables. Used to set jellies and jams

pipe To force meringue icing, savoury butter, potato purée, etc., through a forcing bag fitted with a nozzle, to decorate various dishes

poaching Cooking food in simmering liquid, just below boiling point

praline Sweet consisting of unblanched almonds caramelised in boiling sugar

preserving Keeping food in good condition by treating with chemicals, heat, refrigeration, pickling in salt or boiling in sugar

pudding Baked or boiled sweet dessert

purée Sieved raw or cooked food

A to Z of Cookery Terms

R

ratafia 1. Flavouring made from bitter almonds. 2. Liqueur made from fruit kernels. 3. Tiny macaroon

reducing Concentrating a liquid by boiling and evaporation

rennet Substance extracted from the stomach lining of calves. Used to coagulate milk for junket and for making cheese curd

rice paper Edible, glossy white paper made from the pith of a tree grown in China. Used for macaroon base

S

sauté To fry food rapidly in shallow, hot fat, tossing and turning it until evenly browned

savarin Rich yeast cake, which is baked in a ring mould and soaked in liqueur-flavoured syrup

scald 1. To heat milk or cream to just below boiling point. 2. To plunge fruit or vegetables in boiling water to remove the skins

sifting Passing flour or sugar through a sieve to remove lumps

simmering Cooking in liquid which is heated to just below boiling point

skimming Removing cream from the surface of milk, or fat or scum from broth or jam

sorbet Water ice made with fruit juice or purée

soufflé Baked dish consisting of a sauce or purée, which is thickened with egg yolks into which stiffly beaten egg whites are folded

spring-form mould Baking tin with hinged sides, held together by a metal clamp or pin, which is opened to release the cake or pie

starch Carbohydrate obtained from cereal and potatoes

steaming Cooking food in the steam rising from boiling water

sterilising Destroying germs by exposing food to heat

straining Separating liquids from solids by passing them through a sieve or through cheesecloth

strudel Thin leaves of pastry, filled with sweet or savoury mixtures, which are rolled up and baked

syllabub Cold dessert of sweetened thick cream, white wine, sherry or fruit juice

syrup A thick sweet liquid made by boiling sugar with water and/or fruit juice

T

timbale 1. Cup-shaped earthenware or metal mould. 2. Dish prepared in such a mould

tube-pan Ring-shaped tin for baking cakes

turnover Pasty made by folding a circle or square of pastry in half to form a semicircle or triangle

tutti frutti Dried or candied mixed fruits, added to ice cream

U

unleavened bread Bread made without a raising agent which, when baked, is thin, flat and round

V

vanilla sugar Sugar flavoured with vanilla by enclosing it with a vanilla pod in a closed jar

W

wafer Thin biscuit made with rice flour; served with ice cream

waffle Batter cooked on a hot greased waffle iron to a crisp biscuit

whey Liquid which separates from the curd when milk curdles. Used in cheese-making

whipping Beating eggs until frothy or cream until thick

whisk Looped wire utensil used to beat air into eggs, cream or batters

Y

yeast Fungus cells used to produce alcoholic fermentation, or to cause dough to rise

yogurt Curdled milk which has been treated with bacteria

Z

zest Coloured oily outer skin of citrus fruit which, when grated or peeled, is used to flavour foods and liquids

Index

A
Almond(s) 77
  blanching 98
  slivered 98
  recipes
    and apple pudding 11
    squares 69
Amaretti 35
American
  cheese cake 60
  stirred pastry 86
Anadama bread 65
Angelica 98
Apple(s) 74
  freezing 96, 97
  storing 74
  recipes
    and almond pudding 11
    and cheese pie 14, 15
    and nut strudel 13
    crumble 14
    flan, French 10
    pie 10–11
    purée 74
    rum meringue 12
    turnovers 12–13
Apricot(s) 74
  freezing 96, 97
  halving and stoning 80
  recipes
    and walnut loaf 71
    croûtes aux abricots 16
    pie 10
    poached 16
    purée 24–5
    sorbet 15
    trifle, with brandy 15
    tutti frutti pudding 49
Avocado fool 17

B
Babas 66
Baked
  custard 83
  oranges 32–3
  stuffed peaches 35
Baking blind 87
Banana(s) 74
  preventing discoloration 75
  recipes
    and rhubarb compôte 17
    fruit salad 30
    fruit salad in a pineapple 38
Baps, floury 73
Barn brack 68

Batter 84
  pancake 84
  recipe
    clafouti Limousin 20, 21
  see also Crêpes
Bilberries 75
Biscuit crust 86
Biscuits
  freezing 96–7
  recipe
    oat 55
Biscuit Tortoni 54
Blackberries 74, 75
  freezing 96, 97
  recipes
    and apple pie 10
    and lemon pudding 18
    charlotte, Swiss 18–19
Black currants 75
  freezing 96, 97
  stripping from stalk 80
  recipes
    and mint pie 19
    brûlée 20
    pie 10
    sorbet 20
    summer pudding 42–3
Blind, baking 87
Blueberries 75
  recipes
    brûlée 20
    pie, 10, 19
    sorbet 20
Brandy
  apricot trifle 15
  grapefruit in 24
  poires flambées 36–7
Bran teabread 72
Brazil nuts 77
Bread
  baking 91
  dough 90–1
  freezing 96–7
  loaf shapes 91, 92
  storing 91
  recipes
    anadama bread 65
    and butter pudding 50–1
    brioches 68–9
    brown bread ice cream 53
    pudding 50
    quick wheatmeal loaf 92
    rolls 92
    soda 70

summer pudding 42–3
wholemeal loaf 91
see also Teabreads
Brioches 68–9
Brown bread ice cream 53
Brûlée
  blackcurrant 20
  blueberry 20
  cherry 20
Buns, Chelsea 67

C Cakes
  baking 94
  cooling 94–5
  freezing 96–7
  ingredients 93–4
  lining tins 94
  storing 95
  types 95
  recipes
    carrot 64
    Danish layer 63
    farmhouse fruit 64
    fruit, soft 44
    gingerbread 61
    potato 68
    strawberry cream sponge
      62–3
    Tyrol 64–5
    Victoria sandwich 60–1
    Yorkshire tea 72
Candied oranges Grand
  Marnier 30–1
Cantaloup melon 77
Caramel
  custard with orange 32
  topping 41
Carrot cake 64
Champagne Charlie 55
Chantilly cream 59, 98
Charentais melon 77
  serving 81
Charlotte, blackberry 18–19
Cheese cake, American 60
Cheesy apple pie 14, 15
Chelsea buns 67
Cherries 75
  freezing 96, 97
  stoning 80
  recipes
    brûlée 20
    clafouti Limousin 20, 21
    summer pudding 42–3
Chestnuts 77

Chinese
  gooseberries 76
  pears 37
Chocolate
  leaves 98
  melting 98
  squares 98
  storing 98
  recipes
    covered pears 36
    cream pie 59
    sauce 58
Choux pastry 59, 88
  faults in 89
Clafouti Limousin 20, 21
Cob loaf 91, 92
Cob nuts 77
Coconuts 77
Coeur à la crème and
  raspberries 42
Coffee
  Granita al caffè 54–5
Compôte, banana and
  rhubarb 17
Confectioner's custard 25
Corn oil 93
Cranberries 75
Cream, pastry 25
  low-fat 25
Crème
  brûlée 52
  caramel à l'orange 32
  pâtissière 25
Crêpes
  Georgette 38
  Suzette 32–3
Crescents 69
Croûtes aux abricots 16
Crown loaf 91, 92
Crumble
  apple 14
  rhubarb 44–5
Currants *see* Black currants;
  Red currants; White
  currants
Custard
  baked 83
  confectioner's 25
  pouring 83

D Damsons 78
  freezing 97
Danish
  layer cake 63

pastries 69, 96–7
Dates 75
Decorations 98
  pastry 87–8
Diets 7–9
  fibre in 9
  gluten-free 9
  low-cholesterol 8
  low-fat 8
  low-salt 7
  low-sugar 8
  wholefood 9
Dough, bread 90–1
Drop scones 71

E Egg custards 83

F Farmhouse fruit cake 64
Fats
  for cakes 93
  in dough 90
Figs 75
  recipes
    and yogurt 22
    pie 22
Filbert nuts 77
Flans
  baking blind 87
  biscuit crust case 86
  finishing edges 87–8
  glazing 88
  lining flan ring 87
  recipes
    apple, French 10
    gooseberry 23
    soured cream 58
Florida cocktail 80
Flour
  for bread 90
  for cakes 93
Floury baps 73
Flowerpot loaves 92
Fool, avocado 17
Freezing
  fresh fruit 96, 97
  pre-cooked dishes 96–7
French apple flan 10
Frosting 98
Fruit cake, farmhouse 64
Fruit salad 30
  in a pineapple 38

G Gantois, hazel nut 41
Garnishes 98
Gâteau, soft fruit 44
Gelatine 82
  leaf 82–3
  powdered 82
Genoese sponge 95
Ginger, peaches with 34
Gingerbread 61
Glacé cherries 98
Glazing
  pastry 88
  with jelly 82
Gooseberries 75
  Chinese 76
  freezing 97
  topping and tailing 80
  recipe
    flan 23
Granita al caffè 54–5
Grape(s) 75–6
  frosted 98
  peeling 80
  removing pips 80
  recipes
    fruit salad 30
    fruit salad in a pineapple
      38
    jelly 23
Grapefruit 74, 76
  freezing 97
  peeling 80
  preparation 80
  storing 74
  recipes
    Florida cocktail 80
    in brandy 24
Greengage(s) 78, 79
  freezing 97
  recipes
    quiche 25
    with apricot purée 24–5

H Hazel nut(s) 77
  toasting 98
  recipes
    and apple strudel 13
    gantois 41
    Hungarian torte 62
Honey ratafias, Miriam's 55
Honeydew melon 77
  preparing 81
Hungarian hazel nut torte 62

I Ice cream 83, 84
  freezing 96–7
  making in freezer 84
  recipes
    brown bread 53
    champagne Charlie 55
    melon 29
    peach Melba 34
    strawberry 47
    tangerines, iced 48
    vanilla 53

J Jam
  recipes
    sauce 50–1
    steamed pudding 50–1
    strawberry cream sponge 62–3
  Japanese medlars 76
  Jellies 82–3
    recipe
      grape 23

K Kiwi fruit 76
  Knocking back (dough) 91
  Knocking up (pastry) 86, 87
  Kumquats 76

L Lemons 74, 76
  freezing 97
  spirals 98
  storing 74, 76
  twists 98
  recipes
    meringue pie 28
    mousse 26
    soufflé 28–9
    syllabub 26–7
    tart, glazed 26–7
  Limes 74, 76
  Linzertorte 56–7
  Litchis 76
  Loaves *see* Bread
  Loganberries 76
  Loquats 76
  Lychees 76

M Macaroons 12
  recipe
    Biscuit Tortoni 54
  Mangoes 76
    serving 81
  Medlars, Japanese 76
  Melba, peach 34

Melons 76–7
  freezing 97
  preparing 81
  recipes
    fruit salad 30
    ice cream 29
Meringues 83
  recipes
    apple-rum 12
    pie, lemon 28
    topping, Swiss 18
Mint leaves, frosted 98
Miriam's honey ratafias 55
Moulds 82–3
Mousses 82–3
  freezing 96–7
  recipes
    lemon 26
    raspberry 42–3

N Nectarines 78
  recipe
    in wine 34
  Nuts 77

O Oat biscuits 55
  Ogen melon 77
    serving 81
  Oranges 74, 77
    freezing 97
    peeling 81
    spirals and twists 98
    storing 74
    recipes
      and caramel custard 32
      baked 32–3
      candied, with Grand Marnier 30–1
      crêpes Suzette 32–3
      Florida cocktail 80
      foam sauce 49
      fruit salad 30
      fruit salad in a pineapple 38
      soufflés 30
  Ortaniques 77
  Oven scones 70

P Pancakes
  basic batter 84
  cooking 84
  freezing 96–7
  reheating and storing 84
  recipes see Crêpes

Papayas 78
  preparing and serving 81
Paradise pudding, apple and almond 11
Paris–Brest 59
Passion fruit 77–8
Pastries, Danish 69
  freezing 96–7
Pastry
  American stirred 86
  baking blind 87
  biscuit crust 86
  choux 59, 88, 89
  covering a pie dish 86–7
  cream 25
  decorations 87–8
  double crust pie 86, 87
  faults in 89
  flowers 88
  freezing 96–7
  glazing 88
  gluten-free 10
  knocking up 86, 87
  lattice pattern 88
  leaves 87, 88
  lining a flan ring 87
  lining a pie plate 87
  low-fat 23
  pâte sucrée 86
  puff 89
  sealing edges 87
  shortcrust 85–6, 89
  tassels 87, 88
  recipes
    apple flan, French 10
    apple pie (shortcrust) 10–11
    apple turnovers (puff) 12–13
    black currant and mint pie (shortcrust) 19
    cheesy apple pie 14, 15
    chocolate cream pie (biscuit crust) 59
    fig pie (shortcrust) 22
    gooseberry flan 23
    lemon meringue pie (shortcrust) 28
    lemon tart, glazed (shortcrust) 26–7
    Linzertorte 56–7
    Paris–Brest (choux) 59
    plum and cinnamon pie (American stirred) 40

profiteroles (choux) 58
quiche Reine-Claude (shortcrust) 25
shoo fly pie (shortcrust) 57
soured cream flan (shortcrust) 58
treacle tart 56
Pâte sucrée 86
Pawpaws 78
  preparing and serving 81
Peaches 78
  freezing 96, 97
  peeling 81
  recipes
    and hazel nut gantois 41
    baked and stuffed 35
    in wine 34
    Melba 34
    pie 10
    with ginger 34
    with soured cream 35
Peanuts 77
Pears 78
  poaching 78
  storing 78
  recipes
    Chinese 37
    fruit salad 30
    in chocolate jackets 36
    paradise pudding 11
    poires flambées 36–7
Pecans 77
Peel 94
Persimmons 78
Pies
  covering 86–7
  decorations 87–8
  double crust 86, 87
  freezing 96–7
  glazing 88
  knocking up 86, 87
  lining plate 87
  sealing 87
  recipes
    apple 10
    black currant and mint 19
    blueberry 10, 19
    cheesy apple 14, 15
    chocolate cream 59
    fig 22
    lemon meringue 28
    plum and cinnamon 40
    shoo fly 57

Pineapple 78
　freezing 97
　jelly 82
　preparing 81
　recipes
　　and plum flambé 39
　　crêpes Georgette 38
　　fruit salad in 38
Pinwheels 69
Pistachio nuts
　blanching 98
Plums 78–9
　freezing 97
　recipes
　　and cinnamon pie 40
　　flambé with pineapple 39
　　in wine 39
　　pie 10
Poached apricots 16
Poires flambées 36–7
Pomegranates 79
Poppy-seed plaits 92
Potato cakes 68
Profiteroles 58
Proving (dough) 91
Puddings 82
　recipes
　　apple and almond
　　　paradise 11
　　blackberry lemon 18
　　bread 50
　　bread and butter 50–1
　　hazel nut gantois 41
　　jam, steamed 50–1
　　summer 42–3
　　tutti frutti, with orange
　　　foam sauce 49
Purées, fruit 82
　freezing 96
　recipes
　　apple 74
　　raspberry 34, 79
　　strawberry 79

Q Quiche Reine-Claude 25
Quinces 79

R Raising agents 93
Raisins 94
Raspberries 74, 79
　freezing 97
　recipes
　　and hazel nut gantois 41
　　and yogurt sorbet 40, 41

gâteau 44
mousse 42–3
purée 34, 79
summer pudding 42–3
with cream cheese 42
Ratafias, Miriam's honey 55
Red currants 75
　freezing 97
　frosted 98
　stripping from stalk 80
　recipe
　　gâteau 44
Rhubarb 79
　freezing 97
　recipes
　　and banana compôte 17
　　crumble 44–5
Rice
　recipe
　　apple and almond
　　　paradise pudding 11
Rising (dough) 91
Rolls 92
　fancy 92
Rum babas 66

S Sally Lunns 66
Satsumas 79
Sauces
　recipes
　　chocolate 58
　　jam 50–1
　　orange foam 49
Schlagsahne 56
Scones
　freezing 96–7
　drop 71
　oven 70
Shoo fly pie 57
Shortcake, strawberry 46
Shortcrust pastry 85–6
　enriched 86
　faults in 89
　traditional 85
　with oil 85
　for recipes see under Pastry
Soda bread 70
Sorbets 83
　recipes
　　apricot 15
　　black currant 20
　　raspberry yogurt 40, 41
Soufflés
　freezing 96–7

recipes
　lemon 28–9
　orange 30
Soured cream 76
　recipe
　　flan 58
Sponge cake 93, 95
　recipes
　　strawberry cream 62–3
　　Victoria sandwich 60–1
Spun sugar 98
Steamed puddings 82
　recipe
　　jam 50–1
Strawberries 74, 79
　freezing 97
　hulling 81
　recipes
　　cream sponge 62–3
　　gâteau 44
　　ice cream 47
　　purée 79
　　shortcake 46
　　summer pudding 42–3
　　syllabub trifle 45
　　water ice 46, 47
Strudel, apple and nut 13
Suet pudding 82
　recipe
　　jam 50–1
Sugar 90, 93–4
　frosting with 98
　spun 98
Sultanas 94
Summer pudding 42–3
Syllabubs 83
　recipes
　　lemon 26–7
　　trifle, strawberry 45

T Tangelo 79
Tangerines 79
　recipe
　　ice cream 48
Tartlets, baking blind 87
Tarts
　finishing edges 87–8
　lining pie plate 87
　recipes
　　apple 10
　　lemon 26–7
　　Linzertorte 56–7
　　treacle 56
　see also Flans

Teabreads
　freezing 96–7
　recipes
　　apricot and walnut loaf 71
　　barn brack 68
　　bran 72
　　Sally Lunns 66
Tea cakes, Yorkshire 72
Treacle tart 56
Trifles 83
　recipes
　　brandy apricot 15
　　strawberry syllabub 45
Turnovers, apple 12–13
Tutti frutti pudding with
　orange foam sauce 49
Tyrol cake 64–5

U Ugli fruit 79

V Vanilla ice cream 53
Victoria sandwich 60–1

W Walnuts 77
　recipes
　　and apple strudel 13
　　and apricot loaf 71
Water ices
　recipes
　　granita al caffè 54–5
　　strawberry 46, 47
　see also Ice cream; Sorbets
Watermelon 77
Wheatmeal bread, quick 92
White currants 75
　freezing 97
　stripping from stalk 80
Wholemeal bread 91
Whortleberries 75
Wine
　peaches in 34
　plums in 39

Y Yeast 90
Yogurt
　recipes
　　and fresh figs 22
　　and raspberry sorbet 40,
　　　41
Yorkshire tea cakes 72

Z Zabaglione 52

The Good Health Cookbooks

The Publishers wish to express their gratitude for major contributions by the following people:

Editor: URSULA WHYTE   Art Director: MICHAEL McGUINNESS   Designer: SANDRA DEON-CARDYN

Diet Consultant: MIRIAM POLUNIN   Home Economist: VALERIE BARRETT   Additional Photography: PHILIP DOWELL

The Publishers also wish to acknowledge the help of the following:

Gilly Abrahams for editorial help; Fred and Kathie Gill for proof reading; Mary-Anne Joy for help with calorie counting;
Terri Lamb and Carole Perks for design assistance; Vicki Robinson for indexing; and Michelle Thompson for food preparation.
Additional photographic props were supplied by Graham and Green. The recipe for gluten-free pastry on page 10
is based on one from Rita Greer's Gluten-free Cooking (Thorsons Publishers Ltd, 1983).
The recipe for low-fat pastry on page 23 comes from Miriam Polunin's The New Cookbook (Macdonald & Co Ltd, 1984).

The Good Health Cookbooks are based on THE COOKERY YEAR, **to which the following made major contributions:**

Editorial Adviser: ELIZABETH POMEROY
Photographer: PHILIP DOWELL
Home Economist: JOY MACHELL

Writers:

Ena Bruinsma
Margaret Coombes
Derek Cooper
Margaret Costa
Denis Curtis
Theodora FitzGibbon
Nina Froud
Jane Grigson
Nesta Hollis
Kenneth H. C. Lo

Elizabeth Pomeroy
Zena Skinner
Katie Stewart
Marika Hanbury Tenison
Silvino S. Trompetto, MBE,
 Maître Chef des Cuisines,
 Savoy Hotel
Suzanne Wakelin
Kathie Webber
Harold Wilshaw

Artists:

Colour:
 Roy Coombs
 Pauline Ellison
 Hargrave Hands
 Denys Ovenden
 Charles Pickard
 Josephine Ranken
 Charles Raymond
 Rodney Shackell
 Faith Shannon, MBE
 John Wilson

Black and white:
 David Baird
 Brian Delf
 Gary Hincks
 Richard Jacobs
 Rodney Shackell
 Michael Woods
 Sidney Woods
Black and white photography:
 Michael Newton

Typesetting: Tradespools Ltd, Frome   **Printing:** W. S. Cowell Ltd, Ipswich   **Binding:** Dorstel Press Ltd, Harlow

RGHCD–16-003